GREAT BOOKS AND
BOOK COLLECTORS

GREAT BOOKS AND BOOK COLLECTORS

ALAN G. THOMAS

SPRING BOOKS

First published in Great Britain in 1975 by
Weidenfeld and Nicolson Ltd

This edition published in 1988 by Spring Books
An imprint of Octopus Publishing Group PLC
59 Grosvenor Street
London W1

Distributed by the Hamlyn Publishing Group Limited
Bridge House, London Road,
Twickenham, Middlesex, England

ISBN 0 600 55927 0

Printed by Mandarin Offset in Hong Kong

CONTENTS

PREFACE

'OF MAKING MANY BOOKS there is no end,' wailed the Preacher. To what organ roll of prophetic lamentation would the author of *Ecclesiastes* have been inspired by the situation today? Nobody knows how many different books there are in the world, but the number has been estimated at between thirty and forty million. To deal with them all in the space available to me here would allow one word to about each thousand books.

Seven years ago I wrote a small book, *Fine Books*, with four chapters on Manuscripts, Early Printing, English Books with Coloured Plates and Private Presses. Those four chapters have here been revised, expanded and wherever possible provided with different illustrations. The book is now enlarged with new chapters on Bookbinding, the Bible, Early Books in Hebrew, Herbals and Colour-Plate Flower Books, Books on Architecture, The New World, First Editions, Fakes and Forgeries and the Great Book Collectors.

By selecting these twelve aspects of the book I hope to give some details of interest, some human anecdotes: to add flesh, as it were, to the skeleton. And if many subjects of supreme importance have been omitted, the books described range from the *Cottonian Genesis*, written in the first half of the fifth century, to work of craftsmen who are still alive. However inadequate my treatment may be, at least the subject represents one of the most glorious achievements of Western civilization.

It is now forty-seven years since I first went to work in a bookshop, and I cannot imagine any life that would be more rewarding. Not only is there the privilege of handling, sometimes even temporarily owning, the great books themselves, but all the lifelong friendships which grow out of mutual enthusiasms. So it is now my gratifying duty to thank the following great scholars who have given so generously of their time in reading and commenting upon the chapters in this book: Derek H. Turner, Manuscripts; George D. Painter, Early Printing; Howard M. Nixon, Bookbinding; Josef Rosenwasser, Early Books in Hebrew – all on the staff of the British Museum; A. N. L. Munby, Librarian of King's College, Cambridge, who read Great Book Collectors and provided illustrations from his unique collection; John Carter, Fakes and Forgeries; John Harris of the Royal Institute of British Architecture, Books on Architecture; and Charles Ede, Founder of the Folio Society, Private Press Books. The Atlantic unites rather than divides the English-speaking bibliographical community, and Charles C. Ryrie of Dallas Theological Seminary read the chapter on the Bible; David Sandler Berkowitz of Brandeis University, that on Early Hebrew Books; and James Hart of the

University of California at Berkeley, The New World. Lord John Kerr, Director of Sotheby's, has given me a number of photographs. I would also like to thank my polyglot, polymath friend, Dr Theodore Stephanides.

Finally I thank my wife, Shirley. To say that she typed the text would mention but a small aspect of her part in creating this book. She has been at my side both in the writing and also in my activities as a bookseller. And to her I dedicate *Great Books and Book Collectors*.

ALAN G. THOMAS

NOTE In these days of change hardly a week goes by without some country or institution calling itself by a new name. While I have been writing this book the British Museum Library has become the British Library. I am too old to change and, having loved the British Museum for so long, I have not altered phrases such as 'now in the British Museum'.

CHAPTER ONE

MANUSCRIPTS

I N THESE DAYS when the world is flooded with books (in Britain alone about thirty-five thousand new volumes were published last year and a further thirty-nine thousand in the United States), it is difficult to think oneself back into an age when there were not only no *printed* books, but very few books of any kind, and when most people could neither read nor write.

By the Dark Ages of the sixth century AD the barbarian hordes had swept across Europe, destroying both the classical world of Greece and Rome and, to a great extent, the early Christian civilization. At this time nearly all educated men were in the Church, and indeed our word 'clerk', one who earns his living with a pen, derives from 'cleric', a clergyman.

At that time the standards of peace and security, without which it is difficult to achieve progress, were mostly found in the monasteries, where dedicated men led a communal life. The monasteries themselves might be compared to a chain of castles holding the line in a dark and savage land. Most religious houses possessed libraries in which were preserved not only the Bible and the great texts of Christendom but also, in some fortunate cases, the books that contained practically everything that has come down to us from the ancient world in the way of spiritual teaching, philosophy, literature, history, medicine and science. Our knowledge of the classics is almost entirely due to work done in the *scriptoria* of Carolingian monasteries.

Our debt to these men is incalculable. Let us now consider how they created these manuscripts. We are used to borrowing or even buying books without difficulty; but in those days a rich man or a wealthy institution would employ a scribe and an illuminator, perhaps for years on end, to write books for them.

Although there was already a flourishing book trade in Oxford by the twelfth century, the only course open to a poor scholar was to buy the necessary equipment and set to work himself. Chaucer's Clerk of Oxenford probably produced the 'twenty bokes, clad in blak or reed' that 'stodd above his beddes heed' in this way – though the thought of writing out the whole Bible single-handed must have seemed intimidating. Many such humble manuscripts are still in existence.

In the early days, before the thirteenth century, the majority of books must have been written in monasteries, and especially in Benedictine and Cistercian houses. The really great centres were comparatively few in number; in England at Winchester, St Albans, Canterbury, Durham, Peterborough, Glastonbury and Bury St Edmunds. The *scriptorium* in a

Benedictine house was generally over the chapter-house or, perhaps, the scribes worked in carrels in the cloister, as at Gloucester. Strict rules were applied. Artificial light was forbidden for fear of fire. Absolute silence was enjoined and, to avoid the mistakes that so frequently follow interruption, only the highest monastic officials were allowed to enter the *scriptorium*. Communication was by signs. If a scribe needed a book he extended his hands and turned over imaginary leaves; a missal was signified by the sign of the cross; a psalter by placing the hands on the head in the shape of a crown (a reference to King David); a lectionary by wiping away imaginary grease fallen from candles; and a pagan work by scratching the body in the manner of a dog.

At first all books were written on vellum (the skin, generally, of sheep, goats or calves), washed, dressed and rubbed smooth. Smaller books or more delicate works were written on the finer uterine vellum, which is the skin of an unborn calf or lamb. Vellum is one of the best materials ever used in book production. It is smooth, white, tough and lasting, the only disadvantage being its high cost.

'How many sheep,' I asked, rhetorically, in the first edition of this book, 'would be needed for a Bible?' The question has since been answered, with Teutonic thoroughness, by Bonifatius Fischer, in the learned introduction to a splendid manuscript facsimile, *Die Bibel von Moutier-Grandval* (Berne: Verein Schweizerischer Lithographiebesitzer 1970). This is British Museum Add. MS 10456, often known as the 'Alcuin Bible', since it was once claimed, by a vendor who hoped to sell it to the King of France, to be the Bible that Alcuin produced for the coronation of Charlemagne. Today, Fischer argues, the sheet of vellum derived from a full-grown goat or sheep measures 100 × 55 centimetres; but the sheet of vellum from a 'half-year' animal will be only 84 × 45 centimetres – and animals were probably smaller in the ninth century. A book the size of the 'Alcuin Bible' would need sheep that had been kept alive through the winter by stable-feeding *(Stallfütterung)*, which shows that the monks of Tours, or their tenants, were good agriculturalists. Each Bible would require from 210 to 225 sheep – and this would not include animals that were diseased or had been injured. From the first fifty years of the ninth century we have records of forty-six large Bibles and eighteen Gospels produced at Tours. A sure cure for insomnia.

Those of us who have lived through two world wars are accustomed to the production of ersatz materials in times of shortage. A similar crisis was responsible for the production of vellum. In about 150 BC Eumenes II, the cultured King of Pergamum, was building up one of the world's great libraries, the fame of which began to rival that of Alexandria. In order to defend the prestige of their own library the Ptolemies forbade the export of papyrus. The intelligence of the Greeks overcame this setback by producing a superior material – and the Latin name for vellum is still *pergamena*.

To avoid the cost of vellum men turned to paper. First manufactured (outside China) in Samarkand in about AD 750, it continued to be imported until the first European paper was produced in the twelfth century.

The scribe wrote on lines ruled with a blunt scriber, making hollows on one side of the leaf, ridges on the other, the spacing of the lines having first been pricked out down each margin with an awl. The pen was a reed or quill, cut with a penknife; the ink was made of soot, gum and water or, alternatively, galls, sulphate of iron and gum.

Scribes were held in high honour; it is always profitable to be able to do what nobody else can do. In Ireland in the seventh and eighth centuries the penalty for killing a scribe was fully equal to that for killing a bishop, and it was considered an honour to St Patrick himself that he was so good a scribe.

The mention of St Patrick brings us to an interesting and curious situation. While the rest of Europe wallowed in the Dark Ages, Ireland was a blaze of light; the barbarians exhausted their impetus attacking England, and Ireland was left in peace. From that peace there emerged one of those inexplicable creative periods in history similar to those of England under Elizabeth I or Florence under the Medici. Scholarship flourished and Europeans travelled to Ireland in order to learn Greek, which, when one considers what travel must have been like in the Dark Ages, is no mean tribute to Irish civilization. From Christian Ireland missionaries set out to reconvert pagan Europe to the faith, and marked each stage of the journey by founding a monastery in which they produced manuscripts: first at Iona in Scotland [1] and Lindisfarne in northern England; then through what is now Germany and Switzerland to St Gall; and across the Alps to Italy, where they established a monastery at Bobbio that was to become famous for its manuscripts.

In 635 King Oswald invited St Aidan to come from Iona as missionary to Northumbria. He came, and made his headquarters on Holy Island, or Lindisfarne, where he founded a monastery on an Irish plan. Here, a little before AD 700, was produced (probably to celebrate the translation of St Cuthbert) the most splendid surviving example of Northumbrian

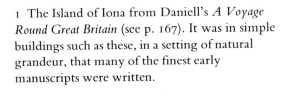

1 The Island of Iona from Daniell's *A Voyage Round Great Britain* (see p. 167). It was in simple buildings such as these, in a setting of natural grandeur, that many of the finest early manuscripts were written.

The Cathedral at Iona

illumination, the *Lindisfarne Gospels*. The text is written in an insular majuscule hand developed from the script that the monks had brought from Iona. About 250 years later Aldred, son of Alfred and Tilwin, added a gloss in English. Fortunately for us, he also wrote a note about the origin of the book that, for a brief moment, draws aside the curtain that hides life on that storm-swept island:

Eadfrith, Bishop of the church of Lindisfarne, he at the first wrote this book for God and for St Cuthbert and for the whole company of the saints whose relics are on the island. And Ethilwald, Bishop of those of Lindisfarne Island, bound and covered it outwardly as well as he could. And Billfrith the anchorite he wrought, as a smith, the ornaments that are on the outside and adorned it with gold and with gems and gilded silver, unalloyed metal. And Aldred, an unworthy and most miserable priest, with God's help and St Cuthbert's, over-glossed it in English. . . .

Plates II and III represent the opening of *St Mark's Gospel* and the 'carpet page' that precedes it. The 'carpet page' contains an interlacing pattern of incredible complexity, completely Celtic in feeling. It is carried out with breathtaking accuracy, every twist and interlacing of the complex pattern being depicted in perfect detail; heads of fantastic animals bite the ribbons as they go by, while the subtle colour may well be described as magical.

Another aspect of the *Lindisfarne Gospels* bears fascinating witness to the international character of the Church in those early days for (and this is about the last thing one would have imagined) it exhibits strong Neapolitan traits in the liturgical directions which, with tables of lessons proper for festivals and so on, precede each Gospel. This appears to have been the result of an exchange of ideas and experience.

Benedict Biscop, a Northumbrian nobleman who founded the twin monasteries of Wearmouth-Jarrow, made more than one journey to Italy, travelling right down nearly two hundred miles beyond Naples to the south. Here he visited a Benedictine house famous for its manuscripts, founded about the end of the fifth century by Cassiodorus near his birthplace, and called by him Vivarium, because of its fishponds. Biscop must have spent much time following the rites practised there, and he also acquired manuscripts, which he carried home to Northumberland. On the other hand Bede tells us of Hadrian, Abbot of Nisida, near Naples, who came on a mission to Northumbria in 669 and later spent some years in Canterbury. These travels explain the extraordinary phenomenon of a Neapolitan liturgy being written in a monastery in the far north of England.

In 875 the Danes invaded Lindisfarne and destroyed the monastery. The monks fled, taking their more portable treasures, including the relics of St Cuthbert and this book. It was carried from place to place and, during a journey to Ireland, was washed overboard in a storm. It was recovered, miraculously uninjured, at low tide.

After many wanderings the *Lindisfarne Gospels* came to rest in Durham, where it was seen by a certain Simeon of Durham in the twelfth century, as he records in his history of the cathedral. But in all probability the

2 St Matthew from the *Book of Kells*. On either side behind the throne is the head of the lion of St Mark; behind the arms of the seat are the ox of St Luke and the eagle of St John. The spreading ornament in the spandrels of the arch is modelled on the *flabellum* used in the Eastern Church in early days to keep flies from the altar. Dublin, Trinity College Library.

book was later returned to the refounded priory on Lindisfarne, for the inventory of 1367 records: '*Liber S. Cuthberti qui demersus in mare*'. After the sack of the monasteries the manuscript disappears until, in the seventeenth century, it was acquired (stripped of its jewelled binding) by Sir Robert Cotton. It eventually passed, with the rest of his library, to the British Museum on its foundation in 1753.

'That man is little to be envied,' said Dr Johnson, 'whose patriotism would not gain force upon the plain of Marathon, or whose piety would not grow warmer among the ruins of Iona!' It was here, in 563, that St Columba founded the monastery that rapidly became the centre of Celtic Christianity and sent forth missionaries to pagan Europe. And it was here, in the second half of the eighth century, that the supreme masterpiece of the Celtic school, one of the world's greatest books, was written – the *Book of Kells*.

A few years later the Abbot Cellach and his monks, fleeing from the Norsemen and carrying the unfinished manuscript with them, took refuge in the Abbey of Kells, about forty miles from Dublin. Here the precious book remained until it was given to Trinity College, Dublin, in the seventeenth century. It contains the four Gospels decorated with an unusual wealth of illumination, all but two of the pages being painted. Experts have detected the work of four different artists of unequal talent, and an exceptionally wide series of European and Near-Eastern influences. It is hopeless to summarize a book of such richness in the few words available to me here, except, perhaps, to make one point. In the *Lindisfarne Gospels* the upsurging Celtic imagination is kept within almost classical control as if the wild romantic spirit were held within the Roman discipline of the Catholic Church. In the *Book of Kells* there is far less restraint; the Irish temperament is given free rein.

The exuberance of the *Book of Kells* is well displayed in the three opening words of *Matthew* 1:18, 'Christi autem generatio', with 'Christi (XPI)' and 'autem' contracted [1]. Irish scholars claim that this is 'the most elaborate specimen of calligraphy which has ever existed' – and who can contradict them? Towards the left-hand side, almost hidden in the pattern, there are three angels, two of whom hold books. The third grasps a pair of blossoming sceptres with all his might, as if he were frightened lest the swirling pattern in which they have become entangled were about to snatch them out of his hands. Crouching under the tail of the P a couple of rats are surreptitiously nibbling at the Host, while two cats, with reprehensible languor, look on. There is some dispute as to whether Figure 2 represents St Matthew.

The Amiatino Bible is not only the most important codex of the Vulgate in existence but also the supreme example of English uncial writing, its splendid script marching majestically across the pages like the assured tramp of the Roman legions. It was written in the twin monasteries of Wearmouth-Jarrow, the home of the Venerable Bede, the heart of Northumbrian civilization. The Abbot Ceolfrid commissioned three copies of the Bible, one for each of the monasteries, another as a present for the pope. Armed with his precious burden Ceolfrid set out for Rome in 716, but died at Langres, in France, without having accomplished his mission. We do not know how the Bible reached Italy and the monastery on Mount Amiata, but the presentation inscription was faked by erasing the name 'Ceolfridus Anglorum' and substituting 'Petrus Langobardorum'. The book remained on Mount Amiata until the monastery was suppressed in 1782. It then went to its final home, the Biblioteca Laurenziana in Florence. The fraudulent inscription remained undetected and the book was assumed to be Italian until it was examined, in the 1880s, by the great scholar Giovanni Battista de Rossi. Not only was the deception exposed, but F. J. A. Hort discovered that the verses which head the codex were identical with those recorded by the eighth-century *Historia Abbatum* as having been inscribed in Ceolfrid's Bible [3].

The Northumbrian civilization, which did so much towards relighting the lamps all over Europe, was overrun and destroyed by the Danes, and we must turn to the Anglo-Saxon world of southern England. Here a distinguished group of kings, bishops and abbots promoted a remarkable

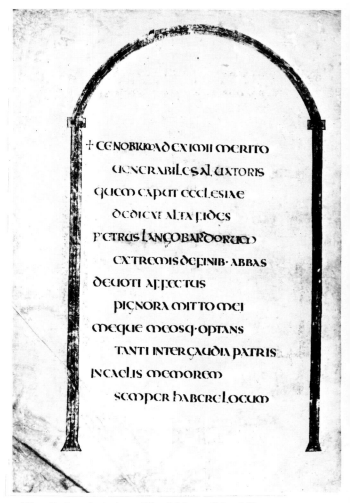

3 The *Codex Amiatinus*. The faking of the fifth line can be clearly seen: the name '*Petrus Langobardorum*' was written in the space where that of the Abbot Ceolfrid had been erased. Northumbria, eighth century. Florence, Biblioteca Laurenziana.

RIGHT 4 St Etheldreda, patron of Ely
Cathedral, in the Benedictional written for
St Ethelwold, Bishop of Winchester (AD 963–84),
during the last great upsurge of Anglo-Saxon
civilization. British Museum, Add. MS 49598.

OPPOSITE ABOVE 5 The Holy Spirit, in the form
of a dove, held by the hand of God, inspires
St John while writing his Gospel. Abbot Wedric,
for whom the manuscript was written, holds out
the inkhorn. The eagle, symbol of St John, is in
the opposite roundel. The others contain scenes
from the life of St John. France, twelfth century.
Avesnes, Société Archéologique.
OPPOSITE BELOW 6 David slays first the bear
and then the lion in the *Beatus* initial of the
great Winchester Bible. Twelfth century.
Winchester, Cathedral Library.

culture. This lasted only a little more than a hundred years, beginning with
the accession of King Edgar in 959 and ending at Hastings in 1066.

A major factor of this upsurge was a revival of monasticism; new
houses were founded and old foundations revived. No man did more
in this field than St Ethelwold, who served as Bishop of Winchester
from 963 to 984. He began the rigorous reformation of his own cathedral by installing monks and driving out the non-monastic clerics. The
latter did not like this and almost succeeded in poisoning their bishop.

One of the most important elements in this civilization found expression in the production of splendid manuscripts, especially at Winchester and Canterbury, generally known as the Winchester School.
The *Benedictional of St Ethelwold* is among the greatest of these manuscripts. A benedictional contains blessings that can be pronounced, at
mass, only by a bishop. Only two really important illuminated benedictionals of this period have survived, and both of them were created
by the Winchester School: the *Benedictional of St Ethelwold* and the

Benedictional of Archbishop Robert of Jumièges, now in Rouen. There was no comparable development of benedictionals elsewhere.

Even today the cathedral at Ely is dedicated to St Etheldreda, the Abbess who died in 679, and it seems that St Ethelwold held her in special veneration. At any rate, he refounded her abbey at Ely and chose her as the subject of one of the illuminations in his great book [4]. The inscription reads: '*Imago Sanctae Ætheldrythae Abbatissae ac Perpetuae Virginis*' ('The representation of St Etheldreda Abbess and perpetual virgin').

Plate IV reproduces a page from a psalter probably written at Winchester in the latter part of the tenth century under St Ethelwold. King David gave medieval illuminators great opportunities by beginning the *Psalms* with the letter B *(Beatus Vir qui non abiit in consilio impiorum)* and the '*Beatus* page' is a great feature in many splendid manuscripts.

The work and achievement of St Ethelwold was shared by his two great friends, St Dunstan and St Oswald, Bishop of Worcester and Archbishop of York, so it is interesting to note that the *Ramsay Psalter*, written in Peterborough, was almost certainly produced for St Oswald.

A superb example of bookbinding executed during the Saxon period is described in Chapter Three [XL]. The popular conception of the Saxons at the time of the Norman Conquest is of a lot of louts with tow-coloured hair wearing belted tunics and held down by an élite of semi-fascist house-carls; and yet they could produce works like this, superior to anything being done on the Continent at the time.

During the last years of Anglo-Saxon rule a proto-Romanesque style was developing in England, but this was entirely smashed by the Conquest and there is no English miniature between 1066 and the *Albani Psalter* of 1123.

With the twelfth century we come to a series of splendid folio Bibles produced under the influence of yet another revival of the monastic spirit. They were not intended for study but rather for ceremonial use on great occasions. These manuscripts are similar in character to the Romanesque cathedrals and abbeys for which they were created. They are austere yet rich, severe but filled with an omnipresent power, and their illumination has much in common with the sculpted Last Judgements found on the tympana of many pilgrim churches.

This illumination was strongly influenced by Byzantine art, for there was considerable contact with the remarkable Byzantine civilization flourishing under the Norman kings in Sicily and some contact with Constantinople itself. However the great impact came with the second crusade. So many Englishmen took part that, according to a contemporary chronicler, 'you would imagine that England would be emptied and exhausted by the movement'. The crusade was a disaster, but on their way home the defeated crusaders were entertained by Roger, King of Sicily, who consoled them with gifts that must have included manuscripts and works of art. Here, too, they saw the stupendous mosaics in Palermo and Monreale. The parallels between these and subsequent English art are far too close to be coincidental.

OPPOSITE I The opening words of *Matthew* 1:18 from the *Book of Kells,* written on the Island of Iona in the second half of the eighth century – the supreme example of Celtic illumination. Dublin, Trinity College Library.

FOLLOWING PAGES II and III The 'carpet page' facing *St Mark* in the Gospels written by Eadfrith, Bishop of Lindisfarne (Holy Island) in Northumbria, probably in connection with the translation of St Cuthbert, AD 698. *St Mark* opens with the words: '*Initium euangelii Ihu XPI [Iesu Christi] fili d[e]i sicut scribtum est in Esaia propheta.*' 'The beginning of the Gospel of Jesus Christ, the Son of God. As it is written in Isaiah the prophet.' British Museum, Cotton MS Nero D IV.

BELOW 7 The mouth of Hell from the *Winchester Psalter,* executed at the Cathedral Priory probably for Bishop Henry of Blois (1129–71), brother of King Stephen. British Museum, Cotton MS Nero C IV.

The Lambeth Bible was produced, almost certainly, at Canterbury. Here, although we do not know his name, it appears that the artist was a layman and that he moved about in the world. The similarities to the Sicilian mosaics are so close that he may well have seen them with his own eyes. Further, there is strong reason to suppose that the same artist illuminated a book for Wedric, Abbot of Liessies in what is now France. Unfortunately this book was a victim of the Second World War, having been destroyed at Metz, but two remarkable detached leaves survive in the possession of the Société Archéologique in Avesnes.

Figure 5 reproduces a page from one of these leaves in which St John is seen writing his Gospel, inspired by the Holy Spirit in the form of a dove which, held by the hand of God, whispers in his ear. Very touchingly, Wedric holds the inkhorn into which the saint dips his pen.

The greatest English Bible of the twelfth century (some say the greatest of all twelfth-century manuscripts) is the Winchester Bible, still in the Cathedral Library. Walter Oakeshott has distinguished the hands of six artists who worked on this supreme book over tens of years. In some cases one man drew an illumination while another painted it. Figure 6 reproduces the *Beatus* initial, in which David slays first the bear and then the lion. This is by the 'Master of the Genesis Initial', painting over a design by the 'Master of the Leaping Figures'. It is interesting to observe the monastic tradition preserving features from previous ages. The interlacing strapwork derives from Hiberno-Saxon manuscripts, while the struggle with the lion not only reflects Byzantine art but harks back to classical images of Hercules.

The long production of the Winchester Bible probably extended into the early years of the thirteenth century, and even then it was never finished. This very passage of time enables us to watch, in the later miniatures, the emergence of a new spirit: the age of stern Romanesque austerity changing into the age of Gothic grace.

The Winchester Bible was probably produced to the order of Henry of Blois (1129–71, a splendid character and a munificent patron), Bishop of Winchester and brother of King Stephen. He made several visits to Rome, and was familiar with Mediterranean and, perhaps, Sicilian art; and it was he who commissioned the *Winchester Psalter.* Most of the Psalter's illuminations are distinctly English, but two (not reproduced here) are strongly Byzantine. Figure 7, it is hardly necessary to add, depicts the mouth of Hell. This manuscript, too, was rescued by Sir Robert Cotton and passed to the British Museum.

During the same period great Bibles were also produced on the Continent. One of these, in two volumes (Harley MSS 2798–99), came from the Premonstratensian Abbey of Arnstein near Coblentz on the Rhine. Figure 8 shows the initial P at the opening of *Proverbs.* This manuscript contains a contemporary injunction: '*Liber sancte Marie sanctique Nycolai in Arrinstein, quem si quis abstulerit, morte moriatur, in sartagine coquatur, caducus morbus instet eum et febres et rotatur et suspendatur. Amen.*' ('This book [belongs to the Abbey of] St Mary and St Nicholas in Arnstein. Which if anyone take away, may he die the death, be cooked in a

34

ħGENERATIO

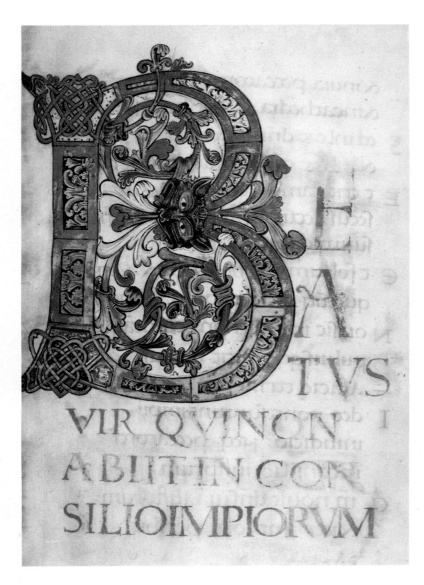

frying-pan, may the falling sickness and fevers draw near him, may he be hung up and twisted around. Amen.') This curse did not achieve its purpose, for the manuscript had already left the monastery when it was purchased by Robert Harley in 1721. This is the more to be regretted, for the curse might otherwise be used against those who, in our own day, have turned the stealing of books from national, and other, collections into a *modus vivendi*.

The monastic *scriptoria* of Bury, Canterbury and Winchester produced splendid Bibles and liturgical manuscripts over several centuries, but the most interesting *scriptorium* during the first half of the thirteenth century, St Albans, is famous for its chronicles and historians.

The historiographers wrote the *St Albans Chronicle*, commencing with the Creation of the World. This ambitious history was continually up-dated by the addition of events as they occurred. In the first half of the thirteenth century St Albans produced two historians who are of the greatest importance for our knowledge of medieval history, Roger of Wendover (d. 1236), who wrote *Flores Historiarum*, and Matthew Paris.

Matthew Paris (*c.* 1200–59) entered the monastery at the age of seventeen. In his youth he assisted Roger of Wendover and, on the latter's death, took over the duties of historiographer and head of the *scriptorium*. By this time there must have been an outstanding historical library at St Albans – but Matthew Paris did not confine himself to documents. He took every opportunity to talk to men of affairs, to mingle with courtiers and talk with the king when, from time to time, he stayed at St Albans, and to gather information at first hand. Nor was he confined to the cloister; he travelled in England and observed and wrote of historical events. His vivid observations on court life include an entertaining account of an elephant that some potentate had presented to the king.

In our own day we see politicians attempting to ingratiate themselves with television interviewers, and it is amusing to note that Henry III and his court were much the same. When, for example, the Holy Blood was to be translated from St Paul's to Westminster – and carried by the king – Matthew Paris was invited to watch the ceremony from the steps of the throne. It is much to his credit that he maintained an independent position and, when he felt it necessary, never hesitated to criticize the king.

Matthew Paris was an active head of the *scriptorium*. He wrote and illustrated books with his own hand and produced volumes of maps. We may with confidence credit Matthew Paris with the beautiful signed drawing in which he depicts himself at the feet of the Virgin [9]. Having rounded off his *Chronica Majora* at the year 1250, Paris intended to retire and take life more easily. However, his enthusiasm apparently proved too strong, for he made the last entry in his own hand shortly before his death. At the end of the chronicle there is a drawing, by a disciple, of the old chronicler on his deathbed. He rests his head on his arm, which lies upon an open manuscript, '*Liber Cronicorum Mathei Parisiensis*'. Above is the inscription: '*Hic obit Matheus Parisiensis*'.

One English thirteenth-century illuminator who has emerged from the

ABOVE 8 Solomon writing Proverbs in the initial P of a splendid twelfth-century Bible from the Abbey of Arnstein on the Rhine. For the great curse, intended to protect this book from theft, see p. 16.
British Museum, Harley MS 2799.

OPPOSITE ABOVE LEFT IV The '*Beatus* page' from an Anglo-Saxon psalter, probably written for St Ethelwold, Bishop of Winchester AD 963–84.
British Museum, Harley MS 2904.
OPPOSITE ABOVE RIGHT V St Katherine, the name saint of his mother, presents Henry VI of England to the Virgin and Child. Paris, fifteenth century.
British Museum, Cotton MS Domitian A XVII.
OPPOSITE BELOW VI The Missal written for the Carmelites in London in the fourteenth century was desecrated in the nineteenth century by children who were allowed to cut out the initials to make scrapbooks. Inside this initial T a bishop is conducting the ceremony for the dedication of a church.
British Museum, Add. MS 29704–6, 44892.

9 Matthew Paris was a monk at St Albans. His *Chronica Majora* is a prime source for medieval English history. Here he has drawn a portrait of himself at the feet of the Virgin. British Museum, Royal MS 14 C VII.

encircling gloom (by courtesy of Sir Sidney Cockerell) is William de Brailes, a little tonsured cleric who appears, tucked away in three miniatures, holding a scroll with: '*W. de Brailes me fecit*'. In one of these, now in Cambridge, the angel of the Last Judgement is seen herding the naked souls with a large and menacing sword. William de Brailes, looking none too sure of his chances, presents his scroll with the air of a man whose passport has expired but who is hoping for the best. Another leaf, also at Cambridge, depicts the Fall of Man [10].

William de Brailes appears to have worked in Oxford. The villages of Upper and Lower Brailes lie ten miles west of Banbury, and his name is to be found among the illuminators who lived in Cat Street, Oxford, in about 1260. Connoisseurs of esoteric information may care to follow this up in Graham Pollard's *Notes for a Directory of Cat Street, Oxford, before 1500* (unpublished manuscript in the Bodleian).

The first manuscripts to have survived in any quantity, and to be still available in private hands on a considerable scale, are the Bibles written – especially in France – during the hundred years following 1175. Europe had settled down, to some extent, after the Dark Ages, and the strong hand of Philip Augustus (1180–1223) had effected a considerable degree of security in France, enabling the arts of peace to flourish and allowing Paris to assume that position as the intellectual capital of Europe which she has so often held since. With the reign of Saint-Louis (1226–70) the Middle Ages reached the apogee of artistic achievement and spiritual fervour. Intellectual leadership was now moving from the monasteries to the universities where the friars, and especially the Dominicans, played a great part. In due course the monks, feeling rather left out, moved into the universities too.

It was the enthusiasm of Louis himself that firmly established Paris as the spiritual power-house of Christendom. Geoffroi de Beaulieu tells us that, while abroad on the crusades, the King learned of a great Saracen ruler who had formed what virtually amounted to a national library. Shamed by this spectacle of spiritual and intellectual superiority on the part of an infidel, Louis determined to set matters right and on his return to Paris scoured all the abbeys in his realm for important texts, and established schools of scribes to multiply them. His private library was thrown open to all *savants* and *réligieux,* and he gathered an important theological library in the treasury of the Sainte-Chapelle, remarking that a church without books was like an army without weapons. All this created a far greater demand for books than had ever existed before, but whereas most previous manuscripts had been written in monasteries, production now passed mainly to commercial workshops, which were to be found near the universities in Paris and elsewhere. However a few really superb manuscripts were still produced in monasteries.

Robertus de Bello was Abbot of St Augustine's, Canterbury, from 1224 to 1253 and his Bible [VII] was probably written there. The *Book of Genesis* opens with a long initial I, which extends the full length of the page and contains a series of roundels depicting the Days of Creation.

10 William de Brailes was one of the very few English illuminators who signed his work. In this example we see the Fall of Man, from Adam's 'The Woman gave it me' (top right), to Cain accidentally killed by his grandson. Cambridge, Fitzwilliam Museum.

The opening words, IN PRINCIPIO CREAVIT DEUS, are embodied in the illumination, while there are six more roundels, with scenes from *Genesis*, at the foot of the page.

In addition to the splendid books treasured by wealthy institutions and private patrons, an immense quantity of quite humble Bibles poured from the workshops. These were modest in size, more sparsely illuminated and generally written in a script which, though tiny, was very neat and regular. These were compact books, fitting easily into the wallets of itinerant preachers to provide the texts for those sermons that were to have so significant an influence on European civilization.

Probably the favourite book, before the appearance of the Breviary and the Book of Hours, was the Psalter – and some of the richest were produced by the so-called East Anglian School. I use this phrase because no better definition has received general acceptance. It has been employed in the past because many of the most important examples are connected with Norfolk, the Gorleston, Ramsey, St Omer and Ormesby Psalters, among others. Yet even its firmest advocates are forced to extend East Anglia by the inclusion of Peterborough, and it seems probable, now, that some of the major Psalters were produced in other parts of the country. East Anglia was then a rich and flourishing centre of agriculture and the wool trade; Norwich was the second largest city in England, while populous towns existed and great churches were built in places where there are now only a few cottages.

These Psalters were planned on a large scale and the spacious margins gave full opportunity to the riotous imagination of the illuminators. In addition to religious pictures there were fabulous beasts and vigorous scenes from daily life: bear-baiting, juggling, ploughing, sowing, harrowing, harvesting, cooking and feasting – they were a sort of fourteenth-century illustrated magazine, to be idly leafed through when wet weather confined ladies to castle or manor.

One of the most famous is the *Luttrell Psalter,* whose pictures have become especially well known over the last eighty or so years with the spread of interest in the history of everyday life. In Figures 11 and 12 the artist has depicted a coach for four queens – a sort of ancestor of the 'royal train'. A small chest (which may well be a tool-box) hangs underneath, and the horses have spiked shoes, like athletes. There is some doubt as to whether Sir Geoffrey Luttrell actually received the manuscript, for the decoration was not entirely completed and certain portions are by a much inferior hand.

Queen Mary's Psalter derives its name from the action of a watchful customs officer who prevented its export and, seizing it, presented it to Queen Mary I in 1553. This manuscript, executed during the first quarter of the fourteenth century, has been described by Eric Miller as

BELOW LEFT AND RIGHT 11 and 12 The mode of travel of the ruling classes in the fourteenth century is delightfully presented in these pages from the *Luttrell Psalter,* one of the prime sources of our knowledge of English medieval life. It is a manuscript so lavish that it has been described as 'expense account art'.
British Museum, Add. MS 42130.

the 'central manuscript of the East Anglian group'. It is one of the most fully illustrated of manuscripts, with hundreds of miniatures. Old Testament scenes are generally two to a page, but with the New Testament there is generally a large miniature at the top of the page, then a few lines of text followed by grotesques in the lower margin. In all there are tinted drawings of religious and secular subjects in the lower margins of 464 pages [13]. All of this appears to be the work of one artist of supreme ability.

Throughout the ages linear draughtsmanship has been the foremost feature of English art, and here the exquisite outline drawing has been touched in, but only touched, by delicate, translucent colour washes that leave the drawing clear.

To compare the Winchester Bible with *Queen Mary's Psalter* (the two consummate examples of English Romanesque and English Gothic art) is not merely to compare two different styles of drawing; it is to apprehend two very different approaches to life. The great and severe strength of the Winchester Bible is that of a man who has looked with clear, unflinching eyes into the depths of the human tragedy, yet kept his faith. The exquisite grace of *Queen Mary's Psalter* represents the beauty of the world as it might be, were it governed by Christian love.

A book which, in its time, must have been among the most beautiful of English manuscripts was the Missal written during the late fourteenth century for the Carmelites of Whitefriars, London. Certain portions of this already imperfect book came into the possession of Philip Augustus Hanrott, an early nineteenth-century collector. His children, believe it or not, cut up the Missal to make scrapbooks, sticking in favourite pictures and spelling out their own names with a series of illuminated initials. A title-page was spelled out with further fragments: INITIAL LETTERS. The younger children made further scrapbooks from

ABOVE 13 *Queen Mary's Psalter*, so named because a customs officer seized and presented it to Queen Mary I in 1553, was written in the first quarter of the fourteenth century. Here we see the Marriage at Cana.
British Museum, Royal MS 2 B VII.

14 The killing of a pig in preparation for the grim medieval winter may be seen in this early sixteenth-century Flemish Book of Hours. British Museum, Add. MS 24098.

the 'leftovers', and the text and humbler fragments of decoration were thrown away.

At the Hanrott sale in 1833 the major scrapbooks were acquired by Sir William Tite, and soon after his death in 1873 they passed to the British Museum. Here the scrapbooks remained intact, greatly admired and often exhibited until, in 1933, an American scholar, Margaret Rickert, conceived the idea of reconstructing the Missal from the surviving fragments. The solution of this colossal jigsaw puzzle took about five years, most of the clues coming from such fragments of text as could be read on the backs of the scraps.

The Reconstructed Carmelite Missal now consists of three very large volumes measuring $28\frac{1}{2}$ by $22\frac{1}{2}$ inches. The great size of the original book, so inconvenient in a modern private library, may have contributed to its dismemberment.

One of the many illustrations of the *Carmelite Missal* is reproduced here. The initial T [VI] comes from the opening of the service of dedication for a new church: *Terribilis est locus iste* ('This is a fearsome place: it is the house of God, the Gate of Heaven'). Before entering the church the bishop – preceded by a religious procession and followed by the wealthy lay patrons who have paid for the building – walks round it three times. He stops at the main door on each circuit, knocking with his crozier and saying, '*Aperite portas principes vestras.*' In the miniature the bishop is sprinkling the church with holy water, an act that drives out the devil, who is seen leaving, in haste, by the roof.

In the fourteenth century many scribes were kept busy producing Psalters, but during the remaining years of the Middle Ages their patrons demanded illuminated copies of the *Horae,* or Hours of the Virgin. This was not a church service book but a manual of private devotions, a shortened version of the Breviary. A large proportion of *Horae,* it must be stressed, were produced for laymen and, perhaps more often, laywomen. They contained a calendar of saints' and feast days, gospel lessons, certain hours or services, the penitential psalms, prayers for the dead and so on. Almost all these books must have been produced in commercial workshops, the quality and scale of the illumination varying according to the purse of the patron. At the top of the scale these were royal and princely persons such as John, Duke of Bedford, brother of Henry V and Regent of France – while more humble examples were written for small merchants or craftsmen.

The more sumptuous books were regarded as precious works of art rather than as books to be read and have generally survived in fine condition. The lesser ones sometimes show great signs of use, like any other prayer-book, and the majority must have been read out of existence. The general run became rather stereotyped with six, twelve or twenty-four full-page miniatures, mostly of the same subjects, which, in the more mediocre books, were hackneyed copies of copies of copies. The best had miniatures by some of the finest artists of the period, Van Eyck, Jean Fouquet, Perugino and certain masters who (although they can be identified by their style) are unknown by name.

A charming feature of *Horae* is the calendar, which contains a series of twelve miniatures depicting the occupations of the months and giving a vivid insight into late medieval life. In the winter the lord and lady are generally sitting by the fire while Tom bears logs into the hall; in spring and summer they indulge in field sports, make music out of doors or go on pilgrimages, the sheep are shorn and, later on, the crops are cut. In autumn come sowing and harrowing, wood is stacked and, lastly, beasts are killed and salted down against the grimness of the forthcoming winter [14]. Very often the occupations of the month are accompanied by the signs of the zodiac, which give considerable scope to a decorative artist. The calendar is of great use to the student in determining the origin of the manuscript. The major saints and the great feasts of the Church are, of course, universal; these days are entered in colour and

15 The *Bedford Book of Hours* was probably executed to celebrate the marriage of John, Duke of Bedford, Regent of English rule in Paris, to Anne, daughter of the Duke of Burgundy, in 1423. This miniature shows the building of the Tower of Babel.
British Museum, Add. MS 18850.

give us the phrase 'red-letter days'. However, the presence of a group of minor Breton saints unknown outside north-western France, or the dedication of a church in Norwich, must indicate that the book was written for a patron living in those places. Certain differences in the liturgy – Use of Paris, Use of Sarum, Use of Sens, Use of Tours and so on – are also a help in identification.

When the *Bedford Book of Hours* [15] was produced the Duke of Bedford was lording it in Paris as Regent, at a time when the English domination of France was at its peak. A key factor in that domination was the Burgundian alliance, to further which, in 1423, Bedford married Anne, daughter of John, Duke of Burgundy. This manuscript was probably written in celebration of that marriage, and may well have been a wedding present to the bride, for it contains a portrait of Anne opposite the *Memoria* of her name saint, her arms and her motto. The Harleian manuscripts were purchased by the Nation in 1753, but this manuscript was 'reserved' and had to wait almost a hundred years, passing through several collections, before reaching the British Museum in 1852.

Plate V represents most people's idea of a Book of Hours: a good-sized miniature and three lines of text surrounded by an ivy-leaf border with a few grotesques. Actually, this is the *Psalter of Henry* VI of England, originally executed in Paris for someone else (we don't know for certain whom) quite early in the century and subsequently adapted. It may well have been for 'little Louis' (d. 1415), the eldest son of King Charles VI of France, for in one miniature the surcoat originally covered with the fleur-de-lys of France has been quartered by adding the leopards of England, and here the patron is Saint-Louis. In 1430, ten days after his ninth birthday, Henry was crowned King of France in Paris. It may well have been at this time that the book (having by now been adapted for him) was given to him by his mother, Queen Katherine. Among the added miniatures is one which shows St Katherine, identified by her wheel, presenting the little king to the Virgin.

'Webster was much possessed by death/And saw the skull beneath the skin,' says T. S. Eliot. So, for that matter, was the Master of the Rohan Hours. In his earlier years this artist worked in the *atelier* that produced the *Bedford Book of Hours,* but later he had the good fortune to be taken up by Yolanda of Aragon, the wife of Louis II, Duke of Anjou and King of Sicily. Blessed with a sympathetic patroness who gave him a workshop of his own, the Rohan Master now developed into the most remarkable miniature painter of his day.

An artist of such perception cannot have been unaware of the new techniques of perspective and the new Renaissance spirit that were beginning to permeate art – qualities that, with his abilities, he could have mastered with ease. Instead he ignored them entirely. No man could have been further from the elegant, gay Gothic of the early fifteenth century. Rather, one might say, he was a Romanesque spirit born out of his due time. Jean Porcher has suggested that the Rohan Master may have been a Spaniard, and this is a very plausible hypothesis, for in addition to the character of his work, which, like that of so many Spanish artists,

OPPOSITE VII This thirteenth-century *Biblia Latina* was executed for Robertus de Bello, Abbot of Canterbury. The *Book of Genesis* opens with a long initial I containing the Seven Days of Creation, with six other scenes in roundels at the foot of the page.
British Museum, Burney MS 3.

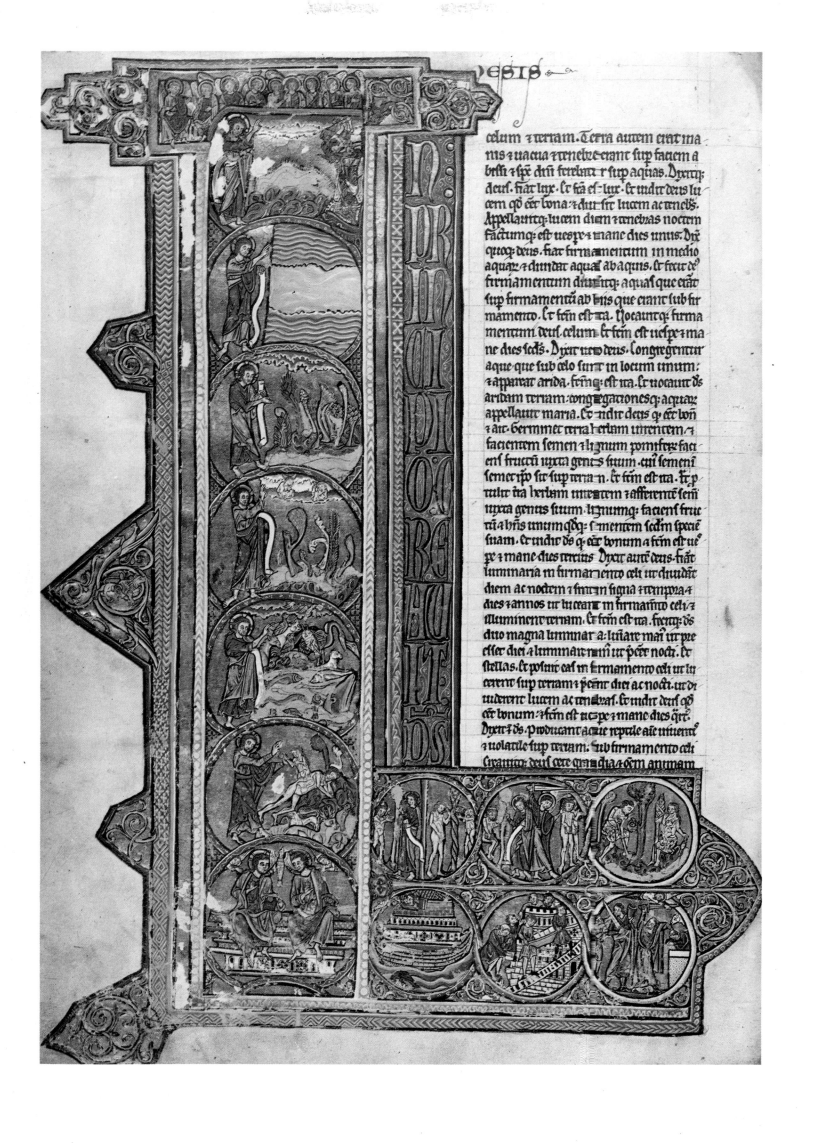

celum ⁊ terram. Terra autem erat ina-
nis ⁊ uacua ⁊ tenebre erant sup faciem a-
byssi ⁊ spc dei ferebatur sup aquas. Dixitq;
deus. fiat lux. Et fca est lux. Et uidit deus lucem qd eet bona ⁊ diuisit lucem ac tenebs.
Appellauitq; lucem diem ⁊ tenebras noctem
factumq; est uespe ⁊ mane dies unus. Dixit
quoq; deus. fiat firmamentum in medio
aquaꝝ ⁊ diuidat aquas ab aquis. Et fecit de
firmamentum diuisitq; aquas que erant
sup firmamentu ab hiis que erant sub firmamento. Et fcm est ita. Uocauitq; firma
mentum deus celum. Et fcm est uespe ⁊ ma
ne dies secds. Dixit uero deus. Congregent
aque que sub celo sunt in locum unum:
⁊ appareat arida. factumq; est ita. Et uocauit ds
aridam terram. congregationesq; aquaꝝ
appellauit maria. Et uidit deus q eet bon
⁊ ait. Germinet terra herbam uirentem ⁊
facientem semen ⁊ lignum pomifeꝝ faciens fructu iuxta gen⁊s suum. cui semeni
semetipo sit sup terra. Et fcm est ita. Et p-
tulit ita herbam uirentem ⁊ afferentem sem
iuxta genus suum. lignumq; faciens fructu ⁊ hns unumquodq; sementem secdm specie
suam. Et uidit ds q eet bonum ⁊ fcm est ue
spe ⁊ mane dies tercius. Dixit aut deus. fiat
luminaria in firmamento celi ut diuidat
diem ac noctem ⁊ sint in signa ⁊ tempora ⁊
dies ⁊ annos ut luceant in firmamto celi ⁊
illuminent terram. Et fcm est ita. fecitq; ds
duo magna luminar⁊a. lu̅iare mai ut pre
esset diei ⁊ luminare min ut preeet nocti. Et
stellas. Et posuit eas in firmamento celi ut lu
cerent sup terram ⁊ preeent diei ac nocti. ut di-
uiderent lucem ac tenebras. Et uidit deus q
eet bonum. ⁊ fcm est uespe ⁊ mane dies quartꝰ.
Dixit ⁊ ds. pducant aque reptile aie uiuentis
⁊ uolatile sup terram. sub firmamento celi
creauitq; deus cete grandia ⁊ oem anima

ARTIVM·AVRELI·CORNELI·CELSI·LIBER·
QVAE·RATIO·MEDICINE·POTISSIMA·SIT·
ET·QVEMADMODVM·SANOS·AGERE·CO̅
VENIAT·LIBER·PRIMVS·INCIPIT·FELICIS

T ALIMENTA SA
NIS CORPORIBVS
AGRICVLTVRA SIC
SANITATEM EGRIS
medicina promittit. Hactenusq; quidem no̅ est: si qui
dem etiam imperitissime
gentes herbas aliaq; promp
ta in auxilium uulnerum.
morboru̅q; nouerunt. Ve
rutamen apud grecos ali
quanto magis q̅ in ceteris nationibus exculta est: ac ne a
pud hos qdem a prima origine. sed paucis ante nos seculis
utpote cum uetustissimis auctoribus esculapius celebretur.
Qui quoniam ad hodiernam et uulgarem hanc scientiam pau
lo subtilius accessisset in deorum numeru̅ receptus est. Huius
deinde duo filij podalirius et machaon bello troiano ducem
Agamenonem sequuti non mediocrem opem co̅militonibus
suis adtulerunt. Quos tame̅ homerus non in pestilentia. ne
q; in uarijs generibus morborum aliquid adtulisse auxilij. sed
uulneribus tantu̅modo ferro et medicamentis mederi solitos
esse proposuit. Ex hoc apparet: has artes medicine solas ab
his esse probatas easq; esse uetustissimas. et deinq; auctore
disci potest. morbos tum ad iram deoru̅ immortalium rele

is obsessed with the fate of death that awaits us all, it seems likely that Yolanda would have been sympathetic to an artist of her own people.

The *Rohan Hours* (so named from the arms of a later owner, subsequently painted into the book) must have been executed in about 1418–25, probably for Yolanda's eldest son, who became Louis III, Duke of Anjou. In Figure 17 we see the Dead Man face to face with his Judge. The corpse is depicted with gaunt realism, thin and emaciated by suffering. The devil already bears away his soul to perpetual torment; but God the Father looks down with infinite compassion, prepared to forgive until seventy times seven – and beyond. The scroll from the dead lips reads: 'Into Thy Hands I Commend My Spirit', and not in vain, for the Archangel Raphael flies swiftly to the rescue, sword in hand.

With Figure 16 we pass from Gothic to Renaissance, from an artist obsessed by the next world to a cardinal very comfortable in this. This Book of Hours was executed for Bona of Savoy in about 1490, at which time she was the widow of Galeazzo Maria Sforza, Duke of Milan. St Gregory, one of the four historic Doctors of the Church, is seen as a Renaissance cardinal in a gorgeous setting, attended by elegant young acolytes, while as he writes the Holy Spirit (in the form of a dove) whispers divine wisdom into his ear. In all probability one of the illuminators was Gian Pietro Birago who, in a letter that has survived, speaks of an 'Officiol imperfecto' (the manuscript was completed only in later years and by different hands) on which he was working. Birago was also responsible for the border to the *Sforziada* [XII] executed for Bona's brother-in-law, Ludovico il Moro.

Before turning to printing we must retrace our steps to fourteenth-century Italy, where the momentum of the medieval spirit was beginning to lose its force and the best minds were turning for inspiration to the ancient world. This was the dawn of the Renaissance when Petrarch (1304–74) and other poets and Humanists were rediscovering the Greek and Latin classics that, during the later Middle Ages, stood forgotten on the monastic shelves. They eagerly copied these precious works for their own libraries. In so doing they would have dearly loved to write like 'the ancients' – if only a single example of Roman handwriting had survived. They hated reading classical texts in what they had come to regard as a barbarous gothic script. To them 'gothic' was a term of contempt – so they produced a new handwriting of their own. For the capitals they turned to Roman lapidary inscriptions, of which a wealth of examples lay all round them, and derived their lower case from the minuscule manuscripts of the School of Charlemagne.

The great majority of fine Humanist manuscripts were created under the patronage of popes, cardinals, Italian despots and so forth. However, one very remarkable Humanist library of the highest order was formed outside Italy by Matthias Corvinus, King of Hungary (1440–90).

Matthias ascended a very insecure throne in 1458, threatened by the magnates who were led by his uncle and guardian. By means of brilliant abilities and force of arms he not only secured his position but entered

OPPOSITE VIII Aulus Cornelius Celsus, a Roman of the first century AD, wrote an encyclopaedia of which only the medical section has survived. Nicknamed 'Cicero Medicorum', his style became a model during the Renaissance. This manuscript, written in Florence *c.* 1460–70 and illuminated in the 'white vine' style, bears the arms of Matthias Corvinus, King of Hungary. Munich, Bayerische Staatsbibliothek, Cod.Lat. 69.

16 The Holy Spirit, descending as a dove, whispers into the ear of St Gregory, last of the four great Doctors of the Church. He lived in the sixth century but is here depicted as a comfortable Renaissance cardinal in the *Hours of Bona of Savoy*, Duchess of Milan. Executed about 1490, but completed later. British Museum, Add. MS 34294.

therefore, are to be found in the great trading cities and, above all, in Venice. The Venetians had worked out banking systems, double-entry book-keeping and the technique of commerce at a time when most Britons were still living in mud huts. They had depots and agents everywhere and Venetian galleys made their way to all parts of the known world. Venice in the fifteenth century was not unlike England in her greater days: governed by an oligarchy, with traditions of independence and a comparative freedom from the Inquisition that favoured the expression of thought. Here printing first really developed as a business, and about 150 presses had been founded in the city by 1500. The first men to work in Venice were John and Wendelin of Speier, who set up in 1469. In order to satisfy the demands of the Humanists they produced the first really satisfactory roman type. However, the most important for our purpose were two printers of genius: Jenson and Aldus.

Nicolaus Jenson, a Frenchman born near Troyes, is the first really important printer who was not a German. As Master of the Royal Mint (once again the connection with metalwork) he was sent to Mainz, in secret by his king, to spy on the secrets of the new invention of printing. That was in 1458; after which we lose sight of him until he set up on his own in 1470 at Venice, where he continued to print until his death, ten years later.

Although Jenson's was not the first Humanist type, it is by far the best. Each letter is beautiful in itself, but not *too* perfect (absolute perfection sometimes results in deadness) and, what is far more important and difficult to achieve, the letters combine well to produce a harmonious whole. This type has been the admiration of printers ever since, and those who have sought to revive printing in later days have often turned to it for inspiration. It is to be found in a considerable number of books, but by general consensus the Pliny of 1472 is regarded as Jenson's masterpiece. It is hard to believe that such perfection was a prentice effort. In the twelve years between 1458 and 1470 Jenson may have designed types for others, but of these dark years we know nothing [20].

Jenson was primarily a craftsman of genius. Aldus Manutius, a scholar with a passion for the classics of Greece and Rome, was consumed by a desire to produce accurate texts and to put them into as many hands as possible. Born in 1450 at Bassiano near Velletri, Aldus studied at Rome under two famous scholars, Gaspar of Verona and Domizio Calderini. From 1482 to 1484 he was the guest of Count Pico della Mirandola, the brilliant champion of Florentine Platonism, who filled his house with scholars who had fled from Greece. The friendship of this noble family brought unforeseen advantages and proved a major factor in the life of Aldus, for he was appointed tutor to Pico's nephews, Albertus and Leonellus Pius, Princes of Carpi. He so inspired these pupils with his own enthusiasm for the classics that in later years the elder, Albertus, provided the money with which to found the Aldine Press.

There was no rush to get into print. In 1490 an academy of scholars was founded in Venice, manuscripts were collected and collated, the best possible texts were prepared. The first books came out in 1494.

By that time many of the Latin classics were already in print; therefore the majority of Aldus's first books were in Greek. In the course of his career he printed the first Greek editions of Aristophanes, Aristotle, and then, from 1502 onwards, of Thucydides, Aeschylus, Sophocles, Plato, Demosthenes, Herodotus and Pindar. No other publisher has ever made such a staggering contribution to the human spirit.

The first half of his ambition had been nobly achieved, but these books, like the great majority of contemporary publications, were large and expensive to buy. Aldus next revolutionized publishing itself: he produced the pocket edition. In place of the stately folios, fit for the library of a cardinal, he printed small books, half a dozen of which would pack into the saddle-bag of a wandering scholar. In order to do this he commissioned an entirely new type, an italic based on the chancery hand used by the Vatican scribes. The first small book in the new type

CAIVS PLYNIVS SECVNDVS NOVOCOMENSIS DOMITIANO
SVO SALVTEM.   PRAEFATIO.

IBROS NATVRALIS HISTORIAE NO
uitium camœnis quiritium tuorum opus natum
apud me proxima fœtura licentiore epistola nar
rare constitui tibi iucundissime imperator. Sit.n.
hæc tui præfatio uerissima:dum maxio cösenescit
in patre. Náq; tu solebas putare esse aliqd meas
nugàs:ut obicere moliar Catullum conterraneu
meum. Agnoscis & hoc castrése uerbum. Ille eni
ut scis:permutatis prioribus syllabis duriusculu
se fecit:q uolebat existimari a uernaculis tuis:&
famulis. Simul ut hac mea petulätia fiat:quod
proxime nö fieri questus es:i alia procaci episto
la nostra:ut in quædam acta exeät. Sciantq; omnes:q ex æquo tecum uiuat impium.
Triumphalis & censorius tu sextumque consul ac tribuniciæ potestatis particeps. Et
quod iis nobilius fecisti:dü illud patri pariter & equestri ordini præstas præfectus præ
torii eius:omniaq; hæc reipub. Et nobis quidem qualis in castrési contubernio? Nec
quicq mutauit in te fortunæ amplitudo in iis:nisi ut prodesse tantundem posses: &
uelles. Itaq; cum cæteris in ueneratione tui pateant omnia illa:nobis ad colendum te
familiarius audacia sola superest. Hanc igitur tibi imputabis:& in nostra culpa tibi
ignosces. Perfricui faciem:nec tamen profeci. Quando alia uia occurris ingens. Et
longius etiam submoues ingenii facibus. Fulgurat in nullo unq uerius dicta uis elo
quentiæ. Tibi tribuniciæ potestatis facüdia. Quäto tu ore patris laudes tonas? Quä
to fratris amas? Quantus in poetica es? O magna fœcunditas animi. Quéadmodü
fratrem quoq; imitareris:excogitasti. Sed hæc quis posset intrepidus æstimare:subi
turus ingenii tui iudicium:præsertim lacessitum? Neque enim similis est conditio
publicantium:& nominatim tibi dicantium. Tum possem dicere:quid ista legis im
perator? Humili uulgo scripta sunt: agricolarum: opificum turbæ: deniq; studioru
ociosis. Quid te iudicem facis? Cum hanc operam condicerem:non eras in hoc albo.
Maiorem te sciebam:q ut descensurum huc putarem. Præterea est quædam publica
etiam eruditorum reiectio. Vtitur illa &.M. Tullius extra omnem ingenii aleam po
situs. Et quod miremur:per aduocatum deféditur. Hæc doctissimum omniü Persiü
legere nolo. Lælium Decimum uolo. Quod si hoc Lucillius qui primus cödidit stili
nasum:dicédum sibi putauit. Si Cicero mutuandü:præsertim cum de repub.scribe
ret:quanto nos causatius ab aliquo iudice deffidimur? Sed hæc ego mihi nunc patro
cinia ademi nuncupatione. Quáplurimü refert:sortiatur ne aliquis indicé:an eligat.
Multumque apparatus interest apud inuitatum hospitem & oblatum. Cum apud
Catonem illum ambitus hostem:& repulsis tanquam honoribus ineptis gaudentem:
flagrantibus comitiis pecunias deponerent candidati:hoc se facere:pro inocétia:quod
in rebus humanis summü esset:profitebat. Inde illa nobilis.M.Ciceronis suspiratio.
O te fœlicem.M.Porti a quo rem improbam petere nemo audet. Cum tribunos ap
pellaret.L.Scipio Asiaticus:iter quos erat Gracchus:hoc attestabat:uel inimico iudici
se approbare posse. Adeo summum quisq; causæ suæ iudicem facit:quécunq; eligit:
Vnde prouocatio appellatur. Te quidem in excelsissimo humani generis fastigio po
situm summa eloquentia summa eruditione præditum religiose adiri etiam a salutä
tibus scio. Et ideo immensa præter cæteras subit cura ut quæ tibi dicätur:cum digna

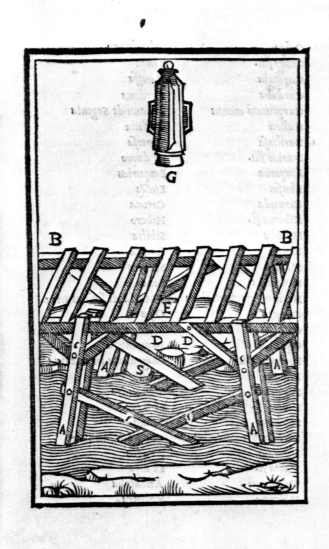

Libro quarto.

Pontem, eadem forma & ratione, bis fecit Cæsar supra
Rhenum flumen latissimum, rapidissimum, & al=
tissimum, Primum in Menapijs contra Sicambros.
Deinde paululū supra eum locum in finibus Treui
rorū, ex quo trāsitus erat ad Vbios Cæsaris amicos·

a Tigna bina sesquipedalia paulum ab imo præacu-
ta dimensa ad altitudinem fluminis. & c.

b Trabes bipedales immissæ super utraq; tigna, quæ
binis utrinq; fibulis ab extrema pte distinebantur.

c Fibulæ quæ disclusæ distinent bipedales trabes.

d Vbi fibulæ disclusæ in contrariā pte reuinciūtur·

e Materia directa, quæ iniecta supra bipedales trabes totum opus contexebat.

f Sublicæ obliquæ ad inferiorem partem fluminis ad
actæ, quæ pro ariete subiectæ, & cum omnia opere
coniunctæ, uim fluminis exciperent·

g Fistuca, qua adigebantur tigna in flumine.

Hæc utraq; insuper bipedalibus trabibus immis
sis· Hunc locum sic corrigendum puto· Hæc utraq;
insuper, bipedales trabes immissæ, hac ratione, ut
insuper sit præpositio, & hæc utraq; sit accusandi
casus. Quod si duriusculum hoc quisquam existima
rit, sciat Cæsarem ipsum simul usum constructione
in secundo de bello ciuili in expugnatione Massiliæ
his uerbis· Hanc insuper contignationem, quantum
tectum plutei, ac uinearum passim est, laterculo
astruxerunt, sciat et Vitruuium in quinto, ubi agit de

was the Virgil of 1501 and this was followed by a high proportion of the classics [21 and 22].

The Aldine italic was cut by Francesco Griffi. In general we know very little about the early craftsmen and designers, but Griffi emerges from the prevailing anonymity because he hit his son-in-law over the head with an iron bar, and killed him. For this very understandable act he was hanged in Bologna in 1518. He seems to have been a somewhat irascible character who quarrelled with Aldus as well as his son-in-law, and in 1503 he claimed to have designed *all* of the Aldine types.

In 1515, at the funeral of Aldus, the mourning Humanists piled round him, as he lay in state, the books he had printed and to which he had devoted his life.

William Caxton, the first English printer, born in Kent in about 1422, spent a great part of his life in Bruges working as a merchant and 'governor of the English colony' – a kind of consul. He was one of that

21 Aldus Manutius, the greatest scholar-printer, was the first to publish 'pocket editions' of the great classics for which he created italic type. This is his Caesar of 1519, with the bridge over the Rhine – the terror of generations of schoolboys.

OPPOSITE 20 This *Natural History* of Pliny was printed by Jenson in Venice in 1472 in type which is often considered the most beautiful ever designed and which has had the greatest effect on the modern revival of fine printing. British Museum.

F elice faffo, che'l bel uifo ferra :
Che poi c'haura riprefo il fuo bel uelo;
Se fu beato, chi la uide in terra;
H or che fia dunque a riuederla in cielo ?

Impreffo in Vinegia nelle cafe d'Aldo Romano,
nel anno . M D I . del mefe di Luglio, et tolto con
fommiffima diligenza dallo fcritto di mano me
defima del Poeta, hauuto da M . Piero Bembo
Con la conceffione della Illuftriffima fi
gnoria noftra , che per . x . anni
neffuno poffa ftampare il
Petrarcha fotto le
pene, che in lei
fi conten
gono .

ABOVE 22 The Aldine Petrarch (1501), one of the first books to be printed in italic type. The long-standing misconception that italic is based on the handwriting of Petrarch stems from this colophon '. . . *tolto con sommissima diligenza dallo scritto di mano medesima del Poeta*', which really means that the *text* is transcribed from a manuscript in the poet's hand.
RIGHT 23 *The Dictes or Sayengis of the Philosophers*, the first book to be printed in England by William Caxton at Westminster (1477).

BELOW 24 Before the introduction of the title-page printers signed their books in a colophon at the end of the volume, often with a woodcut device. This, the first, was used by Fust and Schoeffer from 1462.

sympathetic type, not unknown in English life, the sensitive man of affairs who devotes his leisure to literature; he was akin to Chaucer, who for the greater part of his life worked as a civil servant. Encouraged by his patron, Margaret of Burgundy, sister of Edward IV, Caxton translated Raoul le Fèvre's *Recuyell of the Hystoryes of Troye*. The picture of Troy that filled the minds of Le Fèvre and Caxton was probably like Bruges itself, a medieval walled city, with belfries and red tiled roofs.

Caxton's translation was a great success among the English colony and his friends clamoured for copies. 'And for as moche as in the wrytyng of the same my penne is worn,' he says, 'myn hand wery and not stedfast, myn eyen dimmed with overmoche lokyng on the whit paper. . . .' There was only one way out of this impasse, a rather desperate one: he went to Cologne and learned how to print. On returning to Bruges he set up his own press, starting with *The Hystoryes of Troye* (1474), the first book to be printed in English. In the autumn of 1476 he crossed into

England, rented premises in Westminster and set up his press where, in 1477, he printed *The Dictes or Sayengis of the Philosophers* [23].

Caxton was one of the first men other than a German to introduce printing into a new country. It must be admitted that his technical abilities were not as high or his types as beautiful as those of his continental *confrères*; his interests and abilities lay in another direction. Nearly all the other first printers were craftsmen primarily interested in printing itself, or businessmen interested in making money. Caxton was a man of letters who would be remembered for his services to English literature even if he had never printed at all. Of the 103 editions known to have been printed by him, twenty were in his own translations. He printed the first editions of Lydgate, Malory [248] and Chaucer and many books contain prefaces in his vivid and racy style.

Since the idea of a title-page had not yet been conceived, information regarding the name of the printer, the place of printing and other data was given in the colophon, a final paragraph that is generally found at the end of the text or the end of the book. In 1462 Fust and Schoeffer began to sign their work regularly with a woodcut printer's device consisting of two shields with their respective coats of arms hanging from a bough and printed near the colophon [24]. This was a development of the medieval merchant's mark with which other craftsmen had long put a seal on their own work. Many printers followed suit and the resulting wealth of woodcut designs forms an attractive feature of early printing. Aldus, too, had his printer's device, perhaps the most famous of them all. It was based on a coin of the Roman Emperor Titus, given to him by Cardinal Bembo; the dolphin and anchor symbolize Aldus's motto, 'Hasten Slowly'. Figures 25 and 26 show the first state of this device with the border that was subsequently cut away. Caxton's device [27] consists of his initials surrounded by a little elementary decoration.

The printing of individual woodblocks preceded the production of books by means of movable types. Textile printing had been established in Egypt by the sixth century AD, while the Chinese used block printing by the eighth century. In addition to the decoration of textiles, European craftsmen produced individual pictures and playing-cards during the fourteenth century. There are references to playing-card manufacture in the German cities of Ulm and Augsburg, which afterwards became famous for book illustration, while in 1430 a Florentine artist, filling in his income-tax returns, mentions the woodblocks from which he printed playing-cards.

During the fourteenth century there had been a great increase in pilgrimages. Woodcut pictures of the saints were on sale at favoured shrines, and no doubt Chaucer's Wife of Bath collected quite a batch of these in the course of her peregrinations. One of the finest woodcut portraits of a saint, and the first to bear a date, 1423, depicts St Christopher carrying the Christ Child across a river. Only one example has survived, pasted into a manuscript written in 1417, which was once in the Charterhouse at Buxheim and is now preserved in the John Rylands

TOP 25 The device of Aldus, the dolphin and anchor, symbolizes his motto 'Hasten Slowly'. Here it is in the first state, before the border was cut away, from *Poetae Christiani* (1501).
ABOVE 26 The second state of the Aldine device from *Valerius Maximus* (1502).
BELOW 27 William Caxton's bold initials sufficed to sign the first books printed in England.

Cristofori faciem die quacunque tueris·
Illa nempe die morte mala non morieris·
Millesimo cccc°
xx° anno·

44

Library, Manchester. As will be seen in Figure 28, this has two lines of text that are an integral part of the woodcut itself and are therefore not printed from types:

Christofori faciem die quacunque tueris
Illa nempe die morte mala non morieris
[with the date 1423].
(On whatsoever day you see the face of Christopher,
On that day you will not die an evil death.)

Observe the cunning of this wording, which has something in common with all soothsayers from the Delphic oracle to modern clairvoyants and astrologers. Supposing a purchaser of the woodcut, having looked upon St Christopher, died the same day, the reply to any irate widow would be: 'But I feel quite sure your husband did not die an *evil* death.'

It was an obvious step from printing single pages with a little text to the production of rudimentary books in which each page, containing both text and illustrations, was printed from a single woodblock. A handful of these early block-books has survived, the dating of which has been a matter for more or less scholarly conjecture and discussion since the history of printing first became an object of study, and many learned monographs and essays have been written with varying conclusions. The problem has recently been solved beyond doubt, by Allan Stevenson. He has shown, by accurately dating the paper used in block-books, that the first edition of the earliest of these, the *Apocalypse*, appeared towards 1451 (a little before the Gutenbergian *Indulgences* of 1454, which are the earliest known type-printed pieces), while the earliest editions of the *Biblia Pauperum* and *Ars Moriendi* were produced towards 1462 and 1466 respectively.

The public at whom the block-books were aimed is sufficiently shown by the title later invented for one of them: *Biblia Pauperum, The Bible of the Poor*. In this book parallel incidents from the Old and New Testaments are placed side by side in order to illustrate spiritual truths. Thus in Figure 30 the Entombment is flanked by Joseph being dropped into the well and Jonah being thrown to the whale. All three are good men being dropped (as it seems) into the jaws of death, from which all three will rise again. The verse reads: '*Jonas glutitur/tamen illesus reperitur*' ('Jonah is swallowed yet found again unharmed') – a Leonine hexameter with internal rhymes. This form of versifying calls for a degree of ingenuity (hardly justified by the generally ugly results) that is equalled only by the tortuous parallels of medieval sermonizing. In Figure 29 the Crucifixion is shown between Abraham about to sacrifice Isaac and being restrained in the nick of time by the angel and Moses with the brazen serpent saving his people from real serpents *(Numbers* xxi), as examples of God's mercy at the brink of death to those who obey him. Here the verses read: '*Eruit a tristi/barathro nos passio Christi*' ('Christ's Passion raises us from the dismal abyss') and: '*Lesi curantur/ serpentem dum speculantur*' ('The wounded are healed when they look upon the serpent').

OPPOSITE 28 St Christopher bears the Christ Child safely across a river in the earliest woodcut portrait of a saint to be dated, 1423. This, the only surviving example, is in the John Rylands Library in Manchester.

OVERLEAF 29 and 30 Before the invention of movable types a few rudimentary books were produced in which text and illustrations were cut on the same block of wood. The *Biblia Pauperum* consists of parallel incidents in the Old and New Testaments from which moral lessons could be drawn.

with vigorous little figures of Biblical characters surrounded by well-drawn foliage [x].

It has been remarked that the railway timetables in Burgundy read like a wine catalogue. For the bibliophile, as he drives along the auto-bahn through Western Germany, the signposts might almost be the index to a library of incunabula: Cologne, Mainz, Bamberg, Nuremberg, Augsburg and Ulm. Ulm was another city that produced remarkable woodcut books, a city already noted, as mentioned above, for the production of playing-cards. It is rather sad to have to record that the Ulm printers did not meet with much worldly success. Perhaps they had more difficulty in distributing their books, since Ulm was a less powerful commercial city than Augsburg, and printing there lacked a powerful patron like Melchior von Stamhaim. Moreover the city was cursed by frequent visitations of the plague. Yet all these troubles did not in any way prevent Johann Zainer (a kinsman of Günther's) from producing some of the best of all woodcut books, especially Boccaccio, *De Claris Mulieribus* (1473) and Aesop, *Vita et Fabulae* (1476–77), both works lending themselves admirably to illustration, as can be seen from the picture reproduced here [34]. Johann Zainer's books are remarkable for their borders and initials decorated with curling leafy sprays drawn with remarkable vigour and sense of design. Two hundred years later they were to influence Morris when he drew the decorations for the Kelmscott Press.

Once the production of illustrated books had been throughly mastered it was natural that printers should turn their attention to the Bible, and particularly to those editions printed in the vernacular; the first Bible in the German language had been produced in Strassburg in 1466. Lay readers, especially those fired by the already dawning Reformation, were more likely than the clergy to have an appetite for pictures, and especially pictures of Old Testament stories. It is not surprising, therefore, that the most influential of all illustrated Bibles, that printed at Cologne in

OPPOSITE ABOVE LEFT IX The Gutenberg Bible, the first book printed with movable types (Mainz 1455) with the illuminated decorations added by hand.
British Museum.
OPPOSITE ABOVE RIGHT X Woodcut initial coloured by hand from the Bible printed in German by Günther Zainer at Augsburg (1475).
OPPOSITE BELOW XI The decorated initial of the 'Beatus page' is printed in red and blue in the Psalter of Fust and Schoeffer (Mainz 1457).

RIGHT 34 Boccaccio's stories of famous women are transformed by the Gothic conception of the German artist in this edition of *De Claris Mulieribus* printed by Johann Zainer (Ulm 1473).

Frater ambrosius tua michi munuscula perferens detulit simul et suauissimas litteras: que a principio amicicias fide probate iam fidei et veteris amicicie preferebant. Vera eni illa necessitudo est et xpi glutino copulata: qua non vtilitas rei familiaris non presencia tantu corpm no subdola et palpas adulacio: sed dei timor et diuinaru scripturaru studia conciliant. Legim in veteribz historijs quosdam lustrasse puincias nouos adijsse ppls maria transisse: vt eos quos ex libris nouerant coram qz viderent. Sic pitagoras memphiticos vates sic plato egiptum et architam tarentinu: eamqz oram ytalie que quonda magna grecia dicebat: laboriosissime peragrauit: et vt qui athenis mgr erat et potens: cuiusqz doctrinas achademie gignasia psonabant: fieret peregrinus atqz discipulus: malens aliena verecunde discere: qm sua impudenter ingerere. Deniqz cum litteras quasi toto orbe fugientes persequitur captus a piratis et venudatus: tyranno crudelissimo paruit: ductus captiuus vinctus et seruus: tamen quia philosophus maior emente se fuit: ad tytumliuiu lacteo eloquentie fonte manantem de vltimis hispanie galliarumqz finibus quosdam venisse nobiles legimus: et quos ad contemplacionem sui roma non traxerat: vnius hominis fama perduxit. Habuit illa etas inauditum omnibus seculis: celebranduqz miraculum: vt vrbem tantam ingressi: aliud extra vrbem quererent. Apollonius siue ille magus vt vulgus loquitur: siue phus vt pitagorici tradunt: intrauit plas: pcrtrasiuit caucasum albanos scithas massagetas opulentissima indie regna penetrauit: et ad extremum latissimo physon amne transmisso venit ad bragmanas: vt hyarcam in throno sedentem aureo et de tantali fonte potantem: inter paucos discipulos de natura de moribus ac de cursu dieru et sideru audiret docentem. Inde per elamitas babilonios chaldeos medos assirios parthos syros phenices arabes palestinos reuersus ad alexandria: perrexit ad ethiopiam: vt gignosophistas et famosissimam solis mensam videret in sabulo. Inuenit ille vir vbiqz quod disceret: et semp proficiens semper se melior fieret. Scripsit super hoc plenissime octo voluminibus phylostratus.

Quid loquar de seculi hominibz: cum apostolus paulus vas electionis et magister gentium: qui de consciencia tanti in se hospitis loquebatur dicens. An experimentum queritis eius qui in me loquitur cristus: post damascum arabiaqz lustratam: ascendit iherosolima vt videret petru et mansit apud eum diebus quindecim. Hoc enim misterio ebdomadis et ogdoadis: futurus gentium predicator instruendus erat. Rursumqz post annos quatuordecim assumpto barnaba et tyto: exposuit cum apostolis euangelium: ne forte in vacuum curreret aut cucurrisset. Habet nescio quid latentis energie viue vocis actus: et in aures discipuli de auctoris ore transfusa: fortius sonat. Vnde et eschines cum rodi exularet: et legeret illa demostenis

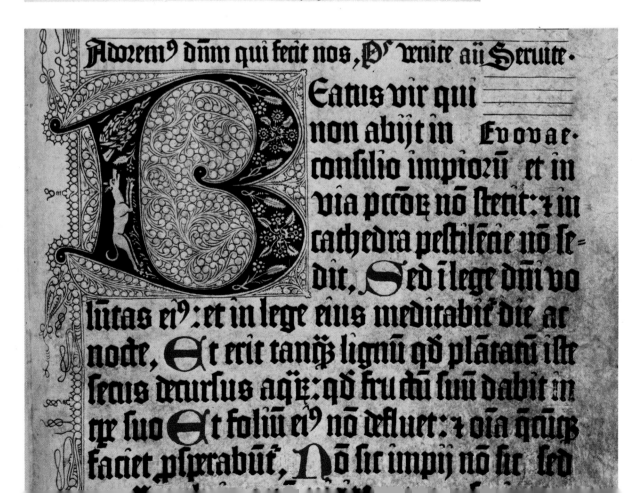

LIBRO PRIMO DELLA HISTORIA DELLE COSE FACTE DALLO INVICTISSIMO DVCA FRANCESCO SFORZA SCRIPTA IN LATINO DA GIOVANNI SIMONETTA ET TRADOCTA IN LINGVA FIORENTINA DA CHRISTOPHORO LANDINO FIORENTINO.

FRAN. SFOR. VIC
DVX
M II II

PATER PATRIAE

NE TEMPI CHE LA REGINA GIOVANNA SEconda figliuola di Carlo Re regnaua:perche era succeduta nel regno Neapolitano a Latislao Re suo fratello:elquale parti di uita sanza figliuoli:Alphonso Re daragona con grande armata mouendo di Catalogna uenne in Sicilia: Isola di suo Imperio. La cui uenuta excito gli huomini del Neapolitano regno a uarii fauori:& a diuersi consigli:& non con piccoli mouimenti di quel regno:Impero che Giouana Regina per molti & uarii suoi impudichi amori era caduta in soma infamia. Et desperandosi che lei femina potessi adempiere lofficio del Re:& administrare tanto regno:fece a se marito Iacopo di Nerbona Conte di Marcia:elquale per nobilita di sangue:& belleza di corpo:ne meno per uirtu era tra Principi di Francia excellente. Ma accorgendosi in breue che quello desideraua piu essere Re: che marito:& quella non molto stimaua:mosso da feminile leuita lo rifiuto:& priuo dogni administratice. Questo fu cagione chel suo regno:elquale per sua natura e prono alle dissensioni & discordie:arrogendouisi e nö honesti costumi della Regina: ritorno nelle antiche factioni & partialita:& comincio ogni giorno piu a fluctuare & uacillare.Erano alcuni a quali nö dispiaceua la signoria della döna:perche benche il nome fussi in lei:loro nientedi meno comädauono.Altri desiderauano che Lodouico tertio Duca dangio: figliuolo di Lodouico elquale era nomato Re di Puglia:& di uiolante nata della Reale stirpe daragonia:fussi adoptato dalla Regina.Costui poco auäti pe conforti di Martino tertio sömo Pontefice:& di Sforza Attendolo excellentissimo Duca in militare disciplina: & padre di Francesco sforza de cui egregii facti habbiamo a scriuere era uenuto a liti di Campagna:Et cögiuntosi Sforza:hauea mosso guerra alla Regina. Ma quegli che repugnauano a Lodouicho:metteuano ogni industria: che Alphonio fussi adoptato in figliuolo della Reina: accio che in Napoli fussi tal Re:che con le sue forze & di mare & di terra potessi resistere alla possa de Franciosi. Adunque in cosi uehemëte contentione de baroni:& piu huomini del regno:Alphonso chiamato dalla Reina in herede & compagno del regno:diuene nö solo illustre: ma anchora horribile: Et el nome Catelano elquale insino a quegli tempi nö era molto noto & celebre se non a popoli maritimi:ma inuiso & odioso: comincio a crescere: & farsi chiaro. Ma & da Lodouico & da Sforza tanto ogni giorno piu erono oppressi:el Re & la Regina:che diffidädosi nelle proprie forze: conduxono Braccio Perugino: elquale era el secondo Capitano di militia in Italia in quegli tëpi cö molte honoreuoli cöditioni:& maxime

1478 by Heinrich Quentell, was produced in two editions, each in a different German dialect. By means of river transport up and down the Rhine Cologne was in constant touch with the Low Countries, and this may account for the striking Netherlandish quality of the woodcuts in this famous book. Alternatively, the artist may have copied a manuscript of this type [35].

Few German woodcut books are better known than the *Nuremberg Chronicle,* printed by Anton Koberger in 1493. This large folio contains woodcuts illustrating the Bible, ecclesiastical and other history, topography, maps and views of towns. There are actually 645 different blocks, but as these are repeated at intervals the total is swelled to 1,809 pictures. Naturally there can be no claim to individual portraiture, the same cut being used again and again to depict different bishops or saints. The large double-page pictures of cities bear considerable resemblance to reality and are only used once, but twenty-two other blocks of cities and countries are repeated to represent sixty-nine different places. These blocks were produced by Michel Wolgemut (who was Dürer's master) and Wilhelm Pleydenwurff. They vary in merit, but some of them are of considerable quality. Nevertheless the great variety of size ensures that there is very little balance of pages or consistency of style. One feels that this is a commercial or made-up book, the first *édition de luxe,* giving rich burgher customers the greatest possible value for their money [36].

Koberger founded an immense, well-organized and successful

ABOVE 35 The most influential of all early Bible illustrations appear in the edition printed in Cologne by Heinrich Quentell (*c.* 1478). This one is from the *Book of Judith.*

OPPOSITE XII The *Sforziada* is a glorious tribute to the ruling family of Milan. What at first appears to be an illuminated manuscript is a printed text on vellum lavishly illuminated by hand. Dibdin called this 'the loveliest of membranaceous bijoux'.
British Museum.

business. He kept twenty-five presses and a hundred pressmen working simultaneously, while other printers produced books for him on commission and he had agents and commercial outlets everywhere.

The German Humanist Sebastian Brant (1457–1521) satirized the follies of his time, indeed of all times, in his *Narrenschiff (The Ship of Fools)*, (first edition in German, Basle 1494; first Latin edition, *Stultifera Navis*, Basle 1497). Fifteen editions were called for by the end of the century and much of the success was due to the delightful and vigorous woodcuts. Many leading authorities believe these to be by Albrecht Dürer, an attribution discussed by A. M. Hind in *A History of the Woodcut* (1935).

The Ship of Fools laden with and steered by fools, sails to the Fools' Paradise of Narragonia. With a few timely additions, it might well sail today [37]. All manner of folly is depicted. In Figure 38, for example, we observe the irate building workers taking leave of a patron who, having ordered a building beyond his means, is unable to complete it or pay them.

Considering the enthusiasm with which the religious public supported illustrated Bibles and lives of the Saints and Fathers, one might have expected the Italian Humanists to demand similar editions of the

OPPOSITE 36 The *Nuremberg Chronicle* (Koberger 1493) contains 645 different woodcuts swollen by repetition to 1,809 pictures. This one shows Adam and Eve.

37 and 38 The German Humanist, Sebastian Brant, satirized the follies of mankind in his *Narrenschiff* (*The Ship of Fools*) (1494). On the left, the fools set sail for the Fools' Paradise, Narragonia; on the right, irate building workers take leave of a patron who has ordered a building beyond his means and is unable to pay them.

FOLIO

Nauis focialis mechanicorum.

XXVI

De fatuis edificandi incœptibus.
Qui vult nunc edificare:
Et quid magnum attentare:
Sumptus debet penfitare:
Quibus poffit hoc parare.

De fatuis edificandi inceptibuf

Quifquis opus magnū tentat cōponere: fumptus   xxii. q. ii. fa ciat
Antea nec reputat: nec tempus cōputat ipfum:
Eft fatuus plane. fapiens vero extruit illud
Quod potis eft: tentatqʒ nihil quod ferre recufent   d. ii.

ABOVE 39 Fearsome military engines, such as this mobile siege-engine designed by Robertus Valturius, may be seen in his *De Re Militari* (Verona 1472).
BELOW 40 The profession of medicine has never been more nobly depicted than in the woodcuts (sometimes even attributed to Mantegna) which illustrate Ketham's *Fascicolo di Medicina* (1493).

classics. Surely the *Iliad* or the *Odyssey* could inspire pictures as charming as anything in *Genesis,* and what grave and noble woodcuts depicting Roman heroes might have been produced by the pupils of Mantegna! But the fifteenth century brought forth no illustrated Homer because the austere, not to say pedantic, nature of the Humanists considered illustrated books to be almost vulgar, unworthy of the *gravitas* of the ancients.

On the contrary, the first Italian book to be illustrated with woodcuts was of a severely practical nature, Robertus Valturius (1413–84), *De Re Militari* (Verona 1472). This work was written at the court of, and dedicated to, Sigismondo Malatesta, perhaps the most fascinating combination of culture and cruelty that even the Italian Renaissance could produce. It combines wide knowledge of military science among the ancients with practical experience in the fifteenth century, and is illustrated by eighty-two large woodcuts [39]. In some ways Valturius was a precursor of Leonardo da Vinci in that he designed all manner of war machines, submarines and even rudimentary tanks of an ingenuity far beyond anything previously conceived. Leonardo is known to have possessed a copy of Valturius, for it appears in the autograph list of his books, and he imitated some of its designs.

The genius that Venetian artists could bring to bear on a book may be seen in the woodcuts that illustrate Johannes de Ketham, *Fascicolo di Medicina* (Venice 1493–94) [40]. Surely no other textbook has ever achieved such grave dignity. Artist and engraver have combined to catch the finest spirit of a noble profession. We know hardly any more about the artists who designed book illustrations than we know about the men who illuminated manuscripts, but such important authorities as A. M. Hind and Friedrich Lippmann considered that the Ketham woodcuts might have been designed by Mantegna or Gentile Bellini.

Two books printed in Ferrara are notable for their illustrations. The *Epistles of St Jerome,* printed by Laurentius de Rubeis (1497), opens with a fine woodcut border and a picture of the saint seated in a Renaissance study. But the main attraction of the book lies in the series of small woodcuts depicting incidents in the life of the saint. The artist must have been a man with a considerable sense of humour, which he expresses through St Jerome's lion, who often sits unnoticed in a corner looking on with an expression that leaves little doubt of his feelings: he is bored, sceptical, warmly approving or angry as the occasion demands. Later in the book a series of cuts depicting the lives of nuns give a vivid insight into fifteenth-century conventual life. In one illustration an earnest group is busily engaged in burning scientific textbooks, '*De la vanita de la scientia mundiale',* while in another three sisters, stripped to the waist and kneeling by the altar, passively await the cat-o'-nine tails about to be wielded by their superior [41 and 42].

The other Ferrara book, *De Claris Mulieribus,* 1497, by Jacobus Philippus Foresti (Bergomensis), a history of famous women throughout the ages, is illustrated with a series of portraits. The woodcuts, which portray women from ancient times, have no more claim to accuracy, of

do o ueio e concupifcentia di occhii o cōcupifcentia di carne .o fuperbia di uita per cioche in tale modo gli fimplici & humili cuori fi acoftauano a le ueftigie de la obedientia & d̄ la humilita che quafi pareua effere uerifichata in loro la oppinione de alcuni philofophi gli quali ponghono neli huomini una anima fola. Percioche gli abbati & padri niente al poftuto fapeuano uolere fe non quello che gli fubditi & gli fubditi innanzi fi sforzauano di adimpire gli commandamenti che fuffeno proferti & in alcuno modo per certi inditii fi sforzaueno di prophetare de la uolunta del commandante.

De la uanita de la fcientia mundiale:

Capitulo .xi.

Sancta ftoltitia laq̄le gli huoi nati ale fatiche nel mūdo meriti di trāfportare ala gloria tratti d̄ le pene.quefta doctiffima ftulticia non iparo plato ad athene:nō Ariftotile :nō anaxagora:non la turba de gli altri ftolti fauii del mundo la comprefe :nō certo io mifero Hieronymo feguitatore de ftulti fauii innāzi che io patiffe le fancte batiture benche la citta Romana acciocb̄ io fcopra lemie miferie:innā ci che io fuffe peruenuto al uigefimo anno dela mia eta me haueffe electo in fuo maeftro quafi in tutte le arte liberali.nō ancho ra haueua intraro le fcuole del fancto fpirito : non anchora io ciecho ero potuto per uenire ala difciplina de la fancta uerita .nō

in achademia :non certo in Roma rifonarono gli ftudii di quefta docta ftoltitia li quali el fancto heremo ritiene :ueramente non fenza faticha imparafti la tua ftolta fapiētia o plato elq̄le el mōdo nō poteua ritenere perfeguitante la fapientia del mundo per parti di diuerfe natione & genti & regioni cō infinite neceffita & innumerabili fatiche difcorrendo:nientemeno non fapefti trouare in tutto elmundo el fine dela ftoltiffima fapientia elquale e il fummo bene & alquale la intentione dela natura ti moueua elquale quefti fancti ruftici.quefta fu gendo trouarono nafcofti ne gli heremi.at tendi anchora tu o p̄incipe de ftolti fauii Ariftotile fe tu anchora fe ftato fenza dubitatione uno monftro & grande miraculo in tutta la natura alquale quafi pare infufo tutto ciò di che e capace la humana gene ratione.perciò che la fapientia del mundo e ftultitia apreffo adio.Se la carita non la informa fe lo intellecto non e riducto ala fede.   Se ilcuore ala feruitu di chrifto non e inclinato.ilquale a iudei e fcandalo a pagani ftulticia.ma anui credenti honore & gloria.nelquale folamente la poftolo fi gloria dicendo .chi fi gloria nel fignore fi glorii.

De la prontitudine di adimpire gli commandamenti impofti.

Capitulo.xii.

L iii

course, than those in the *Nuremberg Chronicle,* but several women contemporary with the book are actually depicted from life. This precedent is all the more interesting because the ladies in question come from the little courts that formed so fascinating a feature of Renaissance life [43].

The most important Florentine woodcut book is the *Epistole e Evangelii,* printed by Morgiani in 1495. Only two copies have survived and one of those has been damaged by fire. However while the latter copy was in the possession of C. W. Dyson Perrins he reproduced it in facsimile for the Roxburghe Club. It opens with a splendid frontispiece followed by numerous smaller cuts of great charm [44].

Another Florentine woodcut of exquisite beauty is to be found in the first edition of the *Laude* of Jacopone da Todi, printed by Francesco Bonaccorsi in 1490 [45]. Jacopone da Todi (1230–1306) was a Franciscan mystic who wrote lovely devotional poetry including, especially, the

⊏ Epiſtole ⁊ Euangelii ⁊ Lectioni vulgari in lingua toſchana

44 The most important Florentine woodcut
book is the *Epistole e Evangelii*, printed by
Morgiani in 1495.

45 Jacopone da Todi, author of the *Stabat Mater*, in adoration before the Virgin. The frontispiece to his *Laude* (Florence 1490).

Stabat Mater. The author, having laid down his book, kneels in adoration before the Virgin, who appears in a mandorla. The skill and artistry with which both wood-engraver and artist have combined to express the religious ecstasy of Jacopone is beyond praise. Lippmann rightly compared this woodcut with the silver-point drawings of the Florentine school.

But Florence was not one of the greatest printing centres. Some Florentine scholars had their work produced in Venice and many of the Florentine books were tracts, small volumes of poetry or romances, such as the *Novella della Figliuola del Mercante* [46]. These were works of an ephemeral nature, not collected by connoisseurs or preserved in great libraries, but read to pieces and thrown away; consequently, they are now very scarce.

Prominent among these Florentine publications is the spate of tracts by Savonarola. Often fanatical, these too are frequently illustrated by

ABOVE LEFT 46 Many ephemeral Florentine tracts, novelettes, and so forth, were illustrated with charming woodcuts. Here we see domestic discipline in fifteenth-century Florence in *Novella della Figliuola del Mercante*.
ABOVE RIGHT 47 Sermons and other tracts by Savonarola usually contained at least one woodcut in the 'outline style'. Here he harangues a congregation in *Compendio di Revelazione* (1496).

BELOW 48 This portrait of the Albanian hero in the fight against the Turks is from M. Barletius, *Historia de Vita et Gestis Scanderbegi* (1510).

SIGNOR SCANDER BEGO

woodcuts of striking beauty that are immediately recognizable as being of the Florentine 'outline style'. Issued during the time when Florence was dominated by this formidable friar [47], they were probably designed by the lesser painters, though Berenson has attributed some to his Alunno di Domenico.

At this time Venice was engaged in a life-and-death struggle, defending her empire against the ever-advancing Turks. Any man who made a successful stand against the common enemy was a hero, and none more so than George Castriota (1403–67), dubbed Scander-beg, the Dragon of Albania. After twenty years in Ottoman service he revolted and took his native city, Kroia, by surprise. For the next quarter of a century he fought a ruthless guerilla struggle among the mountains, and is remembered to this day as a hero, the 'Albanian Alexander'. His exploits are commemorated in Marinus Barletius, *Historia de Vita et Gestis Scanderbegi* (1510). Although the book was printed in Rome the portrait [48] is, naturally enough, Venetian in style.

Aldus did not normally illustrate his books, but in 1499 he produced a work that may well claim to be among the most beautiful printed books of all time, a black tulip in the midst of his classical texts: the *Hypnerotomachia Poliphili* by Francesco Colonna. In post-Renaissance times the text of this extraordinary book has generally been regarded as a jumble of mystical nonsense that owed its reputation solely to the woodcut illustrations, just as some really bad poems have achieved immortality because Schubert set them to music. But in the last few years there has been a revision of this view. George Painter (probably the only man capable of being at once a leading authority on fifteenth-century printing and the definitive biographer of Proust) has analysed the text in a brilliant and perceptive essay. The *Hypnerotomachia*, which means 'The Strife of Love in a Dream', is an allegory of remarkable subtlety in which Poliphilo's pursuit of his lost love in a dream symbolizes man's striving after unattainable spiritual ideals [49, 50 and 51].

The artist who designed the superlative woodcuts has never been identified, though many great names in Italian painting have been put forward. Discussing this mystery (in his Introduction to the Eugrammia Press facsimile, 1963) Painter says:

Some have argued that he was a painter, others that he was a sculptor, a medallist, a niellist, or that the question is unimportant. The very variety of the solutions, and the over-simplification and neglect of conflicting evidence involved in any one identification, suggest that these hypotheses are on the wrong track. The individuality of the *Hypnerotomachia* illustrator is surely so striking that his identity with a known artist would leap to the eye if any such identity existed. . . .

Whoever he may have been, he was deeply influenced by Mantegna and Giovanni Bellini, and may well have worked in their studios as a pupil, but his individual manner is splendidly his own. His work is to be found in only three books printed within four years. Did he, like Giorgione, die in his twenties?

As George Painter has further remarked:

Gutenberg's Forty-two-Line Bible of 1455 and the *Hypnerotomachia* of 1499 confront one another from opposite ends of the incunable period with equal and contrasting pre-eminence. The Gutenberg Bible is sombrely and sternly German, gothic, Christian and mediaeval; the *Hypnerotomachia* is radiantly and graciously Italian, classic, pagan and renascent. These are the two supreme masterpieces of the art of printing, and stand at the two poles of human endeavour and desire.

Finally, before we leave early printing let us look at a book that combines the best of both worlds, printing on vellum and gorgeous illumination: Giovanni Simonetta's *Sforziada,* printed in Milan by Antonio Zarotto in 1490 [XII]. This book brings vividly to life the brilliant, art-loving though Machiavellian world of the Italian Renaissance despots, and contains portraits of two of them. Francesco Sforza, the founder of the family, began life as a *condottiere,* inheriting a small band of mercenaries from his father. While in charge of the Venetian armies he was induced to change sides in the middle of a war by the offer in marriage of Bianca, illegitimate daughter of Filippo Maria Visconti, Duke of Milan – she was eight years old at the time. In due course Francesco Sforza secured the dukedom of Milan for himself, and among the often unscrupulous and vicious rulers of the Renaissance (the Visconti had, only too rightly, chosen the viper as their emblem) this robust, rough-mannered, able soldier of fortune stands out as a ruler of unusual integrity. Milan prospered and lived happily under his rule. As the founder of the dynasty and the hero of the *Sforziada,* his portrait has been painted by the illuminator at the beginning of the text.

The portrait on the right is that of his younger son, the brilliant and sinister Ludovico, nicknamed 'Il Moro', for whom this book was illuminated. His emblem, the Moor, appears in the top margin and his arms, with the fleur-de-lys of France on an escutcheon of pretence, are

RIGHT 49 The *Hypnerotomachia (The Strife of Love in a Dream)* by Francesco Colonna, printed by Aldus (1499), is an allegory in which Poliphilo's pursuit of his lost love symbolizes man's striving after unattainable spiritual ideals. The woodcut illustrations are among the most beautiful ever created. 50 *(below)* represents a triumph. In 51 *(below right)* the lovers are, at last, united.

POLIPHILO QVIVI NARRA, CHE GLI PARVE AN-
CORA DI DORMIRE, ET ALTRONDE IN SOMNO
RITROVARSE IN VNA CONVALLE, LA QVALE NEL
FINE ERA SER ATA DE VNA MIR ABILE CLAVSVRA
CVM VNA PORTENTOSA PYRAMIDE, DE ADMI-
RATIONE DIGNA, ET VNO EXCELSO OBELISCO DE
SOPRA. LA QVALE CVM DILIGENTIA ET PIACERE
SVBTILMENTE LA CONSIDEROE.

L A SPAVENTEVOLE SILVA, ET CONSTI-
pato Nemore euaso, & gli primi altri lochi per el dolce
somno che se hauea per le fesse & prosternate mébre dif-
fuso relicti, me ritrouai di nouo in uno piu delectabile
sito assai piu che el præcedente. Elquale non era de mon-
ti horridi, & crepidinose rupe intorniato, ne falcato di
strumosi iugi. Ma compositamente de grate montagniole di non tro-
po altecia. Siluose di giouani quercioli, di roburi, fraxini & Carpi-
ni, & di frondosi Esculi, & Ilice, & di teneri Coryli, & di Alni, & di Ti-
lie, & di Opio, & de infructuosi Oleastri, dispositi secondo laspecto de
gli arboriferi Colli. Et giu al piano erano grate siluule di altri siluatici

at the foot of the page. In 1490 Ludovico was acting as regent for his young nephew, but he soon seized power for himself. There are certain qualities of the Greek tragedy about Ludovico; few men can have been blessed with more splendid worldly opportunities than he. He ruled one of the richest states in Italy for about twenty-four years, and his wife was the beautiful, intelligent and charming Beatrice D'Este. A generous and perceptive patron, he had Leonardo da Vinci as his court painter and engineer, while Bramante served as his architect – and these were but the peers in a galaxy of genius and talent. The gods, it must have seemed, were lavishing their gifts upon him. But all the time he was, unconsciously, promoting his own catastrophic downfall, for his tortuous and unscrupulous political policies brought nemesis in their train at last.

The French invaded Italy and sacked Milan. The cold and imperturbable Leonardo, it is said, sat unmoved, sketching the spirals of smoke that rose from the burning city, while Ludovico was dragged off to France as a captive. He spent his last nine years at Loches, the latter part of them in a dark and subterranean dungeon cut out of the solid rock. Louis XII carried home an unparalleled treasure of artistic loot, including, there is little doubt, this copy of the *Sforziada*. It later passed through a number of celebrated collections: Charles Rohan, Prince de Soubise, Count MacCarthy-Reagh, George Hibbert, P. A. Hanrott and the Hon Thomas Grenville, who bequeathed it to the British Museum. In an ecstasy of enthusiasm the irrepressible Dibdin* exclaimed: 'We have here the loveliest – or at any rate, and without question or doubt ONE of the loveliest – of membranaceous bijoux!'

52 This lovely woodcut forms the frontispiece to the *Letters of St Catherine of Siena*, printed by by Aldus (1500). The few words in the open book and on the sacred heart are the first appearance of italic type.

SANCTA CATHARINA DE SENIS.

---

* For the Rev Thomas Frognall Dibdin (1776–1847) see p. 258.

CHAPTER THREE

BOOKBINDING

53 The Cathedral Library at Hereford shows the manner in which books were shelved during the Middle Ages and Renaissance, with a chain fixed to the foot of the front board. The shelving of books with the fore-edges outwards was normal in England until at least 1650.

WITH THE MAJORITY of books we know the name of the author and of the more important illustrators and printers. When we come to bookbinding we are often faced by masterpieces created by craftsmen who are totally unknown to us. Until the present century, bookbinding history was extremely casual. All early seventeenth-century French bindings with *pointillé* tooling were by Le Gascon; all English Restoration bindings were by Samuel Mearne; all English late eighteenth-century bindings by Roger Payne.

When it came to patrons and owners the most romantic, or even imaginary, names were bandied about on the flimsiest evidence – or on no evidence at all. This brought about the natural reaction of sweeping iconoclasm. Then came the painstaking research by a series of brilliant, learned and patient scholars who have built up the mosaic, tessera by tessera, of our present knowledge. Their findings are scattered through learned journals, *festschrifts*, catalogues of loan exhibitions, private and public libraries. Different craftsmen have been identified by the tools which they used to decorate their bindings, and given names such as the Entrelac Binder, the Medallion Binder, Queens' Binder A and so forth. But even now, to change the simile, all we have is a jigsaw puzzle, with only part of the outline and a little of the centre completed.

These scholars have developed a complex vocabulary in order to describe intricate designs in words. I hope I can utilize this as well as any man, and I fill my catalogues with phrases like, 'fields semés with tear-drops, animal-in-foliage rolls, intersecting lozenges within rectangular two-line fillets'. Indeed an assistant once remarked that my descriptions of bookbindings reminded him of over-rich fruit cake. However, in the present chapter I shall avoid this semi-private language, allow the illustrations to speak for themselves and try to give some idea of the historical settings from which these beautiful books came.

We take it for granted that books should be ranged on shelves with their spines facing outwards. However, this was not the case until the Renaissance and Reformation were well advanced. Earlier books lay flat on shelves or on reading desks. They were often provided with metal bosses on their sides to raise them above the damp surfaces in un-heated medieval buildings. This being so, it was the upper cover that was seen, and the titles were not lettered on the spine but written on labels attached to the upper cover, sometimes protected by transparent horn. Almost all early books were written on vellum and were liable to swell open through either damp or heat. To avert this, catches and clasps were fixed to the fore-edges to hold the book closed.

In certain chained libraries the books stood upright on the shelves, but with the fore-edges (sometimes lettered with the title) outwards, and the chain fastened to the foot of the front board. Indeed the practice of shelving books with their fore-edges outwards was normal in England until at least 1650 [53].

The earliest surviving European decorated leather binding is the Stonyhurst *Gospel of St John* [54]. The manuscript it contains, written at Wearmouth-Jarrow towards the end of the seventh century, was found in the coffin of St Cuthbert, the most venerated Northumbrian saint, who died on the Island of Lindisfarne in 687. Eleven years later the monks reburied him in a more elaborate coffin, the *levis theca,* which has survived to this day, and it seems most probable that the Gospel was placed in his coffin at that time.

During the terrible Danish invasions the monks fled to the mainland, taking St Cuthbert on a veritable Odyssey around the North of England. When the coffin was opened for the veneration of kings and other not-ables Cuthbert's body was found to be uncorrupted. Ælfred Westou, *custos ecclesiae fidelissimus,* made a practice of regularly combing the saint's hair.

After many years St Cuthbert came to rest at Durham, but when William the Conqueror was ravaging the North, in 1069, the monks fled back to Lindisfarne, taking the sacred coffin with them. Finally it was brought back to Durham, and Ranulph Flambard, the bishop who created the Norman cathedral, gave it a place of honour behind the high altar. On this historic occasion the Gospel was removed from the coffin and exhibited to the faithful. At that time it was preserved in a satchel of red leather with a badly frayed sling made of silken threads. One of the monks stole a thread and put it in his shoe, whereupon his leg swelled. He was cured only after the prior had advised him to propitiate the Saint 'by putting on his tomb that which you took away'.

The Gospel remained in Durham Cathedral until the dissolution in 1540. In 1769 it was given, by the Rev. Thomas Phillipps, to the Jesuit community (now called Stonyhurst College) where, it is gratifying to record, it still remains.

The binding is made of goatskin stuck on to boards. This was moulded, while damp, to a pattern that was then enriched by indenting and colouring. It hardly seems necessary to point out the similarity of the interlacing design to the illumination of manuscripts of the same time and place.

The monastery of Admont, in Styria, Austria, was founded in 1074. In the middle of the following century some of the brothers must have studied in the famous theological schools at Paris and, on their return, brought back a number of manuscripts, products of professional scribes and binders. The Benedictines have always been celebrated for their scholarship and learning, and Admont was fortunate in having at least three abbots who were especially devoted to the library and who, one supposes, ensured that the books were well cared for. An interesting account of all this will be found in Anthony Hobson's *Great Libraries.*

54 The Stonyhurst *Gospel of St John* was found in the coffin of St Cuthbert (d. AD 687). It is the earliest European decorated binding. Note the similarity of the design to illuminated manuscripts of the same date and place. Stonyhurst College.

In the eighteenth century the monks rebuilt their library, creating one of those magical Baroque rooms that are the glory of south German abbeys, complete with frescoed ceilings, symbolical statues and so on. The simple bindings of early medieval manuscripts looked out of place in this gorgeous setting, so they were banished to another room and forgotten. As a result a little group of Romanesque bindings, hardly touched since the twelfth century, have survived in breathtaking condition.

The example of these twelfth-century Paris bindings illustrated in Figure 55 (a glossed *Gospel of St John*, *c.* 1150), is in the Broxbourne Library formed by Albert Ehrman, now deposited at the Bodleian Library. For quality and condition the binding is quite unsurpassed. It is

55 This Romanesque binding, covering the *Gospel of St John*, was executed in Paris about AD 1150. Wooden boards are covered with reddish-brown sheepskin and tooled in blind with a central stamp of Samson fighting the lion. From the Benedictine Abbey at Admont, Austria, and now in the Broxbourne Library, deposited in the Bodleian Library, Oxford.

made of reddish-brown sheepskin stretched over wooden boards, each cover differently tooled in blind. The central stamp represents Samson fighting with the lion.

With the invention of printing the production of books increased on a great scale. The wealthy monasteries must have been the best customers of the early printers. Even today, for example, Klosterneuburg still has 885 incunabula. Many monasteries had their own binding workshops and, since numerous monastic books contain a written note of ownership, scholars have been able to isolate the binding tools used and assign other books to their original homes, even in the case of libraries long dispersed. The example illustrated [56] is a copy of Johannes Gerson printed at Strassburg in 1488, and bound in the Celestine monastery at Oybin,

56 Solid bindings, gothic in character, were intended to preserve the books in monastic libraries for all time. This one, covering the *Opera* of Gerson, printed at Strassburg in 1488, was bound in the Celestine monastery at Oybin, Saxony, and is now in the Broxbourne Library, deposited in the Bodleian Library, Oxford.

57 The earliest known printed bookplate was made for Hildebrand Brandenburg, a merchant who retired to the Charterhouse at Buxheim, south Germany, late in the fifteenth century, taking his library with him.

OPPOSITE XIII *The Gospels of St Luke* and *St John* in a Limoges enamel binding of the late twelfth century from the Heiningen Nunnery, Hildesheim, South Germany.
British Museum.

Saxony. The binding is of brown calf over wooden boards, decorated with blind tooling. Solid bindings like this were meant for use and made to last as, indeed, they have done in very considerable numbers.

Hildebrand Brandenburg of Biberach, in southern Germany, must have been one of the best private customers that the early printers ever had, a rich merchant ready to buy every really important book on publication – the sort of man who, even today, warms the hearts of that downtrodden body of men, the *new* booksellers. In the latter part of his life he retired from business and devoted himself to higher things by entering the Charterhouse at Buxheim, taking his library with him.

Hildebrand's claim to fame is that he commissioned the earliest known *printed* bookplate: an escutcheon azure, an ox passant argent with a black ring through its nose. Such examples as have been detached and examined are generally found to have been printed on the reverse side of printer's waste [57]. His library survived in remarkable condition. It seems to have been kept separate from the general library of the Charterhouse. Albert Ehrman owned a book from Buxheim with the shelf-mark, 'Upstairs with the books of Hildebrand'. When the German monasteries were secularized by Napoleon, Buxheim was bought, lock, stock and barrel, as a country house by Count Waldbott-Bassenheim. The library remained intact until 1883, when it was sold by auction.

The earlier collectors of incunabula treasured their possessions so highly that they had them all rebound in contemporary morocco, thus destroying innumerable medieval bindings. By the time of the Buxheim dispersal the importance of contemporary state had been realized, and the books have retained their late medieval bindings.

The Charterhouse at Buxheim is now a school, but most of the monastic buildings are intact. Hildebrand would not recognize them all, for a great deal of Baroque redecoration has altered their appearance since his time. But the little individual houses round the cloister, in which Carthusians lived, may still be seen, and there is a handsome monument to Hildebrand, who is buried there.

The greater cathedrals and mitred abbeys had the bindings of specially important manuscript service books adorned with historiated plaques of gold or silver, studded with precious stones. These were, virtually, hieratic treasures rather than books. Carried in processions or resting on a lectern, they looked gorgeous, vying with gold reliquaries and candelabra, and brought out only on the highest feast days.

Over the centuries most of these ornate bindings became the prey of looters, but one superb example has survived in the Pierpont Morgan Library [XL]. This covers a manuscript of the Gospels written in England during the eleventh century. According to the most recent opinion the binding is English work contemporary with the manuscript. It is constructed of thick wooden boards. The upper, covered with plates of silver, is ornamented with filigrees, engravings and gems, and with silver figures in full relief, cast and chiselled, the whole gilt. The inscription, IESVS NAZAR [ENVS REX] IVDEORVM, is in translucent cloisonné enamel. This book had belonged to Judith, Countess of Flanders

(1032–94), who in 1051 came to England as the bride of Tostig, brother of Harold and Earl of Northumberland. Already, according to some contemporary authorities, sister-in-law of William of Normandy, she was in the extraordinary position of being sister-in-law to the leader of each side at the Battle of Hastings. Tostig, among other activities, was the ally of Malcolm, King of Scotland, whom he helped against Macbeth. In 1064 Judith and Tostig were forced to flee to Flanders, taking this book with them. Two years later, in alliance with the King of Norway, Tostig invaded the North of England. King Harold was occupied with the threatened Norman invasion, but he turned and marched swiftly north and defeated the invaders at the battle of Stamford Bridge, in which both Tostig and the King of Norway were killed.

The battle of Stamford Bridge has always held an evocative place in English history. It was the last great achievement of the Saxon kings, and put an end to two centuries of Scandinavian invasions. It took place on Monday, 25 September 1066; on the following Wednesday William the Conqueror set sail. Harold was not there to dispute his landing, and England was successfully invaded for the last time.

In 1071 the widowed Judith married Duke Welf of Bavaria and became the patroness of Weingarten, to which Abbey she bequeathed her library. It is impossible for any Englishman to regard this precious volume without a throb of emotion.

When Napoleon's troops invaded south Germany, four superb manuscripts (including this one) were looted from Weingarten by General Thiébaultin. In 1818 they were purchased for £100 by the grandfather of the Earl of Leicester who sold them to J. P. Morgan for £100,000.

Once such a book had been stolen the jewels would be wrenched off and the gold melted down to conceal the crime. Any value appertaining to a champlevé enamel plaque, on the other hand, would be in its appeal as an attractive object, the melting value being almost nil. So even if they are not common, a reasonable number of these beautiful plaques have survived.

The art of enamelling reached its apogee at Limoges in the thirteenth century. The spaces to be filled with colour were hollowed out of the basic copper plate with engraving tools, leaving a metal line between them that formed the outline of the design. Pulverized enamel was laid in these hollows and fused. It was then filed with a corundum file, smoothed with pumice stone and polished. The German manuscript of the *Gospels of St Luke and St John* [XIII] has a late twelfth-century Limoges enamel plaque on the upper cover, with the *Majestas Domini* in the centre and the symbols of the four evangelists at the corners of the panel. This came from Heiningen Nunnery in the diocese of Hildesheim, Germany.

In bookbinding, as in so many other fields, to pass from the Middle Ages to the Renaissance is to pass from the age of corporate to the age of private ownership, and henceforth most of the bindings discussed will have been produced for individual patrons.

OPPOSITE XIV The greatest patron in the whole history of bookbinding was King Henri II of France. He possessed the most wonderful books, cost was no object, and he could command the virtually exclusive services of some of the finest craftsmen who ever lived. This example covers Estienne's Greek Testament (1550). Paris, Bibliothèque Nationale.

Jean Grolier (1479–1565) is certainly the best-known patron book-binders have ever had, and one of the most famous of all collectors, so he was a natural selection as the posthumous patron of that distinguished body of American bibliophiles, the Grolier Club.

Born in Lyons and educated in Paris, he succeeded his father as treasurer and receiver-general in Milan at a time when Lombardy was a French colony. In 1520 he returned to France for good and married Isabelle-Anne Briçonnet, whose family virtually controlled the national finances. Indeed for the whole of his life Grolier held lucrative offices in the French treasury.

Grolier was no mere amasser of visually beautiful objects. He was deeply in sympathy with the Renaissance and the Italian Humanists. They dedicated their books to him and valued his friendship as that of an intellectual equal. It is clear that he read his books, for many of them are annotated in his beautiful Humanistic hand. He was a most generous patron – probably the most generous patron – of the Aldine Press.

In Europe the application of gold tooling to leather bindings originated in Italy. French binders began to follow suit in about 1507, and by 1520 they were successfully copying Italian designs based on concentric rectangles. In about 1535 the innate French ability for artistic craftsman-ship was making itself felt; there was a striking leap forward, and Parisian bookbinders surpassed their Italian masters. New designs, based, with sensitive perception, on a wide variety of influences hitherto held to be outside the scope of bookbinding, were brought into play; designs from lacebooks, from architecture and sculpture and, above all, designs that expressed the spirit of the Renaissance, through the School of Fontainebleau. Through improved relations with Turkey coloured goatskins became available and French tool-cutters made use of Near-Eastern motifs.

Having made the breakthrough, all that the binders needed was a patron who was both sympathetic to the new spirit and ready to support them with a bottomless purse. They found that man in Jean Grolier, the great proportion of whose books were both Italian and Humanistic, perfectly suited to the new style.

Claude de Picques, born in about 1510, began to work for Grolier around 1538, and bound almost all his books for the next ten years. We can tell from certain details, common to all of Grolier's bindings and not found elsewhere, that he took the most meticulous interest in the work [58 and 59]. In 1548 de Picques was appointed Royal Bookbinder, and henceforth Grolier no longer received the undivided attention that he no doubt regarded as his due. In subsequent years the majority of his books were bound by the 'Cupid's bow' binder, though an occasional volume still came from Claude de Picques.

Grolier is best known for the legend that appears in gold tooling on the upper cover of his books: 'IO GROLIERII ET AMICORUM' ('For Grolier and his friends'), which has made him the symbol of the man through whose patronage fine books are first printed and bound, and then made available to scholars and friends. A second legend almost always

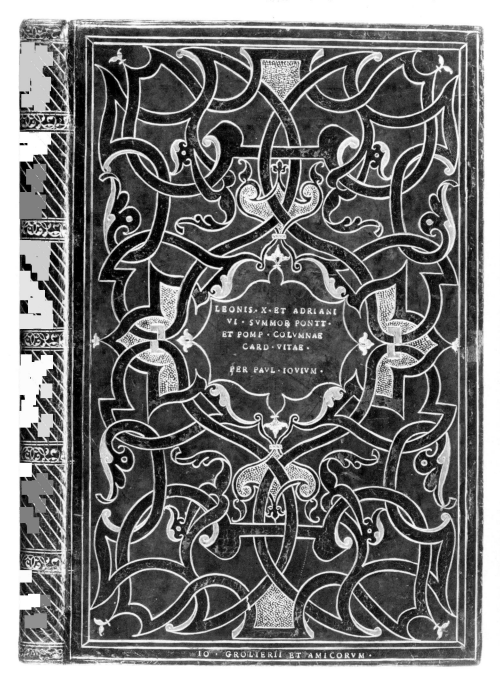

appears on the lower cover: 'PORTIO MEA DOMINE SIT IN TERRA VIVENTIUM', from Psalm CXLI.6, in the Vulgate, 'My portion in the land of the living'.

The pre-eminent fame of Grolier is partly due to the fact that his library has been scattered and that the lovely volumes (quite rightly) have been treasured, shown and boasted about by numerous collectors and libraries. In fact Grolier was surpassed, as every other patron in the whole history of bookbinding has been surpassed, by King Henri II of France. This is less generally known because almost all his bindings, about eight hundred, are still in the Bibliothèque Nationale in Paris, while less than thirty examples are to be found outside Paris.

In the Renaissance sense the French royal library had been founded by François I, 'the only sovereign of all ages [says D. B. Updike] who bestowed upon printing that loving care that a Charles I displayed for his picture gallery and most monarchs reserved for grandiose buildings and the jewellery of their mistresses'. In addition to his patronage and protection of the Calvinist scholar-printer, Robert Estienne, François

ABOVE LEFT 58 At a time when French Renaissance bookbinding reached its peak Jean Grolier (1479–1565) became the best-known patron of bookbinders. His books bear the motto: IO GROLIERII ET AMICORUM ('For Grolier and his friends'). This example is by Claude de Picques, and covers P. Jovius, *De Vita Leonis Decimi Font. Max.* (1549).
Pierpont Morgan Library.

ABOVE RIGHT 59 This set of Cicero, 5 volumes (Venice 1534–36), bound in Paris by Claude de Picques for Jean Grolier about 1545–50, must rank among the supreme masterpieces of bookbinding. It has survived in almost perfect condition while gaining a lovely patina over the years. The central hexagram is copied from Pellegrino, *La Fleur de la science de pourtraicture* (Paris 1530).
Eton College Library.

employed scholars and instructed his ambassadors to collect Greek manuscripts in Italy and Greece. By the time of his death in 1547 he had amassed the astonishing number of 550 Greek manuscripts. For the most part these were still waiting to be bound, a task to which his son, Henri II, immediately addressed himself. No sooner was work on the Greek manuscripts completed than the rest of the royal library was sent to the binder. No wonder Claude de Picques didn't have much time left for Grolier.

By this time, as has been indicated, Parisian bookbinding had reached its apogee. Henri had not, as Grolier had, selected his own books one by one, nor had he followed the progress of each with loving care. But he was the king, he was in possession of the most wonderful books, cost was no object, and he could command the virtually exclusive services of some of the finest craftsmen who ever lived [XIV].

In the starry-eyed days of bookbinding history an undue proportion of Henri's bindings were credited to the patronage of his mistress, Diane de Poitiers. The story of the life-long fascination held over the young

60 Jean de Courcy, *Chronique Universelle,* bound for Diane de Poitiers, mistress of Henri II. Note the interlaced Ds, the crescents of Diana and the crowned Hs of Henri. Only twenty-two bindings are now accepted as having belonged to Diane. (For a faked Diane de Poitiers binding see Figure 225.)
Paris, Bibliothèque Nationale, MS Fr. 15459.

61 The *fenfare* style of binding (so-called from a nineteenth-century revival) flourished in France from about 1570. This very early example covers an edition of Cicero (Paris 1560).
British Museum, Henry Davis Gift.

king by his much older mistress made a strong appeal to bibliophiles and they longed to own a book with this romantic provenance. And the situation was complicated by the fact that Henri's books often bore two Ds interlaced with an H and the crescents usually associated with Diana [60]. The cold eye of modern scholarship has reduced to twenty-two the number of books known, with any real certainty, to have belonged to Diane. Diane's own books sometimes bear two mottoes: '*Consequitur quodcunque petit*' ('She gets whatever she wants'), and '*Nihil amplius optat*' ('She desires nothing further'). The latter sentiment has not always been the guiding principle of royal mistresses, though anyone who has visited the *château* at Anet, built for Diane by Philibert de l'Orme, might regard it as a reasonable frame of mind.

Figure 61 illustrates what has come to be known as a *fanfare* binding. This name has nothing to do with original examples but is derived from a revival of the style in the early nineteenth century by the French binder Thouvenin on a copy of *Fanfares et Corvées Abbadesques*. This style, with its exquisite tooling, took advantage of the growing use of morocco in France. It flourished from about 1570 (an early example is to be found on a binding for Charles IX, who died in 1574) until well into the next century. At one time all examples were attributed to Nicolas and Clovis Eve, the father and son who held the position of Royal Bookbinder from 1578 to 1634. While some of the finest examples, executed for Henri III,

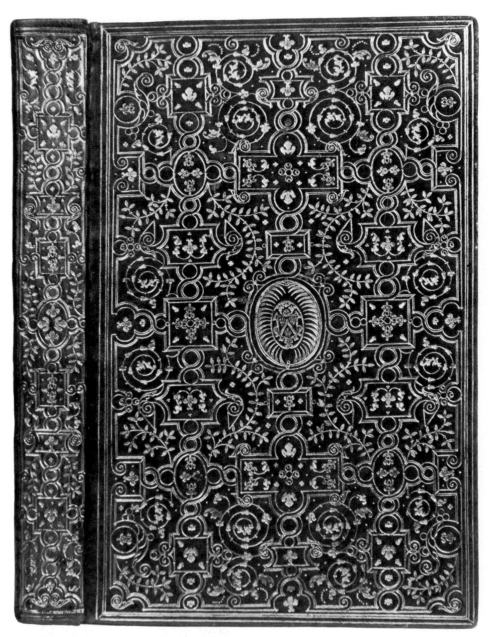

62 The most celebrated exponents of the *fanfare* style were Nicolas and Clovis Eve, the Royal Bookbinders. This more advanced example, on an edition of Herodotus, was bound for Jacques Auguste de Thou (1553–1617) and bears his arms as a bachelor. In later years de Thou incorporated, successively, the arms of his two wives.
Eton College Library.

were undoubtedly the work of the Eves, it seems certain that other Parisian *ateliers* also worked in this style.

The example illustrated was bound for Jacques-Auguste de Thou (1553–1617). It was said that 'the man has not seen Paris who has not looked on the books of De Thou'. His bindings all bear one of three versions of his arms. First as a bachelor [62]; then incorporating the arms of his first wife, Marie Barbançon, whom he married in 1587; she died in 1601, and in the following year he married Gasparde de la Chastre, whose arms he subsequently incorporated. After his first marriage De Thou abandoned elaborate bindings, contenting himself with restrained but beautiful bindings bearing his arms on the sides and his cipher in the panels of the spine. De Thou was very anxious that his library should remain intact. His son was beheaded at Lyons in 1642, but the books remained with the family until 1680. They were finally dispersed by the Prince de Soubise in 1788.

For most of the time, from the age of Grolier down to our own day, the French can rightly claim to have produced the supreme bookbinders.

76

However, during the long reign of Louis XIV French bookbinding dipped into a decline and became rather dull, and the supremacy passed, for a brief period, to England.

Why this unprecedented flowering of English bookbinding should have occurred during the second half of the seventeenth century we cannot say. Had it started in 1660 we should, no doubt, have attributed it to the Restoration of the art-loving Stuarts and an upsurge of art and patronage so long suppressed under the suffocating years of Puritanism; but the revival had already begun, and a number of remarkable bindings had been created during the closing years of the Commonwealth.

Two influences, even if they are not prime causes, may be noted: the introduction of coloured goatskins and the beginning of English trade with the Orient and the Middle East. There is a similarity, for example, between some of the best English Restoration bindings and Persian carpets: the rich colours of these skins with onlays of leathers in other colours, painted 'cottage roofs' and 'drawer-handles', the scattering of gilt detail and a love of flowers. Tulip and poppy tools are omnipresent [63, 64, XV and XVI].

63 The beginning of trade with the Orient and the Middle East had considerable influence on English binders of the Restoration period; echoes of Persian carpets may be noted in this example covering Clarendon's *History of the Great Rebellion* (1704). The term 'cottage roof' is derived from the triangular shape at the head and the foot of the panel.
British Museum.

During the nineteenth century almost all English Restoration bindings were attributed to Samuel Mearne, without any apparent reflection that no one shop could have produced so many bindings, which varied so widely in quality. This brought a reaction, and the ruthless E. Gordon Duff swept away such romantic wishful thinking, declaring that Samuel Mearne was a successful businessman who never bound a book in his life.

Since then a great deal of research has taken place and Samuel Mearne has been reinstated. It has been discovered that in his youth he was apprenticed to a bookbinder, Jeremy Arnold, and that he carried on a bookbinding workshop until his death in 1683. It is unlikely that during his later years he ever worked personally at the bench. He held the official post of Stationer, Bookseller and Bookbinder to the King, was Master of the Stationers' Company and extremely active (I am sorry to add) as a searcher after secret presses. None the less, a man who had been trained as a craftsman and who owned the workshop in which some of the finest bindings ever produced in England were going forward would surely have taken a keen and professional interest in work in progress.

The researches of G. D. Hobson, Howard M. Nixon and others into binders' tools, public accounts and so forth have disentangled a number of different workshops. In some cases the name of the binder, Roger Bartlett or Samuel Mearne, for example, is known, while the anonymous shops have been given names such as the Naval Binder or the Devotional Binder.

G. D. Hobson gave the name 'Queens' Binder' to the craftsman who was thought to have bound for both Catherine of Braganza and Mary of Modena. Howard M. Nixon has now taken this further and shown that three binders were involved: Queens' Binder A, Queens' Binder B [xvi] and Queens' Binder C. Rather like those awful sums in old-fashioned arithmetic books, Queens' Binder A was the more prolific but (and this will rejoice the hearts of all readers of Stephen Leacock) B was the better craftsman of the two. Recent research suggests that Queens' Binder A may well be William Nott 'the famous bookbinder, that bound for my Lord Chancellor's library', visited by Pepys on 12 March 1668/9. Pepys added: 'Here I did take occasion for curiosity to bespeake a book to be bound only that I might have one of his bindings.'

Before we leave English binding, a few other styles and examples may be discussed. William Edwards, of Halifax (1723–1808), and his two sons, James and John, developed an entirely new method of decorating books bound in vellum. After the loose, spongy part of the skin had been scraped, the part to be ornamented was soaked in pearl ash and then submitted to great pressure, making it transparent. Designs, figures, views or coats of arms were then painted on the *underside* of the vellum and backed with white paper. The armorial bearings were frequently coloured, the drawings generally in grisaille. As a result of being on the underside of the vellum, the drawings cannot be smudged or rubbed, and if the binding becomes soiled it can be easily cleaned with a damp cloth [65].

OPPOSITE 64 There was an upsurge in English binding during the second half of the seventeenth century, as may be seen in this Book of Common Prayer with the device of Charles II. Oxford, Lincoln College

ABOVE 65 The name of 'Edwards of Halifax' is especially connected with bindings in which the decoration is painted on the underside of specially prepared transparent vellum. This example, on Wm. Mason, *The English Garden* (1783), is in the Broxbourne Library, deposited in the Bodleian Library, Oxford.

BELOW 66 William Edwards of Halifax (1723–1808) has been credited with the invention of fore-edge paintings although this conceit is a hundred years older.

'Edwards of Halifax' bindings were being produced at least by 1781 and probably before but, after James Edwards had moved to Pall Mall in 1784 and opened what was to become the most important antiquarian bookshop of its day, it was thought wise to take out a patent. Bindings were evidently executed in London as well as Halifax, for Mrs Thrale (Dr Johnson's friend) describes how she saw a lady painting one.

The Edwards family were men of considerable taste and their bindings have very real charm. They have also been credited with the invention of fore-edge paintings, where the gilded fore-edge of a book is splayed open and a painting executed on the slanting surface – the painting disappearing once the book is closed [66]. This amusing conceit, which

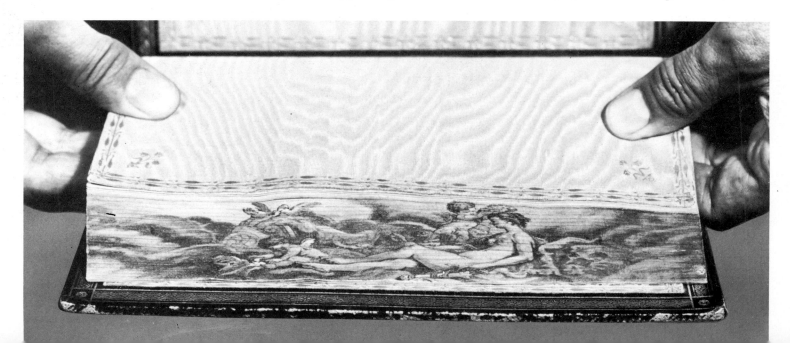

a complete set of rubbings and took a number of photographs. These are now in the National Museum at Dublin [xviii].

But to return to France, any display of eighteenth-century French book-bindings will give visual expression to Talleyrand's remark that no person who had not grown up before the Revolution had experienced *'les douceurs de la vie'* – an ultra-sophisticated Garden of Eden which, if we may judge by *Les Liaisons Dangereuses,* contained an exceptionally high contingent of vipers.

The last years of Louis xiv were a period of restraint, influenced by the dour religion of Mme de Maintenon, the exhaustion following *le grand siècle* and defeat by Marlborough and Prince Eugene in a series of disastrous wars.

With the Regency came a reaction of gaiety and luxury. Life was lived on a more humane scale, the grand style was replaced by Rococo, and the *Grande Galerie* by the *petits appartements* at Versailles.

In the field of binding this new spirit was led by the Regent himself. He designed a series of illustrations for *Daphnis et Chloé,* published in 1718. One of these, *petits pieds,* depicting the feet of a couple engaged in making love, used to be regarded (in days less permissive than our own) as an erotic plate. Six copies of this book were bound by Augustin du Sueil in the mosaic style: the surface of the leather was not cut away, but very thin pieces of shaped leather, in different colours, were pasted on to the covers, after which gilt decoration was added by the use of multiple tools. The Regent's own copy, generally regarded as the masterpiece, is now in the Rothschild Collection at Waddesdon Manor [xvii]. The style was also employed by Antoine-Michel Padeloup (who may, indeed, have anticipated Augustin du Sueil) and reached a peak of perfection in the work of Jacques-Antoine Derôme (1696–1760), one of whose masterpieces, *Teatro Jesuitico* (1654), is illustrated here [71].

This was probably the only age when a considerable body of import-ant women book collectors exercised a strong influence on binding. Several historians have commented on the feminine nature of the *dentelle* style, devised to cover splendid illustrated books such as the *Fables* of La Fontaine. The chief exponent of this style was Derôme le Jeune. Many of his bindings include the backward-looking bird tool, once regarded as being unique to Derôme. It must now be accepted that others used this or, a very similar, tool – but none to greater effect.

The most influential woman book collector was, need I add, Mme de Pompadour [73]. Among others were Horace Walpole's friend, Mme du Deffand, who had a gold stamp of her cat impressed on the spine of her books, and the wife, mistress and three daughters of Louis xv. Each of the princesses had her books bound in her own colour: Mme Ade-laïde (born 1732) in red; Mme Victoire (born 1733) in olive-green; Mme Sophie (born 1734) in citron – all bear the fleur-de-lys in the centre of each cover. It is pleasant to add that these three ladies escaped the guillotine and fled abroad. Mme Adelaïde had a great aversion to the English and planned, so it is said, to destroy the whole nation by inviting

71 French bookbinding reached a peak of perfection in the work of Jacques-Antoine Derôme (1696–1760). In this exquisite mosaic binding the backward-looking bird is made up from small curves. This masterpiece, *Teatro Jesuitico* (1654), is now in the Bibliothèque de Méjanes, Aix-en-Provence.

the men to sleep with her, one by one, and murdering them in the night. It never occurred to her, as a Royal Princess, that anyone would refuse.

Montesquieu's *Le Temple de Gnide* (Paris 1772) in a *dentelle* binding [72], is the copy dedicated to George III. The binder apparently lacked a unicorn stamp. When creating the supporters for the royal arms he substituted a horse and then added a horn.

As the century progressed this surfeit of luxury began to cloy; Marie Antoinette played at being an elegant dairymaid and others read Rousseau. All this simplicity, of course, had to be done with style. It was then that Roger Payne influenced French bookbinding. Indeed in 1798 the young Didot (the greatest French printer and publisher of his day) complained that French patrons were sending their books to England to be bound.

Throughout Europe during the nineteenth century the standards of craftsmanship were high, but original design was virtually non-existent.

BELOW 72 The dedication copy of Montesquieu's *Le Temple de Gnide* (Paris 1772) in a *dentelle* binding. Since the binder lacked a unicorn stamp to support the royal arms he substituted a horse and added a horn.
British Museum.

RIGHT 73 In eighteenth-century France women book collectors exercised a strong influence on binding, especially in the *dentelle* style. This album, now containing Pompadour, *Suite d'Estampes*, was bound for Mme de Pompadour by Louis Douceur (active 1721–69).
Baltimore, Walters Art Gallery.

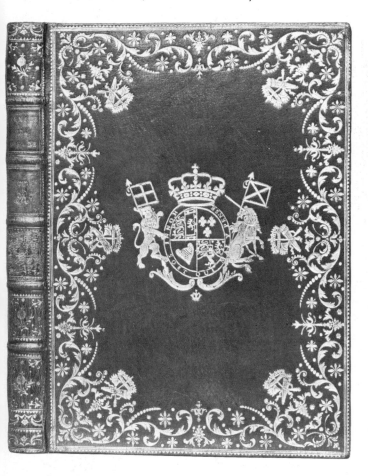

Craftsmen, it has been said, could bind in every style except their own. Mention has been made of Thouvenin reviving *'les reliures à la fanfare'*.

A workshop in England that turned out a large amount of highly competent work was that of Francis Bedford. His bindings look very neat, but they have the disadvantage of being rather too tight for use. Frederick Locker-Lampson took a volume back to Bedford and complained that it would no longer shut properly. Bedford examined the volume and then gasped in horror: 'Why, bless me, sir, you've been *reading* it!'

The first man to bring originality back to the design of bindings was an Englishman, T. J. Cobden-Sanderson (1840–1922), the founder of the Doves Press. Starting life as T. J. Sanderson, he assumed his double-barrelled name upon his marriage rather than (as an early advocate of women's lib.) ask his new wife to abandon hers. He was a barrister who, in middle life and under the influence of Ruskin and William Morris, came to the conclusion that craftsmanship was a more noble human activity than a career in law. While he was looking round for another occupation Mrs William Morris suggested that he take up bookbinding – probably the longest speech that 'silentest of women' is ever known to have uttered.

Cobden-Sanderson bound his first book in 1884 and this, in common with all his work, was profoundly influenced by the Arts and Crafts movement. There is a distinctive Englishness about his designs. Almost all his tools, which he designed himself, are floral, and the freshness and charm of his bindings are reminiscent of a bank of spring flowers [74]. At first he carried out all the work with his own hands, except for the sewing, which was done by his wife. Later, when the Doves Press took up a great part of his time, he employed a few craftsmen, who carried out his designs under close supervision. His impact on bookbinding is akin to that of Morris on printing, where the amateur outsider of genius revolutionizes the whole concept of the craft.

Cobden-Sanderson was an irascible character. When a lady complained at his price for a comparatively simple binding he retorted, 'I charge as much for my restraint as for my elaboration.' In this he resembled his master, Morris, who, when a lady remarked that the colours of his carpets were too bright, flung her out of the shop with, 'If it's mud you want, there's plenty of it in the street.'

However the city where bookbinding was brought into tune with the creative spirit of the twentieth century was, expectedly, Paris. Here the great *livres à peintures,* those books promoted by Ambroise Vollard, with splendid plates by Picasso, Rouault and others, were bound by craftsmen who broke completely with the past in design, and sometimes even with materials.

This school was founded, shortly after the First World War, by Pierre Legrain (1888–1929), and its brilliant standards both of design and craftsmanship are upheld today by P. L. Martin [75]. However, without question the foremost exponent has been Paul Bonet (1889–1971). Bonet, a Belgian by birth, was originally apprenticed to an electrician.

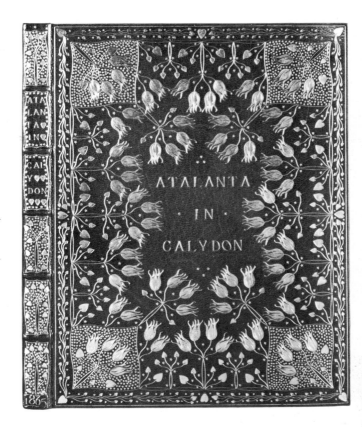

74 Originality of design was brought back to bookbinding by T. J. Cobden-Sanderson (1840–1922). Influenced by the Arts and Crafts movement, he designed his own tools. British Museum.

BELOW 75 André Suarès, *Hélène chez Archimède*, illustrated by Picasso, in a binding by P. L. Martin; a remarkable binding by a living craftsman, proving that fine books are by no means a thing of the past. British Museum.

OPPOSITE ABOVE LEFT XV This fine example of English Restoration binding by John Fletcher covers the Bible and the Book of Common Prayer. British Museum.

OPPOSITE ABOVE RIGHT XVI Many binders who are unknown by name can be distinguished by the tools with which they decorated their work. The 'Queens' Binder' was so designated because he was thought to have worked for Catherine of Braganza and Mary of Modena. We now know that three craftsmen were involved. This superb binding by Queens' Binder B covers Jeremy Taylor, *Antiquitates Christianae* (1675). New York Public Library, Spencer Collection.

OPPOSITE BELOW LEFT XVII The supreme sophistication of eighteenth-century France may be seen in this mosaic binding by Augustin du Sueil on the Regent's own copy of the edition of *Daphnis et Chloé* (1718) for which the Regent had designed the illustrations. Waddesdon Manor, The Rothschild Collection, National Trust.

OPPOSITE BELOW RIGHT XVIII During the sixty years subsequent to 1735 Irish bookbinding rose to unprecedented heights. The series of *Parliamentary Journals*, 1735–1800, 'probably the most majestic series of bindings in the world', was totally destroyed in the civil war in the 1920s. Fortunately a number of photographs had been taken by Sir Edward Sullivan.

He worked for a brief period as a dress designer and turned to bookbinding in 1925. Working in Paris, the friend of the leading painters and poets and supported by the most perceptive collectors, there seems to be no aspect of the École de Paris that he did not express in his designs. Just as, at the Surrealist Banquet, André Breton and his friends consumed boiled shoes, putting the nails, like grape pips, on to the side of their plates, so Bonet onlaid a pair of lady's kid gloves on to the side of a binding. Or on the author's copy of Paul Éluard's *Facile* he onlaid overlapping silhouettes of the hands of Éluard and his wife [76].

Other bindings were Fauvist and Cubist, or reflected the classical spirit of Maillol. Every kind of material was brought into play: duralumin encrusted with nickel; other metals; and numerous leathers. The surface was sculpted, moulded or cut into an endless variety of forms. To use Bonet's own words, a binding is *'une création plastique'*.

For many people Bonet's most beautiful bindings are those in his 'irradiant' style, where apparently parallel lines, varied with almost imperceptible subtlety, create an impression of three dimensions [77]. It was his practice to read and grasp the spirit of a book before he designed the binding. However, when I took this first edition of *Dionysius Halicarnassus* to him he jibbed at the idea of reading through a somewhat solid folio of 1480 and asked me to discuss it instead.

In the bindings that Bonet designed for some copies of Rouault's *Cirque de l'étoile filante* the lines radiate from an oval onlay of white leather; he describes these as 'sunburst' bindings [XIX].

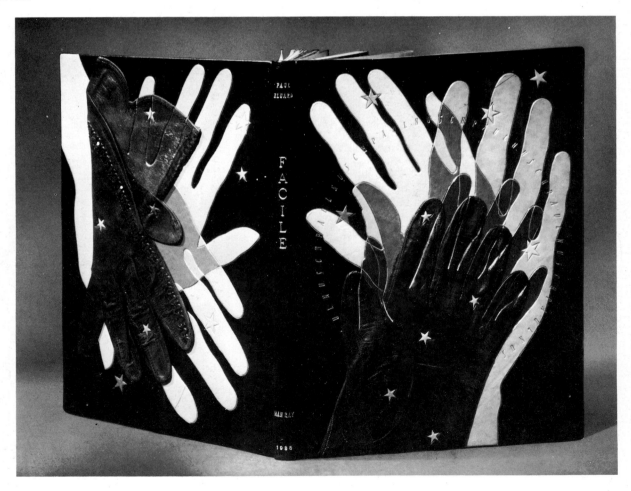

76 In a complete break with the now sterile designs of the past, Paul Bonet (1889–1971) worked in close association with the poets and painters of the École de Paris. On the author's copy of Paul Éluard's *Facile*, Bonet onlaid silhouettes of the hands of Éluard and his wife. Courtesy of Georges Blaizot.

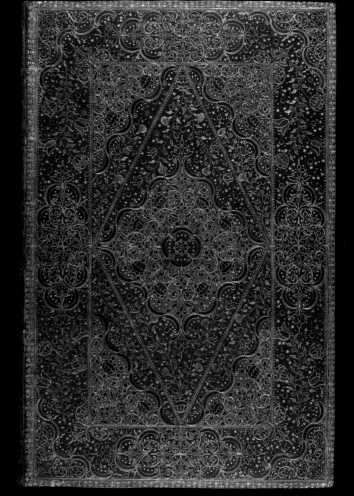

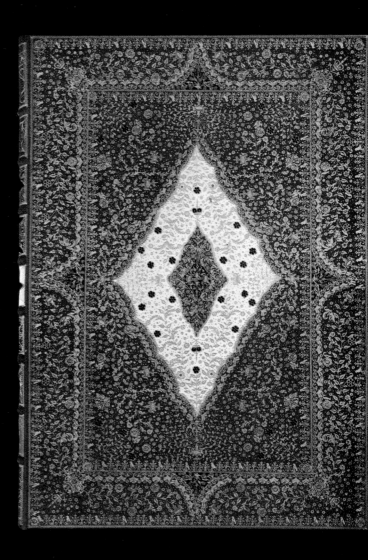

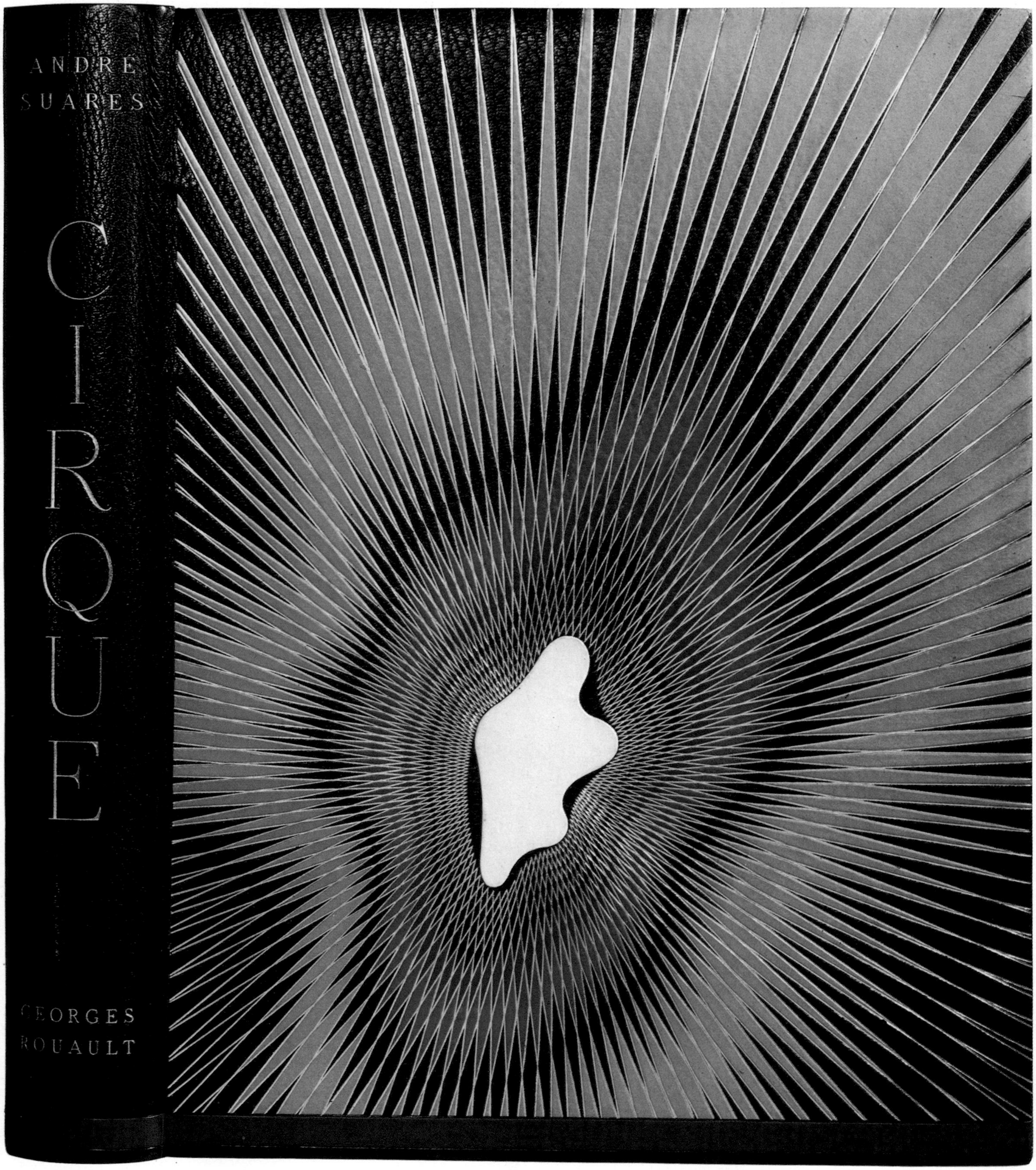

ANDRE
SUARES

CIRQUE

GEORGES
ROUAULT

DIONYSIUS
HALICARNASEUS

MCCCCLXXX

Bonet was a designer, not a gilder. He produced the most intricate drawings, which were carried into effect by the leading Parisian craftsmen. The drawings themselves have been deposited in the Bibliothèque Nationale as a precaution against fakers – like Claude Lorrain's *Liber Veritatis*.

It is pleasant to conclude this chapter*, which has covered the craftsmanship of so many centuries, with praise of masterpieces created in our own time. Most booksellers have had to suffer the fools who point to some binding just back from, say, Sangorski and Sutcliffe, saying, 'Ah, they can't do work like that today.' Paul Bonet is not only the greatest modern designer of bookbindings, he must surely rank among the greatest of all time.

ABOVE 77 Paul Bonet was an outstanding exponent of the modern French school and one of the greatest designers of all time. This first edition of *Dionysius Halicarnassus* (1480) is bound in his 'irradiant' style in which apparently parallel lines, varied with great subtlety, create an impression of three dimensions.

OPPOSITE XIX André Suarès, *Cirque de l'étoile filante* (1933) with coloured plates by Rouault, bound by Paul Bonet; a work of our time worthy to rank with the greatest masterpieces of the past.
British Museum.

* Bookbinding in America is discussed in the chapter on the New World, since it is intimately connected with American printing, and some early American printers were their own binders.

CHAPTER FOUR

THE BIBLE

IT IS WIDELY HELD that a major cause of the Renaissance lay in the determination of the Humanists to study the classics of the ancient world in the original Latin and Greek. But it is perhaps less generally realized that the quickening of the spirit that infused both the Reformation and the Counter-Reformation brought a comparable longing to read the Bible in its original tongues of Hebrew, Greek and Syriac, or, to be more strictly accurate, Aramaic. The important French Humanist, Jacques Lefèvre d'Étaples, based his confident hope for the renewal of faith on the increased knowledge of Greek and Latin that followed the conquest of Constantinople, while Melanchthon, on being appointed professor of Greek at Wittenberg, affirmed, '. . . when we shall have redirected our minds to the sources, we shall begin to taste Christ. His command will become clear to us, and we shall become suffused with that blessed nectar of divine wisdom.'

These men were filled with that unsullied enthusiasm that is possible only during the first glorious days of a new movement – 'bliss was it in that dawn to be alive'; they could no more foresee the Thirty Years' War than Wordsworth foresaw the Terror and Napoleon, or the early socialist idealist foresaw Stalin.

The Hebrew text of the Old Testament had been preserved, naturally enough, by the Jews themselves, and the early printing of the Hebrew Bible is described elsewhere in this volume. The earliest text of the New Testament is in Greek; not because Christ and his apostles spoke and wrote in Greek, but because, as a result of the conquests of Alexander the Great, it was the common language of the Near East. In addition, one of the earliest and most important texts of the Old Testament, the Septuagint, is also in Greek. According to Jewish tradition Ptolemy Philadelphus (308–246 BC), wishing to represent Hebrew law in his great library at Alexandria, engaged seventy-two translators, hence the title. Although one hates to abandon such a good story, it seems more probable that the translation was made over a longer period for the benefit of Greek-speaking Alexandrian Jews.

During the Middle Ages virtually the only biblical text generally available was the Vulgate, the translation into Latin made by St Jerome in about AD 400, one of the pivots of the Roman Catholic Church. But with the passage of the centuries, with endless copying and recopying, mistakes and false readings had crept in, until Erasmus could remark: 'Jerome emended, but what he emended is now corrupted.'

Here, then, was a second vital need for a more advanced scholarship. Every Humanist felt the need to learn Latin, Hebrew and Greek. One is reminded of the Bostonian lady who took up the study of Hebrew in her nineties, so that she could 'greet her Maker in his own language'. To this end new universities were set up and new colleges added to older foundations.

But how and where was all this enthusiasm and scholarship to be combined and embodied in one great work? The imperative need was for a patron of genius, wealth and power; a man who would be able to support the scholars while they worked, to obtain the necessary manuscripts, to cut exotic types, to guide so great and unprecedented an enterprise, and to protect it against all enemies by the strength of his worldly power. (Scholarship had its enemies, then as now. A monk of Freiburg objected that 'those who speak Hebrew are made Jews', while Jews who taught Hebrew to Christians were accused of destroying the faith of their pupils.) For once in history the right man came forward at the right time. Francisco Ximenes De Cisneros (1436–1517), Cardinal Archbishop of Toledo, Primate of Spain, confessor to Queen Isabella.

Behind the outward splendour of his religious and political position – at various times he was virtually ruler of Spain – he led a life of severe austerity. He founded, at his own expense, the University of Complutum (Complutum is the Latin form of Alcalá de Henares, now the University of Madrid). It was here that the Complutensian Polyglot, one of the world's greatest books, was produced [83].

Cardinal Ximenes gathered round him for this task a band of eminent scholars under the leadership of Diego Lopez de Zuñiga, including three converts from Judaism. Ancient Biblical manuscripts were purchased or borrowed.

Work is said to have begun in 1502 in honour of the birth of the child who was to become the Emperor Charles V. The earliest part to be completed was the New Testament, in 1514; the whole work was finished by 10 July 1517.

In the verses that are printed above the cardinal's arms on the title-pages, comparison is drawn between the fifteen divisions of the shield, the fifteen days' visit of St Paul to St Peter and the fifteen years spent in the preparation of the Polyglot. Cardinal Ximenes is said to have lavished fifty thousand gold ducats of his private fortune on the work. He died on 8 November 1517.

In the Old Testament the Latin Vulgate is printed in a column that goes down the middle of the page. On one side of it is the Hebrew text, on the other a new Latin translation of the Septuagint and the Greek text. Beneath these three is the Chaldaic version in Hebrew characters and a Latin translation of this. 'We have placed the Latin translation of the blessed Jerome,' wrote the editors, 'as though between the Synagogue and the Eastern Church, placing them like the two thieves on either side, and Jesus, that is the Roman or Latin Church, between them.' Here, in the Complutensian Polyglot, the Septuagint was first printed and here, also, was the first printing of the Greek New Testament, for which an extremely fine type of an entirely original design was cut.

Rather surprisingly, publication was delayed and the Polyglot does

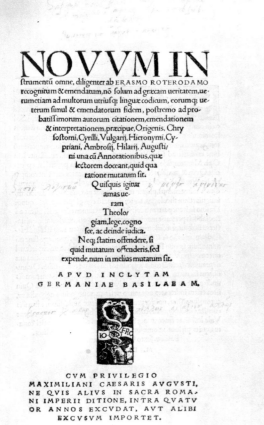

ABOVE 78 The first published edition of the New Testament in Greek was edited by Erasmus and printed by Johann Froben at Basle (1516). Owing to the speed of production the name of Vulgarius appears among the authorities on the title-page, thus a ghost Father of the Church was created.

BELOW 79 The colophon of the Erasmus Greek New Testament (1516) with the device of the printer Johann Froben, a caduceus with the cock of Mercury replaced by a dove.

not seem to have been in general circulation until 1522. The papal sanction to publish is dated 22 March 1520. Even then a further delay seems to have occurred. Dr Rendel Harris suggests that the delay was due to the exclusive privilege for four years granted to Erasmus in 1516 by Maximilian I, which would have been effective throughout the Holy Roman Empire. Whatever the reason, the delay prevented the Complutensian Polyglot from becoming the first published edition of the New Testament in Greek.

ERASMUS NEW TESTAMENT

As we have seen, although the Complutensian Polyglot contained the first edition of the Greek New Testament to be *printed,* it was not the first to be published. The intensive borrowing of manuscripts and similar activity in Spain must have come to the attention of the leading Basle Humanist printer, Johann Froben (1469–1527).

In 1515, with a view to being first in the field, he turned to Erasmus, already the firm's literary adviser. Erasmus was in Cambridge at the time, but he hastened to Basle. Such was the energy of both scholar and printer that their edition of the New Testament in Greek was published a year later, early in 1516 [78]. In the race against time the authorities quoted on the title-page, Augustine, Origen, Jerome *et al.,* include Vulgarius, thus creating a ghost Father of the Church. Erasmus corrected this 'bloomer' in his second edition by replacing Vulgarius with his correct name, Theophylactus, Archbishop of Achris in Bulgaria. In Greek Bulgaria is pronounced Vulgaria, hence, no doubt, the mistake.

Basle, in the early sixteenth century, holds a major place in the history of publishing and many books of outstanding dignity, printed in massive and monumental types, were produced there. Johann Froben, in addition to being the finest printer in Basle, was a leading German Humanist with important friends throughout the movement. He published numerous works by Erasmus, who also edited major editions of Jerome, Ambrose, Tertullian and so on, and lived with Froben while in Basle.

Froben's books were often decorated with woodcut borders and initials, many of them designed by Ambrose or Hans Holbein and Urs Graf. His device embodies a caduceus, the cock of Mercury being replaced by a dove, a reference to *Matthew* x.16: 'Behold, I send you forth as sheep in the midst of wolves: be ye therefore wise as serpents, and harmless as doves' [79].

The illustrated borders in the Erasmus New Testament were designed by Urs Graf (*c.* 1487–1529), who in addition to being a goldsmith and artist was a swaggering soldier of fortune who fought with the Swiss mercenaries in Italy and was often expelled from Basle for brawling. To our way of thinking it is strange that such a man should be chosen to illustrate the Bible, but the Renaissance produced many men who combined brutal cruelty with creative artistic achievement [80].

This is not the place, nor have I the space at my disposal, for an estimate of Erasmus (1466–1536), and his position in the spiritual life of Europe; to evaluate his wide learning, his new conception of scholarship

80 The woodcut borders in the Erasmus Greek New Testament (1516) were designed by Urs Graf (*c.* 1437–1529) artist, goldsmith and swaggering so dier of fortune.

and his genius, which did so much to mould the thought of the modern world. English writers in the nineteenth century tended to disparage him as being pusillanimous. They give the impression that it was rather shameful of Erasmus not to rush out and get himself burned at the stake. These men lived and had their being in the comfortable and safe world of middle-class Victorian England, often in what Johnson described as 'the soft retirement of academic bowers'. For us, who have supped full of horrors, the spectacle of Erasmus setting an example of reasonableness and common sense, tolerance and integrity and, above all, of freedom of the spirit in a blood-torn world is one that commands our humble admiration.

Great scholar though he was, it is hardly to be expected that Erasmus would produce a perfect text working at such speed and not from the oldest manuscripts. In some cases, where the manuscripts he used were imperfect, he completed the text by retranslation back into Greek from the Latin Vulgate, and some of these passages still hold their place in the *Textus Receptus*. He accompanied the Greek text with a new translation into Latin of his own, and completed the volume with a commentary upon which he had been working for some time. Herein lay the importance of his edition: for the first time it was made clear that the Vulgate is not an exact translation from the Greek, and it is fair to say that the Greek Testament of Erasmus is the fountain-head of Biblical exegesis in the modern world.

As an exact text, that of Erasmus is inferior to the Complutensian, but it had far greater influence. Firstly there was the name of Erasmus, famous throughout Europe; his edition came out first, was more compact, cheaper and easier to handle. Then there were the factors of publisher and place. In his masterly studies of nineteenth-century fiction Michael Sadleir pointed out that a book published by a little-known publisher will be scarcer than one coming from a well-established and successful firm. Froben had contacts throughout the European book-trade. Alcala was remote from the main trade-routes of Europe, while Basle stood at the head of the Rhine and was the gateway through which Italian Humanism passed into Northern Europe.

As a result, Erasmus's text, together with his translation, was reprinted many times, thus giving the opportunity for revision and correction. Finally, it formed the basis for Luther's translation into German.

LUTHER'S BIBLE

For Martin Luther (1483–1546) the study of the Bible was the very foundation of his life and faith, the sole key to eternal salvation. His translation of the Bible into German remains his greatest achievement.

There had been about eighteen previous translations into the vernacular, mostly stemming from one made about 1350; but these were medieval translations from the Vulgate, their language archaic and, even in revised editions, somewhat stilted. Luther had already used Greek or Hebrew texts for his lectures and commentaries and there can be no doubt that the idea of a complete translation, direct from the original tongues into the living language of the day, was germinating in his mind.

In 1521 Leo x excommunicated Luther and charged the Emperor Charles v with the task of putting the sentence into effect. But the German nobles, resisting papal pressure, summoned Luther to appear before the Diet of Worms. Here he made his irrevocable stand, refusing to abjure his beliefs or retract his books, ending: '. . . I am held fast by the Scriptures adduced by me, and my conscience is taken captive by God's word, and I neither can nor will revoke anything seeing that it is not safe or right to act against conscience. God help me. Amen.'

As Luther walked from the hall, which was seething with tumult, the Spanish imperial guards shouted: 'To the fire with him.' A group of friends, apprehensive of mortal danger, kidnapped him and carried him to Schloss Wartburg, where he stayed under the protection of the Elector Frederick of Saxony.

OPPOSITE 81 and 82 The first edition of Luther's translation of the New Testament into German is sometimes known as the *Septemberbibel*, since it was completed in September 1522. The woodcuts by Lucas Cranach are of a polemical character, too much so for the mildly reforming Frederick the Wise. Here *(above)* we see the Great Red Dragon of the Revelation wearing the papal triple crown. In subsequent editions *(below)* the two upper crowns were cut away.

'The English House', designated by the authorities for the use of English merchants and given certain extraterritorial privileges. This meant that while inside Tyndale was relatively safe.

In 1535 an ardent Roman Catholic, Henry Phillips, disguising his true faith and pretending to a keen interest in the reformed religion, struck up a friendship with Tyndale, who treated him with kindness and lent him money. Like Trotsky, Tyndale was fatally deceived by this false disciple. Lured by Phillips from 'The English House' he was betrayed to the imperial authorities and imprisoned in the castle of Vilvorde. The English merchants, who had come to love Tyndale as their guest and who were outraged at this breach of their diplomatic privileges, made great efforts to save him. Poyntz carried this to such lengths that he was thrown into prison himself. The help of Cromwell was enlisted, but all in vain. On 6 October 1536 Tyndale was strangled at the stake and afterwards burned. During his last moments he shouted, 'Lord, open the king of England's eyes' [85].

COVERDALE

To Miles Coverdale (1488–1568) goes the glory of having produced the first complete Bible in English. He was a Yorkshireman educated at Cambridge, where he became an Augustinian friar. Coming to London he met Sir Thomas More and became a friend of Thomas Cromwell,

84 The first edition of Tyndale's translation of the New Testament into English, printed by Peter Quentell (Cologne 1525), was suppressed before printing had been completed. Only this single fragment, now in the British Museum, has survived.

RIGHT 85 William Tyndale, to whom the English Bible owes so much, was strangled and burned at the stake in the castle of Vilvorde on 6 October 1536. This woodcut comes from Foxe's *Book of Martyrs*.

OPPOSITE 86 To Miles Coverdale (1488–1568) goes the glory of having produced the first complete Bible in English printed, probably at Marburg, in 1535. About sixty-five copies, all imperfect, have survived. The woodcut title-border contains parallel Old Testament and New Testament scenes. At the foot Henry VIII presents a Bible to prelates while nobles kneel on his left; this scene is flanked by David and St Paul.

The death and martyrdome of W. Tindall. His commendation: Friths testimony of him.

the place of execution, was there tied to the stake, and then strangled first by the hangman, and afterward with fire consumed in the morning at the towne of Filford, an. 1536. cry-

ing thus at the stake with a feruent zeale, and a loude voice : Lord open the King of Englands eyes.
Such was the power of his doctrine, and sinceritie of his

The Martyrdome and burning of maister William Tindall, in Flaunders, by Filford Castle.

who was to prove a powerful patron. As his beliefs moved more and more towards the Reformation he was forced to leave England and spend many years on the Continent. At Hamburg in 1529 he helped Tyndale with his translation of the *Pentateuch*.

Coverdale's Bible was printed, probably at Marburg, in 1535. It was not translated from the original tongues but 'from the Douche [German] and Latyn'. He is quite open about this in his typically modest preface and speaks of 'the five sundry interpreters' from which he had worked. Biblical scholars have identified these as the Vulgate, the German of Luther, the Latin version of Pagnini (very accurate for the Old Testament), Tyndale and, especially, the Zurich or German-Swiss Bible. He reprinted Tyndale's text almost without alteration, but from *Chronicles* to *Malachi* his own translation forms the primary version of the English text. Coverdale's style reflects the gentle nature of his character. He is not so vigorous as the tougher Tyndale, but he writes beautiful melodious prose, especially in the Psalter which, through its use in the Book of Common Prayer (via the Great Bible) has come down to us today [86].

Owing to his unaggressive character, Coverdale had never been officially condemned as a heretic, so his Bible was allowed to circulate freely. In 1537 the second edition became the first complete Bible to be printed in England. Coverdale returned home where, as will appear later, he edited the Great Bible. He was a popular preacher and in 1551 became Bishop of Exeter; but his episcopal career was a short one, for on the accession of Queen Mary in 1553 he was deprived of his see.

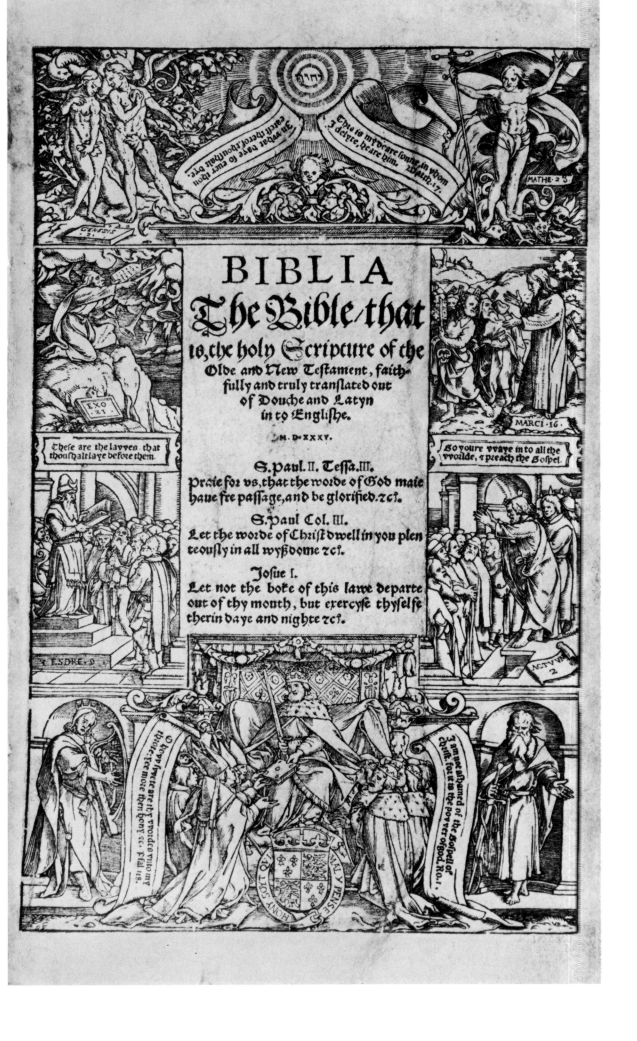

BIBLIA

The Bible, that

is, the holy Scripture of the
Olde and New Testament, faithfully and truly translated out
of Douche and Latyn
in to Englishe.

M. D. XXXV.

S. Paul. II. Tessa. III.
Praie for vs, that the worde of God maie
haue fre passage, and be glorified. zc̄.

S. Paul Col. III.
Let the worde of Christ dwell in you plen
teously in all wyßdome zc̄.

Josue I.
Let not the boke of this lawe departe
out of thy mouth, but exercyse thyselfe
therin daye and nighte zc̄.

At least he escaped the fate of his fellow translator, John Rogers. Curiously enough this escape was made through the intervention of the King of Denmark, at whose request Coverdale was allowed to leave for 'Denmarke with two of his servants [one of them his wife, "a most sober, chast and godlie matron"], his bagges, and baggage without theire unlawfull lette or serche.' After the death of Mary, Coverdale returned and took part in the celebrated consecration of Archbishop Parker.

MATTHEW'S BIBLE

The first Bible in English to receive official recognition was printed at Antwerp in 1537 and is generally known as Matthew's version. Thomas Matthew is the pseudonym of John Rogers (1500?–55), who went to Antwerp as an orthodox Roman Catholic priest, chaplain to the English merchant adventurers. However, living in contact with Tyndale he was converted to the Reformation. After his arrest Tyndale entrusted Rogers with his unfinished translation of the Old Testament and the task of completion. In the resulting edition the Pentateuch and the New Testament follow Tyndale's published versions. *Ezra* to the end of the *Apocrypha* are taken from Coverdale's Bible, but it is generally held that the text from *Joshua* to *Chronicles* consists of the translation that Tyndale had completed before his arrest. Rogers edited these different parts with no little skill and added the notes, thus creating the primary text of what was to develop into the Authorized Version.

Cranmer and Cromwell persuaded Henry VIII to license this edition, curiously ignorant that so much of the translation was really by Tyndale. In short, they now promoted the very book that they had previously ordered to be suppressed and burned [87].

The Act that made this the authorized version is worth reading. To every nobleman and gentleman – being a householder – was extended the privilege of reading 'in his own house, orchards or garden, any text of the approved Bible, so the same be done quietly and without disturbance of good order'. But, lest things should get out of hand, it was enacted that after the first of July, 'no women, artificers, prentyses, serving-men, yeomen or labourers, shall read within this realm, or any other of the King's dominyons, the Bible in English, to himself or to any other, privately or openly, upon payne of one month's imprisonment for every offence.'

Rogers returned to England and, in due course, became a prebend of St Paul's. But on the accession of Queen Mary he was the first martyr to be burned. The French ambassador, the Comte de Noailles, has left an account:

This day was performed the confirmation of the alliance between the Pope and this kingdom, by a public and solemn sacrifice of a preaching doctor who was burned alive for being a Lutheran; but he died persisting in his opinion. At this conduct the greatest part of the people took such pleasure that they were not afraid to make many exclamations to strengthen his courage. Even his children assisting at it, comforting him in such a manner that it seemed as if he had been led to a wedding.

OPPOSITE 87 Thomas Matthew is the pseudonym of John Rogers (1500?–55). 'Matthew's Bible' is often regarded as the real primary version of the English Bible. First printed in Antwerp (1537), Cranmer and Cromwell persuaded Henry VIII to license it. Rogers was the first martyr to be burned by Queen Mary.

The Byble/ whych is all the holy Scripture: In whych are contayned the Olde and Newe Testament truly and purely translated into Englysh by Thomas Matthew.

Esaye.i.

Hearcken to ye heauens and thou earth geaue eare: For the Lorde speaketh.

M, D, XXXVII,

Set forth with the kinges most gracyous lycēce.

88 In the title-border of the 'Great Bible'
Henry VIII, Cranmer and Cromwell are seen
distributing Bibles to the people. The educated
cry 'Vivat Rex'; the common people, 'God Save
the Kynge'. The royal arms and those of Cranmer
and Cromwell were included, but by the time
this edition of 1541 was published, Cromwell
had been executed and his arms deleted,
leaving a round hole.

THE GREAT BIBLE

The Henrican Reformation, as it gained in strength, felt the need of a
dignified Bible of its own, and Cromwell was determined to produce a
version which should, as far as possible, meet the demands of both the
reforming and conservative wings of the Church. Very wisely he handed
the task to Coverdale, who had shown that he possessed those qualities of
moderation and courtesy that are the essence of the Church of England
at its best. He deleted Rogers's somewhat aggressive notes and produced
a revised text with the help of the Complutensian Polyglot, the Greek
text of Erasmus and Munster's Hebrew-Latin Bible of 1535. In general
he moved away from the German idioms derived from Luther and

Zurich, using more phrases based on Latin, a step towards the Author-ized Version. This edition is known as the Great Bible [88 and 89].

In order to achieve a splendid-looking book, diplomatic arrangements were made with François ɪer for it to be printed in Paris. It was also felt that work would progress more speedily when removed from differences of opinion in England. All was going well, a considerable portion of the book had been printed, when suddenly the Inquisitor-General seized the press. Coverdale and the English printer, Grafton, who were in Paris to supervise the work, ran for their lives. Following intervention by the English ambassador, manuscripts, printer's types and paper were allowed to be brought to England, but not the sheets already printed. By good fortune these were sold as waste paper, purchased by a haber-dasher and brought to England in four large vats. Printing was quickly resumed in London, and completed in 1539.

The main title-page is almost filled with a woodcut border, formerly attributed to Holbein and, even if not by him, a splendid piece of work. Henry ᴠɪɪɪ, Cranmer and Cromwell are depicted distributing Bibles to the people. The educated cry *'Vivat Rex'*, the common people, 'God Save the Kynge'. The royal arms and those of Cranmer and Cromwell are also shown, but after the execution of Cromwell in 1540 his arms were deleted, leaving a round white space. Cranmer's own copy, printed on vellum, is preserved in the library of St John's College, Cambridge.

A royal order was issued instructing every clergyman to provide 'one boke of the whole Bible of the largest volume in Englysshe and have the same sett up in summe convenient place within the churche that he has cure of, wherat his parishoners may most commodiously resort to the same and rede yt'. Such was the demand that six more edi-tions were called for by 1541.

GENEVA BIBLE

With the accession of Queen Mary in 1553 the progress of the English Reformation went into reverse. A proclamation prohibited the public reading of the Bible, and no edition was published in England during her reign. Many of the reformers fled to Geneva and there, in 1560, produced a Bible of their own. This is generally known as the Geneva Version, but has a popular nickname, the 'Breeches Bible', owing to a reading in *Genesis* iii.7, '. . . and they sewed figge tree leaves together, and made themselves breeches', even though this is not the first occurrence of 'breeches' in an English translation [90].

The translators were William Whittingham, Anthony Gilbey, Thomas Sampson and perhaps others. William Whittingham is regarded as the chief translator and after the accession of Elizabeth, when the other exiles returned home, he remained in Geneva for some years to complete the work. Later he became Dean of Durham and was responsible (alas) for considerable iconoclasm, so that there is some poetic justice in the fact that his own tomb was destroyed by the Scots in 1640.

The title-page proclaims that the Geneva Bible is 'Translated from the Ebrew and Greeke'. Geneva was the stronghold of Calvinism, described

89 The 'Great Bible', edited and partly translated by Coverdale, represents the qualities of moderation and courtesy which form the essence of the Church of England at its best. In this edition of 1541 the title to the third part is made up from sixteen small blocks.

by Whittingham (said to be Calvin's brother-in-law) as 'the place where God hath appointed us to dwell . . . the store of heavenly judgement'. Certainly the translators had access to the most advanced Biblical and linguistic scholarship of their day. This was the first English Bible to be printed in roman types (all previous versions had been in black letter), the first in which chapters are divided into verses and the first to segregate the *Apocrypha*. Also, it was a handy size, suitable for home reading. An important feature was the addition of marginal notes, often of a bigoted, puritanical character. Some of them sound a note ominously chiming with our own times, such as 'Promes ought not to be kept when the preaching of God's Truth is hindered.' King James I took great exception to these notes and his dislike of them is partly responsible for the

Authorized Version, in which he stipulated that there were to be no notes except those explaining difficult words. Considering the fate of his mother, Mary, Queen of Scots, it has been suggested that he was most offended by the note to *II Chronicles* xv.16, where it is recorded that Asa removed his mother from the throne because she made an idol in a grove. The note runs: 'Herein he showed that he lacked zeal, for she ought to have died.' In our own time a distinguished left-wing poet has hymned the 'necessary murder'.

Although never officially adopted in England, for three generations the Geneva was the most popular of all versions, 140 editions being called for between 1560 and 1640. It became the *textus receptus* for the puritan element in England. It was read by Shakespeare, Bunyan and

90 The Geneva Bible (1560) is the work of reformers who fled to Geneva to escape the persecution of Queen Mary. Strongly Protestant, this version had great influence for a hundred years; the first edition to be printed in roman type, the first in which the chapters are divided into verses. The marginal notes were often of a bigoted, puritanical character.

the soldiers of the Civil War, and is thus of cardinal importance for its influence on the English language, literature and thought.

Some of its phrases were adopted by the Authorized Version and have thus passed into the general consciousness: 'a little leaven leaveneth the whole lump'; 'smote them hip and thigh'; 'cloud of witnesses'; 'childish things'; 'in a glass darkly'.

THE RHEMES NEW TESTAMENT

In some ways the Roman Catholic translation of the New Testament, first printed at Rheims in 1582, is parallel to the Geneva Bible, for both of them were produced by religious refugees who carried their faith and work abroad. Since the English Protestants used their vernacular translations, not only as the foundation of their own faith but as siege artillery in the assault on Rome, a Catholic translation became more and more necessary in order that the faithful could answer, text for text, against 'the intolerable ignorance and importunity of the heretics of this time' [91].

The chief translator was Gregory Martin, an original scholar of St John's College, Oxford, a contemporary of Edmund Campion, 'whom he rivalled, and kept up with in all the stations of academical learning . . . having their meals, their books, and their ideas in common'. He was an important member of the English College at Douai, where he taught Hebrew, and was a colleague of Cardinal Allen, who helped in the revision of this text. Constant study undermined his health and he died of consumption in Rheims.

Whereas the object of Luther and Tyndale had been to render the Gospels into a language within the comprehension of simple people, Martin's aim was to produce the most accurate possible rendering of the Latin Vulgate, 'truer than the vulgar Greek itself'. This extreme exactness made for some incomprehensible passages. For example, *Philippians* ii.10, 'Euery knee bovve of the celestials, terrestrials and infernals.' Hardly a phrase likely to be sung by a ploughboy. Further, by a principle first enunciated by Stephen Gardiner, almost the last Roman Catholic Bishop of Winchester, and Mary's chancellor, technical words were transliterated rather than translated. Thus many new words came to birth, and 'The Explication of Certaine Wordes in this Translation, not familiar to the vulgar reader, which might not conveniently be uttered otherwise', is appended. Many of these words now seem familiar enough to us, such as evacuated, gratis, holocaust, victims, not to mention that most Protestant of words, evangelize.

These new words, however, were not the only contribution that Gregory Martin made to the English language. Not only was he steeped in the Vulgate, he was, every day, involved in the immortal liturgical Latin of his church. The resulting Latinisms added a majesty to his English prose, and many a dignified or felicitous phrase was silently lifted by the editors of King James's Version, and thus passed into the language. Publication of the Old Testament at Douai was delayed until 1609–10 due 'to our poore estate in banishment'.

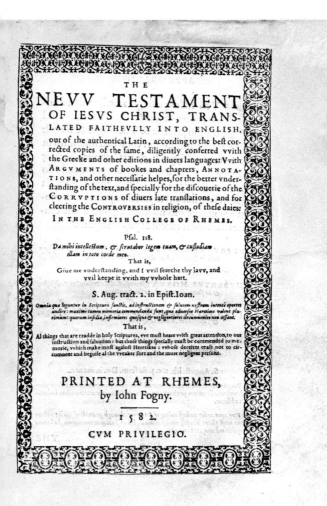

91 The Rhemes New Testament (1582) was the work of Roman Catholic refugees. It contains many splendid phrases which were silently lifted by the editors of King James's Version and so passed into the language. The Roman Catholic Old Testament had to wait until 1609–10 due 'to our poore estate in banishment'.

THE BISHOPS' BIBLE

The popularity of the Geneva Bible was disquieting to the Church of England, held up to scorn as it was in the ferocious notes with which the margins bristled. In an attempt to counter this Matthew Parker, Archbishop of Canterbury, organized a new edition. He 'sorted out' the whole Bible into 'parcels', divided among eight bishops whose work varies considerably in value. B. F. Westcott, that major authority on Biblical texts, considered that their Greek was superior to their Hebrew, and that the alterations in the New Testament showed original and vigorous scholarship. Some of the best and raciest notes were lifted verbatim from the Geneva Bible, but Parker was anxious to avoid sectarian bias.

The result of these labours is generally known as the Bishops' Bible, published in 1568. No trouble was spared in the production. Darlow and Moule remark, 'In typography and illustration this is, perhaps, the most sumptuous in the long series of folio English Bibles' [92 and 93]. It is sometimes called the 'Treacle Bible', from *Jeremiah* viii.22: 'Is there no tryacle in Gilead?', rendered 'rosin' in the Rhemes and 'balm' in the Authorized Version. Or the 'Leda Bible' from a capital letter previously used for Ovid. There is an interesting note at Psalm XLV, 9: 'Ophir is thought to be the Ilande in the west coast, of late founde by Christopher Columbo: from whence at this day is brought most fine gold.'

THE AUTHORIZED VERSION

By the turn of the century a widespread need was felt for another edition. The splendid folio of the Bishops' Bible may have been ideal for the church lectern but it was unwieldy for private use; the steady popularity of the Geneva version was a thorn in the side of the Church of England, and the Puritans were demanding a new translation.

Soon after the accession of James I the Hampton Court Conference was held in order to resolve certain differences within the Church. At this conference the Puritan leader, John Rainolds, President of Corpus Christi College, Oxford, said, 'May your Majesty be pleased that the Bible now be translated, such as are extant not answering to the original.' James agreed, but took the wind out of the puritanical sails by assuming patronage of what is known as the Authorized or King James's Version.

Forty-seven scholars from the Church and the universities were selected. Never since the Septuagint had so many been involved in translating the Bible. They were divided into six companies and the Bible was divided between them: two companies at Westminster, under Lancelot Andrews, Bishop of Winchester, of whom it was said that 'he might have been interpreter-general at Babel'; two at Cambridge under Edward Lively, Regius Professor of Hebrew; and two at Oxford under John Harding, also Regius Professor of Hebrew. Each man of each company was to work on the same chapter, and then the whole company met to discuss the drafts. On completion each book was submitted to the other companies for criticism. Finally a committee of six met daily for nine months to complete the revision. Would it be possible to devise a process less likely to produce the greatest masterpiece of English prose?

92 Stung by the success of the Geneva Bible and held up to scorn in the notes with which its margins bristled, Matthew Parker organized this new edition and 'sorted out' the work among the bishops. The Bishops' Bible was published in 1598. 'In typography and illustration this is, perhaps, the most sumptuous in the long series of folio English editions.'

The seconde part of the Byble conteyning thefe bookes.

The booke of Iofuah.
The booke of the Iudges.
The booke of Ruth.
The firft booke of Samuel.
The feconde booke of Samuel.
The thirde booke of the kinges.
The fourth booke of the kinges.

The firft booke of the Chronicles.
The feconde booke of the Chronicles.
The firft booke of Efdras.
The feconde booke of Efdras.
The booke of Hefter.
The booke of Iob.

ABOVE 93 Queen Elizabeth's favourite, the
powerful Robert Dudley, Earl of Leicester, makes
a surprising appearance on the title of part two
of the Bishops' Bible.

OPPOSITE 94 The aim of those who produced
King James's, or the Authorized, Version of the
Bible was not to produce a new translation,
'but to make a good one better'. It was a
continuation, a refinement, a synthesis of all
that had gone before. The greatest monument of
English prose, no book has had greater influence
on the English language or on the character of
English-speaking people. The engraved title-page
to the first edition of 1611 is shown here.

The aim was not to produce a new translation, 'but to make a good one better'. The Bishops' Bible was taken as a basis and compared with the original tongues and with Tyndale, Matthew, Coverdale, the Great Bible and the Geneva. They also used (though they kept this dark) the Rhemes New Testament. During the previous century immense advances in Biblical scholarship had been made throughout Europe by Protestants, Catholics and Jews. More accurate texts were available, far better grammars and dictionaries had been produced, kindred languages such as Syriac and Aramaic were better understood. In England itself the study of Hebrew had made great strides.

About 90 per cent of Tyndale's work and a great part of Coverdale's survive in the Authorized Version. The Geneva and Rhemes versions, in their different ways, brought a new accuracy to the translation. The Geneva provided pithy phrases, while Latinisms from Rhemes contributed to the majesty of the prose. Whereas Tyndale had deliberately irritated the establishment by choosing words which represented the Reformation, in the Authorized Version the older words were reintroduced, such as 'church' for 'congregation', 'priest' for 'minister' and so forth. Thus it will be seen that the Authorized Version was not a new translation but a continuation, a refinement, a synthesis, of the work of Tyndale, Matthew, Coverdale, the Great Bible, the Bishops' Bible, Rhemes and Geneva. It has been compared to a great English cathedral: not the work of one period alone, but due to the devoted creation of several generations.

It was indeed fortunate that this majestic translation was achieved during one of the most creative periods in English literature, when the English language as we know it was growing out of medieval usage into prose that rolls like a great cathedral organ played by a master musician. Macaulay said: 'If everything else in our language should perish it [the Authorized Version] alone would suffice to show the whole extent of its beauty and power.'

No book has had greater influence on the English language or on the English character. For the next three hundred years the majority of English men and women heard it read aloud Sunday after Sunday and, until within living memory, a very large proportion of people read the Bible with steady, life-long devotion in their own homes. And this great quality was carried to America, where its influence has hardly been less. In how many remote farms and homesteads was it the only book, in how many of the early American communities was it the chief object of study?

The Authorized Version was published by Robert Barker in 1611. It is a stately folio, printed in black letter. In order to meet the anticipated demand two printing houses were set to work and two editions, which differ in some respects, are distinguished by a reading in *Ruth* iii.15. In what is believed to be the first edition this reads, incorrectly, 'and he went into the citie'. Consequently, this is known as the 'He-Bible'. Publication of the other edition, the 'She-Bible', seems to have been delayed until 1613, possibly the result of an accident in which some of the printed sheets were destroyed [94].

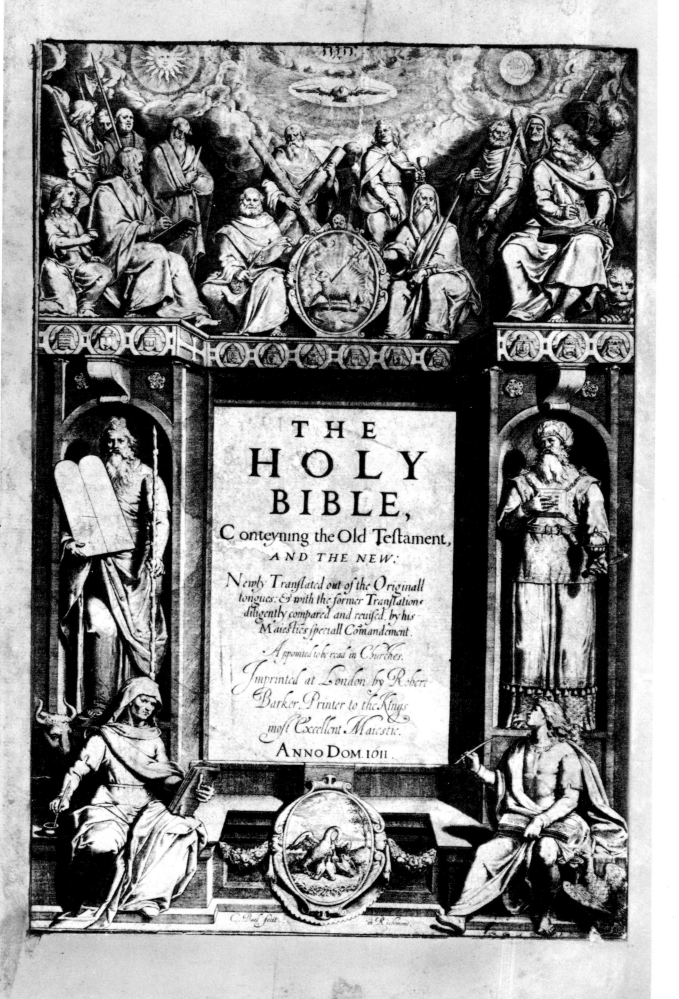

THE
HOLY
BIBLE,
Conteyning the Old Testament,
AND THE NEW:

Newly Translated out of the Originall
tongues: & with the former Translations
diligently compared and reuised, by his
Maiesties speciall Comandement.

Appointed to be read in Churches.

Imprinted at London by Robert
Barker, Printer to the Kings
most Excellent Maiestie.

ANNO DOM. 1611.

CHAPTER FIVE

EARLY BOOKS IN HEBREW

WHEN WE COME TO EXAMINE early books in Hebrew the first point to be stressed is the extreme rarity of surviving examples. Of the rather less than two hundred Hebrew books printed before 1500, a large proportion have survived only in a single copy, some in a single fragment.* How many have disappeared completely? In addition to the normal causes that make for the destruction of books – war, fire, damp, rats, children, spring-cleaning, disposal of the obsolete and so on – Hebrew books have been subjected to two further factors. One, they have been worn to pieces through intense study by generations of devoted scholars. In this some parallel may be found in early editions of the Bible in English. Secondly, they have been subjected to fiendish persecution.

It is not difficult for us, who have witnessed public bonfires of books in our own time, to understand why early Jewish books are scarce. A papal bull of 12 August 1553 decreed the confiscation of Hebrew books. This was put into effect, with great vigour, by Cardinal Caraffa, later Paul IV. Homes were ruthlessly ransacked and, on 9 September, a great quantity of Jewish books and manuscripts was taken to the Campo di Fiori and burned, 'amidst the cries and applause of the populace', while Jews wept 'for the burning which the enemies of the Lord had caused'. (Abraham Berliner.)

David Amram, who records much of this in *The Makers of Hebrew Books in Italy,* wrote in the halcyon days shortly before 1914 when, for a few brief years, it was possible to believe that the world was gradually becoming civilized and humane. How could he foresee that only a generation ahead there was to be persecution and genocide, both in Germany and Russia, far surpassing in evil anything that the world had seen before?

It is not so surprising, then, that many early Hebrew books are worn, soiled and imperfect. One marvels that any have survived at all. To what devotion do we owe the preservation of the books described here? How many of them have been hidden in ransacked homes or carried away from persecution, saved, perhaps, by the sacrifice of objects that some others would have regarded as more precious?

All this is illustrated by events in Spain and Portugal. It was to be expected that a remarkable flowering of Hebrew printing would stem from Iberian manuscript traditions. There was an important school of

---

* This is only an approximate figure. Authorities disagree, thus: *Encyclopedia Judaica*, 175; A. Freimann and M. Marx, 194. No accurate total will be possible until numerous fragments have been more securely located and dated.

Hebrew scribes and illuminators in Lisbon, as can be seen from a fine three-volume Bible on vellum now in the British Museum [xx]. The colophon tells us that this was written by the scribe Samuel b. Rabbi Samuel ibn Mūsā, who wrote the codex for Rabbi Joseph b. Rabbi Yehudah surnamed al-Hakim, and finished in the month of Kislew, on the sixth day of the week AM 5243 (AD 1483–84), in the City of Lisbon. There are richly illuminated titles to each book and, in the Pentateuch, to each weekly section, but the skill of the artist is chiefly displayed in the decoration of the supplementary leaves with Masoretic matter.

One of the most beautiful of all Hebrew editions of the *Pentateuch* was printed in Lisbon in 1491 by Elieser Toledano, who had every right to proclaim in his colophon: 'As for its elegance and preciousness, white marble, alabaster and pearls cannot be compared therewith, nor the gold of Parvim.' A fine copy on vellum that once belonged to George III has passed, with his library, to the British Museum [95].

Iberian Hebrew printing came to an abrupt end with the expulsion of the Jews by Ferdinand and Isabella. A moving memento of those days may be seen in a manuscript Bible, begun in Spain and completed in exile at Constantinople, now preserved in the Jewish Theological Seminary of America [96]. The colophon reads:

This volume . . . was written by the learned Rabbi Abraham Calif in the City of Toledo, which is in Spain. It was finished in the month of Nisan 5252 Anno

95 One of the most beautiful of all Hebrew editions of the *Pentateuch* was printed in Lisbon in 1491 by Elieser Toledano. This fine copy on vellum once belonged to George III and passed with his library to the British Museum.

96 This manuscript Bible was begun by Rabbi Abraham Calif in Toledo (1492), a tragic witness to the expulsion of the Jews from Spain. 'In the self-same year [1492], the exiles of Jerusalem who were in Spain went forth dismayed and banished by the royal edict... And I Chayyim ibn Chayyim have copied...the Masorah [in 1497] in the city of Constantinople....' New York, Jewish Theological Seminary of America.

Mundi [March/April 1492] for the very learned R. Jacob Aboab, the son of the esteemed gentleman R. Samuel. May the Almighty find him and his descendants worthy of meditating in it for ever. And on the seventh day of the month of Ab [31 July 1492], in the self-same year, the exiles of Jerusalem who were in Spain, went forth dismayed and banished by the royal edict. May they come back with Joy bearing their sheaves. And I Chayyim ibn Chayyim have copied therein part of the Masorah and the variants in the year 5257 [1497] in the city of Constantinople. May salvation be at hand.

Meanwhile, in Italy, under the influence of Renaissance Humanism, the situation was less highly charged and in some of the little states there were pockets of what might almost be described as toleration towards the Jews. The more or less pagan Humanists, including Leo x himself, were not so involved in fanaticism that they wished to persecute and destroy men of a different faith, while sincere Christian Humanists were by now infused with a desire to study the Old Testament in its original tongue. Further there was an intense interest in the Cabbala, inspired by Pico della Mirandola, who believed that it provided proof of all Christian mysteries, including the divinity of Christ.

Italy was still 'a geographical expression' divided into innumerable small states, often at war with one another. From the Jewish point of view everything depended on the individual prince, and their situation might change overnight through the death of a tolerant father and the accession of his intolerant son. The Dukedom of Ferrara, for example, is among the most celebrated of the little courts where the arts of the Renaissance flourished. Here Ercole I was not only a highly cultivated prince, he was also perceptive enough to realize the economic advantages that would accrue to his state by toleration of the Jews. In 1473 he relieved them of penal taxation, welcomed refugees from Spain and actually built a new section of his city to house them, an area that became desolated under his less humane successors. The wealthy Jewish community that grew up in Ferrara formed the natural setting for a Hebrew press, and it is here that we meet an interesting figure, Abraham ben Chayyim, de Tintori (the dyer), of Pesaro.

Abraham ben Chayyim is first heard of in Mantua where, in 1476, as the associate of Abraham Conat, he printed a work by Jacob ben Asher. By 1477 he had set up in Ferrara, printed a few books and then moved on. In Bologna, under the patronage of Joseph ben Abraham Caravita, he printed what may well be the first edition of the Hebrew *Pentateuch* (1482),* in which he is described as 'a workman whose equal in Hebrew typography does not exist in the whole world, a man celebrated everywhere' [97].

His typographical work is of high quality, he was among the first to master the complexities of Hebrew printing and is an early example of the practical craftsman who enables other men of scholarly or artistic ability to bring their ideals to fruition. (In later centuries the practical talents of Emery Walker enabled the private presses to function, and that professional architect, Nicholas Hawksmoor, ensured that the buildings of Vanbrugh, an amateur of genius, would stand up.)

Another fascinating example, in minuscule, is Sabbioneta, the tiny state ruled by Vespasiano Gonzaga (1531–91), who had made his fortune fighting as a *condottiere* for Charles V and Philip II. He turned his capital, hardly more than a village, into the ideal Renaissance city in miniature, complete with palaces, a sculpture gallery, a library, a mint, a Palladian theatre designed by Scamozzi and so forth, although inhibitions of space forced him to build his Versailles a mere few hundred yards from his town palace. A Renaissance prince needs a cultivated court and a splendid setting, so Vespasiano formed a remarkable collection of antique sculpture and commissioned the superb bronze statue of himself by Leone Leoni which is, happily, still *in situ*, and he became the patron of a Hebrew press which flourished between 1551 and 1561. Here Tobiah Foà

97 This has long been regarded as the first edition of the Hebrew *Pentateuch*. It was printed by Abraham ben Chayyim under the patronage of Joseph ben Abraham Caravita (Bologna 1482). It is now thought possible (though by no means certain) that two undated editions may precede it.

---

* The Bologna *Pentateuch* of 1482 has long been regarded as the *editio princeps*. Two other editions have emerged to challenge this primacy. One, printed in Italy by Isaac ben Aaron of Este and Moses ben Eliezer Rafael survives in two complete copies only, in the Vatican and at Freiburg. The other is a fragment of twenty-four leaves by an unidentified printer in Spain. Both are tentatively attributed to 1480. If these could be more precisely dated it is possible that the Bologna edition would regain its honoured position.

98 Vespasiano Gonzaga (1531–91), a successful *condottiere,* turned his capital, Sabbioneta (hardly more than a village), into a Renaissance city in miniature. Here Tobiah Foà printed the *Pentateuch* in 1557.

printed the *Pentateuch* [98], Hebrew service and devotional books, festival prayers and works by Jewish authors, including the controversial *Mirkebheth ham-mishneh* by Isaac ben Judah Abravanel.

Vespasiano, having murdered one of his wives and killed his only son by a savage kick to the groin, left no heir, and his capital relapsed into rustic peace.

It was in Italy, then, that Hebrew printing was first achieved, but in talking of the setting we have run ahead of ourselves.

In 1474–75 Meshullam Cusi printed the four volumes of *Arba Turim* by Jacob ben Asher at Pieve di Sacco, a small town near Venice. In the epigraph, printing is personified and delivers this rhythmical soliloquy:

I am wise and the crown of all wisdom; I am hidden and concealed to every mystery; without a pen yet my imprint is easily made out; without a Scribe yet the words are properly ranged; at once the ink goes over it; without rules yet it is straight. If you marvel at the heroine Deborah who governed with the pen of the writer [*Judges* v. 14] assuredly had she seen me at my breaking-in she would have placed me as a crown upon her head.

Meanwhile, at the other end of Italy, Abraham Gorton printed Solomon ben Isaac (Rashi), *Perush 'al hat-Torah (Commentary on the Pentateuch)* at Reggio di Calabria in 1475.

These are the first two Hebrew printed books that are actually dated. There is, however, a group of eight Hebrew books bearing neither date nor place of printing that some authorities believe to have been printed in Rome as early as 1469–72. The arguments are as follows.

There is a reference to early printing in Rome in a Venetian book dated 1566, which interlocks with a passage in one of these books. The books in this group contain the most primitive Hebrew printing to be found in Italy; they do not even contain punctuation marks. The unusually tall and broad pages of the folios and large quartos are similar to the style used almost exclusively by Sweynheym and Pannartz and Ulrich Han, the earliest Christian printers in Rome, who dropped this layout in about 1473. In their earliest days the Christian printers left the opening leaves of the first section blank, a habit that they also dropped in about 1473. The Hebrew books under discussion also contain, or once contained, such blanks. It is unlikely that these two features, the broad and tall areas of type and the early blank leaves, would have been adopted by the Jewish printers after they had been dropped by the Christian.

It seems just possible that at least one of the Hebrew printers in Rome may have served an apprenticeship under Sweynheym and Pannartz or Ulrich Han, and then started on his own in about 1469–72, or even a little earlier.

When advanced Hebraists are not in full agreement among themselves regarding an unresolved problem this is about as far as I can go. However three of the most important books under discussion, all printed by Obadiah, Manasseh and Benjamin de Roma, may be examined side by side in either the British Museum or the Jewish Theological Seminary of America, so the reader may form his own conclusion. They are:

MOSES ben NAHMAN: *Perush 'al hat-Torah (Commentary on the Pentateuch)*

NATHAN ben JEHIEL: *Aruk (Dictionary of the Talmud)*

SOLOMON ben ISAAC (Rashi): *Perush 'al hat-Torah*

The first portion of the Hebrew Bible to be printed was the Psalter, embedded in the *Commentary* of David Kimchi [99]. The date was 1477, and although the place of printing is not mentioned it is assumed to be Bologna, because some of the types were later used in the *Pentateuch* of 1482, mentioned above:

At the time when the art of printing books was invented, that is with moveable types set up in rows, by this process were produced three hundred copies (the choicest of the choice) of the Psalter with Kimchi's *Commentary*, which before the eyes who behold them, shine brilliantly like Sapphires. . . . This is the prayer of those who executed the printing, viz. Meister Joseph and Neriah, Chayyim Mordecai and Ezekiel of Ventura.

Note the word 'Meister'. With the exception of one Spaniard, all early Hebrew printers in Italy were of German origin. It might be asked why they did not print in Germany. The answer lies with the guilds, who would accept only Christian youths as apprentices. The fifteenth-century German guilds excluded Jews from printing as ruthlessly as many trade unions exclude women today.

But for printers who really made an impact we must turn to the family who took the name of Soncino, one of the great names in Hebrew printing, and one of the most remarkable dynasties in the whole history of the craft. The family sprang from Speyer in the Rhineland. Driven thence by a general edict of expulsion in 1435, they migrated to Bavaria. From here they were once again forced to flee, this time from the fanatical, crusading hatred of a Franciscan, Giovani di Capistrano.

From this brutal persecution it is pleasant to turn to the tolerance and protection provided by that bluff and honest soldier of fortune, Francesco Sforza, Duke of Milan. He enabled the family to settle in Soncino (about thirty-five miles east of Milan) in 1454 and, in gratitude, Joshua Solomon, son of Israel b. Samuel changed the family name to that of their adopted home.

At first the Soncini flourished as bankers, but in 1478 the opening of a public loan office (or 'monte di pietà') in Soncino, forced them to turn to other activities. In about 1483 they founded a press and showed wisdom in engaging Abraham ben Chayyim, whom we have previously met in Mantua, Ferrara and Bologna. The prime mover in this activity was Joshua Solomon Soncino, assisted by his nephews, Moses and Gerson. Their first production was a Talmud tract in 1483, but they soon engaged in larger enterprises.

So far other Hebrew presses had printed the *Pentateuch*, the Psalter and the Five Scrolls. This left a major gap, which the Soncini proceeded to fill. They printed the Former Prophets in 1485 [100], followed by the Later Prophets in 1486. With these volumes they established standards of master craftsmanship. The eminently legible type, the skilful

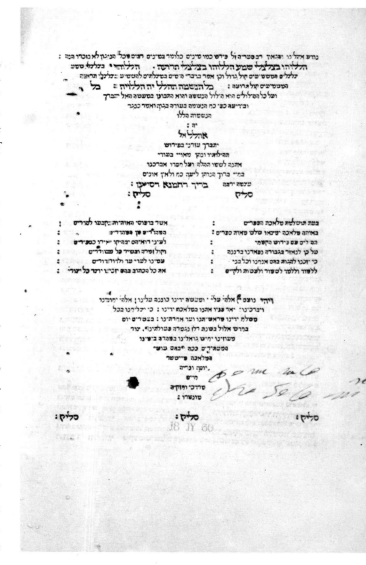

99 The first portion of the Hebrew Bible to be printed was the Psalter, embedded in the *Commentary* of David Kimchi (1477). The place of printing is not mentioned, but it is assumed to be Bologna since some of the types were used later in the *Pentateuch* of 1482. This is the last page, with the colophon.

composition, the attractive woodcut initials and the decorative headings create an atmosphere of dignity. They contain, one is gratified to note, a well-deserved tribute to Francesco Sforza:

Verily it was finished in the year 5246 of the creation of the world . . . here at Soncino in the Province of Lombardy which is under the government of the powerful Duke of Milan: May the Lord preserve him, bless him and strengthen him. Blessed be he who giveth strength to the weary and who multiplieth courage to him who hath no power. May his name be magnified above all blessing and praise.

In 1487 the Soncini printed the *Pentateuch*, of which only a single copy survives in the Jewish Theological Seminary in Breslau.

The Soncini were now in a position to achieve their *magnum opus*, the first complete edition of the Hebrew Bible, based on manuscripts of German and Franco-German origin, with vowel-points and accents but without any commentary. This came from their press in 1488. At the beginning of *Deuteronomy, Judges, Samuel* and *Kings* a space was left for illumination, but elsewhere each book begins with the first word in large ornamental woodcut letters. In the case of *Genesis* the first ornamental word is enclosed in a fine woodcut frame, while the opening of *Joshua* is surrounded by a splendid, full woodcut decorated border [101].

During the last decade of the fifteenth century conditions in Soncino declined. The new Duke of Milan, Lodovico Il Moro, renewed the persecution of the Jews. The turbulent conditions in the duchy, to a great extent the fruit of Lodovico's tortuous political policies, were hardly favourable to printing and Joshua Solomon Soncino moved his press to Naples, the only large city where Hebrew printing was tolerated. There he printed the second Hebrew Bible in 1491 or 1492, 'surpassing all Bible editions not only of this but of latest times in artistic and typographic beauty' [102]. The first pages of individual parts have borders by Ayolphus di Catono, and there are fine woodcut initial words. This is a rare book, only six copies being recorded. Happily there is a superb copy on vellum, which passed through the hands of two major Bible collectors, the Duke of Sussex and the Rev. Theodore Williams, before entering the British Museum.

King Ferrante I of Naples (1458–94), one of the great book collectors, was probably influenced by his Jewish doctor, Guglielmo di Portaleone, in giving protection to a large and prosperous Jewish community. This, no doubt, encouraged a number of printers to settle there, but Ferrante's career as a book collector must not blind us to other aspects of his character.

He was equalled in ferocity [says Burckhardt] by none among the princes of his time . . . he liked to have his opponents near him, either alive in well-guarded prisons, or dead and embalmed, dressed in the costumes which they wore in their lifetime. He would chuckle in talking of the captives with his friends, and made no secret whatever of the museum of mummies. His victims were mostly men whom he had got into his power by treachery; some were even seized while guests at the royal table.

100 The Soncino family, greatest of all early Hebrew printers, took their name from the Italian town where they found refuge from persecution. In 1485 they printed the first edition of the Former Prophets (*Joshua, Judges, Samuel* and *Kings*). Note the legible type, skilful composition, attractive heading and general atmosphere of dignity.

101 The first complete edition of the Bible in Hebrew
(with vowel-points and accents but no *Commentary*) was
printed by the Soncino family in 1488 using manuscripts of
German and Franco-German origin. The opening
of *Joshua* is surrounded by a fine woodcut border.

102 Driven from Soncino by the persecution of
Ludovico Il Moro [XII], Joshua Solomon Soncino
moved his press to Naples. Here, in 1491 or 1492,
he printed the second Hebrew Bible, a fine piece
of printing with Renaissance borders by
Ayolphus di Catono, of which only six copies
are recorded. This superb example on vellum
passed through the hands of two major Bible
collectors, the Rev. Theodore Williams and
the Duke of Sussex, and is now in the
British Museum.

The first Hebrew press at Naples was founded in 1486 by Germans,
their Hebrew name being Ashkenazi, while their surname was probably
derived from their native town of Gunzenhauser. 'Ashkenazi' is a
generic term, distinguishing all non-Mediterranean Jews from 'Sephardi'.
In Naples, where there were, then and later, so many Italian and Spanish
Jews, 'Ashkenazi' as a term identified the 'alien' element. There were
differences in ritual practices and traditions and rivalry in commerce,
much of which was done through a network of cousins.

The Neapolitan haven was short-lived. In 1492 the French invaded the
city 'and put it to the sword. In this misery and tumult the entire Jewish
community of Naples was dissolved and the fate of its printers sealed in
eternal darkness.' (Amram). It is assumed that Joshua Solomon Soncino
was among those who perished, for we never hear of him again. The

Jewish community in Naples was refounded only in the nineteenth century.

Meanwhile Gerson Soncino, who sometimes Latinized his name as Hieronymus Soncinus, moved to Brescia, then within the territory of the Venetian Republic, where he was working by 1491. The most important production of his life came quite early, a complete edition of the Hebrew Bible (1494), which became a standard text [103]. A significant feature was its handy size. Perhaps Gerson got the idea from Johann Froben of Basle (the associate of Erasmus), who in 1491 had printed 'the first poor man's [Christian] Bible'. In the colophon Gerson deplores the suffering and poverty-stricken condition of his Jewish brethren, being driven from place to place and unable to carry the larger Bibles about with them in their exile or to purchase the more costly editions:

I therefore determined to print the Four-and-Twenty books in a small size so that it may be with every man night and day to study therein, that he may not walk four ells without the Bible, but that he may have it by him and read it when he lies down and rises up . . . that he may not rest without it, may carry it about, study therein and reverence it. . . .

This edition achieved an influence even outside the Jewish community, for Luther used it when translating the Old Testament.

Sadly, this was the last major example of Hebrew printing for some time. Persecution increased and the wave of refugees from Portugal and Spain must have taxed the resources of the Jewish community in Italy to the utmost. No further Bible printing took place before 1500, and when the next major editions of the Hebrew Bible were printed (the Complutensian Polyglot [1514] and Bomberg's edition [Venice 1517]) they were the work of Christian printers.

Gerson must rank as one of the most peripatetic printers who ever lived. He worked at Soncino, Brescia, Barco, Fano, Pesaro, Ortona, Rimini, Cesena, Salonica and Constantinople. It is not inappropriate that his name, when divided, Ger-shom, means 'dwelling as a stranger'. Because he did not limit himself to books in Hebrew he was able to survive on his own as a printer for a further forty years and to print 150 books, the last in 1534. He published over a wide range: Humanism and philology, Italian literature, Christian theology, including the Fathers and Pius II's *Hymn to the Virgin,* the *Statutes of Fano* and other state documents. But interspersed with these, throughout his life, he printed a steady stream of Hebrew books.

By 1496 he had moved to Barco and issued a book or two. At this time he was the only Hebrew printer in the world, but there follows a silence of five years in which he printed nothing, and during which he disappears entirely. In 1502 he reappears at Fano. We do not know why he chose this town, which does not appear to have offered any special advantages. At this time Cesare Borgia was carving out a state for himself in Romagna by expelling the hereditary rulers with ruthless ferocity, and Fano formed a part of his dominion. Among the states he had seized was the dukedom of Urbino, causing the most cultured Italian court,

103 Gerson Soncino, himself an exile, realized that his brethren could not carry large Bibles from place to place in their banishment. In 1494 he produced the first pocket Hebrew Bible. This edition was used by Luther when translating the Old Testament.

that of Guidobaldo da Montefeltro (so unforgettably depicted by Baldassare Castiglione in *The Courtyer*), to flee into exile. The artists and Humanists were dispersed, including Guidobaldo's librarian, Lorenzo Astemio of Macerata, who now supported himself in Fano by teaching grammar. He was, no doubt, happy to join Gerson as editor of the books in Latin and Italian, and corrector of the press.

The types used in Fano were cut by the same Francesco Griffi who had created the Aldine italic. The preface to Gerson's Petrarch of 1503 is an interesting typographical document, for it contains an account of the quarrel between Aldus and that irascible type-cutter, expounding the latter's claim to have designed all the Aldine types. Amram gives a full translation.

Gerson and Lorenzo Astemio joined in a strenuous effort to secure the patronage of their overlord, Cesare Borgia. Astemio addressed him in the preface to his *Life of Epaminondas* (Laurentius Abstemius, *Epaminundae vita* [1502]): 'You, Cesare, have also this characteristic of Epaminondas, who though he might have led great armies and could have heaped up the greatest riches desired nothing more than an immortal name.' The Petrarch of 1503 contains a prefatory sonnet concluding:

> O, Godlike Caesar Borgia, whose repute
> E'en now extends unto the farthest land.
> So to thy excellence, thy noble name,
> We dedicate this work, the ripest fruit
> Of Fano's press, imprinted by our hand.

But, what are the hopes of man? Only a few weeks later came the famous supper party in Rome when Cardinal Adrian da Castello entertained Pope Alexander VI and his son, Cesare. The latter had intended to murder his host but, owing to some mix-up on the part of those waiting at table (now we have none, it is pleasant to reflect that servants can be a doubtful blessing), the whole party drank poison. All the guests suffered. Within a week the Pope was dead; Cesare (poetic justice) was too ill to profit by the ensuing chaos and, on recovery, was forced to flee to Spain. Castello recovered, but not before the skin had peeled from his body.

It was in the year of Cesare Borgia's death, 1507, that Gerson completed his finest achievement in terms of book production, *Decachordum Christianum (The Christian Ten-Stringed Harpsichord)*, by Cardinal Marcus Vigerius, dedicated to Julius II [104]. This has ten fine full-page woodcuts with Renaissance borders and many charming vignettes. The beauty of this work so impressed the governor of Fano, a kinsman of Vigerius, that Gerson was engaged to print the *Statutes of Fano* after he had moved to Pesaro some years later.

With the fall of Cesare Borgia the ruling families regained their states and Giovanni Sforza returned as Lord of Pesaro. His wife Ginevra was the daughter of the Venetian nobleman, Marco Tiepolo, who had befriended Gerson Soncino in earlier days. This may be why Gerson moved his press to Pesaro.

It would be interesting to follow Gerson, step by step, as he moved from town to town, up and down the Adriatic coast, but space forbids. However, I cannot resist recording the welcome offered by the City of Rimini to this distinguished printer *(librorum impressore egregio)*. In a document of 24 October 1518 he is exempted from all taxes and customs dues, given a shop on the bridge of St Peter (now the Ponte d'Augusto) and promised, by the City, a year's free rent for his private home.

Yet Gerson's efforts never achieved the financial success they deserved. Aldus and Bomberg, printing in Venice, enjoyed the commercial opportunities provided by that city and, further, must have derived great advantage from the licensing monopolies they were able to obtain.

The final blow to the Jewish community came with the sack of Rome by the Constable of Bourbon in 1527. Even by modern standards this was a revolting and barbaric outrage and the Jews suffered worst. Fearing that the terror would spread, thousands of Jews emigrated and Gerson, then in Cesena, was caught up in the general mood and went with them.

Most of us regard the conquest of Constantinople by the Turks as one of the great disasters of history, bringing with it the final fall of the Roman Empire, the destruction of the great and venerable Byzantine civilization and the enslavement of Greece. For the Jews it provided a refuge and, under Solyman the Magnificent, they enjoyed a toleration denied to them in Christian Europe. Until the German invasion of Greece in 1941 there was a Jewish population of forty to fifty thousand in Salonica who spoke a dialect of Castillian Spanish. At the end of the war only three to four thousand returned.

Gerson's son, Moses, had already left Italy in 1521 and had founded a press in Salonica. The old man joined him and printed an edition of the *Mahzor*. Then, restless as ever, he moved on to Constantinople, set up his press and for the remainder of his life printed entirely in Hebrew. As a centre of printing Constantinople shared the advantage of Venice, Antwerp and London in being an international port, and the books flowed back into Europe.

After the death of Gerson, in 1534, his other son, Eliezer, carried on the press. One of Eliezer's last productions was a polyglot *Pentateuch* in Hebrew, Aramaic, Modern Greek and Spanish, all these languages printed in Hebrew characters, together with the commentary of Rashi. Shortly after this the press passed into the hands of Eliezer Parnas. By that time the Soncino family had, against all odds, been printing Hebrew for almost sixty-five years and the momentum of their press continued, a noble contribution to the culture of their people.

At an international printing conference I once met an Italian Jewish printer who claimed to be descended from the Soncini. 'It is not every family,' he boasted, 'who have been in the printing business for almost five hundred years.'

The other really major early printer of Hebrew Bibles was a Christian, Daniel Bomberg, member of a wealthy merchant family, who was born

104 Gerson Soncino was able to survive through his long career as a Hebrew printer by producing work in other fields. His masterpiece, *Decachordum Christianum (The Christian Ten-Stringed Harpsichord)* by Cardinal M. Vigerius (Fano 1507) is illustrated with fine woodcuts within Renaissance borders.

at Antwerp some time after 1483 and who died there in 1553. In the second decade of the fifteenth century he moved to Venice and established the Hebrew press that made him famous.

All bibliographers of Hebrew accord to Bomberg the high praise that is his due. Amram says of Gerson Soncino and Daniel Bomberg: 'These two men share the highest place in the history of Hebrew typography.' It is natural that Bomberg's name should also frequently be coupled with that of Aldus, 'The Aldus of Hebrew Books'.

In 1515 Bomberg obtained from the Venetian authorities a copyright for books printed in Hebrew types: '. . . *lettere cuneate si in rame come in stagno o in altra materia impronate*'. ('Printed in wedge-shaped [cuneiform] letters in copper, in tin or in other materials.') The Fourth Lateran Council had required all Jews to wear distinguishing marks on their garments, often a yellow cap. In order to protect his workmen from molestation Bomberg also obtained, with considerable difficulty, a further privilege that allowed them to discard this disgraceful badge.

When his privilege to print in Hebrew lapsed in 1526 Bomberg ran into considerable opposition. At first the renewal was refused, 'and this was well done,' records Marino Sanuto (who had voted against it) in his diary, 'for he printed books in Hebrew which were against the faith.' However these conscientious scruples were overcome when Bomberg offered the enormous sum of 500 ducats. To appreciate the size of this sum it may be recalled that the Council of Rimini had paid twelve ducats as the annual rent for Gerson Soncino's house.

Armed with his privilege Bomberg produced his first book in 1515, an edition of the *Psalms* in Hebrew. His editor was a converted Jew, Felix Pratensis (d. 1539), with whose help, in 1516–17, Bomberg printed the first Biblia Rabbinica. Of this noble work, in four volumes folio, C. D. Ginsburg, one of the leading Hebrew scholars of modern times, remarks: 'The importance of this edition can hardly be overestimated.' For the most part it agrees with the Soncino text of 1488, but has been improved by comparison with manuscript Bibles, while various readings and Masoretic glosses are printed for the first time. In addition a number of Targums make important contributions to textual criticism.*

With some effrontery, the dedication describes this as the earliest printing of the Hebrew Bible: 'a truly difficult thing to do, nor, for that reason, heretofore attempted by others.' (*'Rem equidem perdifficilem, nec ob id ab aliis hactenus tentatam.'*) This dedication, incidentally, was addressed to that greatest of all targets for dedications, Leo X, with, in this case, considerable justification; not only for his tolerance to the

---

* The Hebrew word Masoreth means 'tradition'. The Masoretes were Jewish scholars who, between the sixth and the tenth centuries, introduced a system of vowel points and accents with the object of preserving the traditional pronunciation used in the Synagogues, at a time when Hebrew was becoming less and less the daily speech of the Jews. The Hebrew word Targum means 'interpretation', here used for Aramaic translations which preserved oral traditions no longer available in Hebrew. There are Targums to all the Books of the Hebrew Bible except *Ezra, Nehemiah* and *Daniel*.

Bible in Hebrew, but even towards the Talmud which, both earlier and subsequently, was savagely attacked.

In 1524–25, just before the first privilege ran out, Bomberg produced his second Biblia Rabbinica [105]. This really was an innovation, for it contains, for the first time, the extensive and traditional apparatus of the Masorah. It was edited by Jacob ben Chayyim ibn Adonijah, an ultra-orthodox Rabbinic Jew and a profound Masoretic scholar. To him the idea of a Hebrew Bible edited by a Jewish Augustinian and dedicated to the pope must have been anathema, and he persuaded Bomberg to undertake a new edition. In the introduction Jacob ben Chayyim tells us:

> When I explained to Bomberg the advantage of the Masorah, he did all in his power to send into all countries in order to search out what may be found of the Masorah and, praised be the Lord, we obtained as many of the Masoretic books as could possibly be got. He was not backward, and his hand was not closed, nor did he draw back his right hand from producing gold out of his purse to defray the expenses of the books and of the messengers who were engaged to make search for them in the most remote corners and in every place where they might possibly be found.

Amram gives Joseph Justus Scaliger, the sixteenth-century French scholar, as his authority when saying that Bomberg 'lost three or four millions in gold on his printing enterprises'.

The very high standard of editing was worthily presented in a splendid piece of printing in which many typographical difficulties were overcome. C. D. Ginsburg said of this edition: 'No textual redactor of modern days who professes to edit the Hebrew text according to the Masorah can deviate from it without giving conclusive justification for so doing.'

This may be the place to pay tribute to three generations of the Adelkind family, all of whom worked for Bomberg, and especially Cornelio, whose name sometimes appears on title-pages and in colophons. They, too, had fled from Germany. An Adelkind had given up his life for the 'Sanctification of the Name' at Nuremberg; another had recited the Shema on the rack at Weissensee.

Bomberg's Bibles were much used by Reformation translators. Ginsburg, appropriately enough, owned Luther's copy of the 1525–28 edition. Bomberg also printed the first complete edition of the Talmud, and the setting out of the pages that he devised is still in use today. Henry VIII's copy of this edition is in the British Museum.

After his death Bomberg's types passed into the possession of Giovanni di Gara. But in any case with Bomberg the printing of Hebrew had passed out of Jewish into Christian hands: 'Our inheritance has passed to the stranger.'

105 Daniel Bomberg, a Christian from Antwerp working in Venice, produced (with the aid of Jewish editors) Hebrew Bibles of the greatest importance. This, printed in four folio volumes (1524–25) is the first to contain the Masorah. G. D. Ginsburg, the modern Hebrew scholar, said that 'No textual redactor . . . can deviate from it without conclusive justification.'

CHAPTER SIX

HERBALS AND COLOUR-PLATE FLOWER BOOKS

THE HERBALS FIRST PRINTED towards the close of the fifteenth century (though, in some cases, written long before) represent the medical science and botany of the ancient world as it had survived, with accretions and metamorphoses, through the Middle Ages. They are of great interest in scientific history, for they were printed just before the whole conception of nature was revolutionized by Renaissance science.

But for many people the interest lies in their quaintness and charm, especially in the woodcut illustrations of the *Hortus Sanitatis*. And if among my readers there are some, and surely there is at least one, who have never captured a unicorn (much harder today, with the great decline in virginity) [110] or, with infinite precautions, raised a mandrake at midnight (let alone got it with child), dealt with a mermaid or, which is much rarer, a merman, the study of herbals will open up new opportunities. And there can be few who would not eat of the Tree of Life when they shall be 'clothed with blessed immortality, and not fatigued with infirmity, or anxiety, or lassitude, or weariness of trouble'.

One of the most interesting features of early herbals lies in the treatment of the mandrake *(Mandragora officinalis),* a legend at least as old as Pythagoras, who named it *'anthropomorphon'.* The plant, especially to those with a vivid imagination, bears a resemblance to the human form, a resemblance that could be, and often was, doctored by the unscrupulous to deceive the credulous. It was believed that this semi-human plant shrieked when pulled from the soil, a belief recorded by Shakespeare in *Romeo and Juliet:*

> And shrieks like mandrakes torn out of the earth,
> That living mortals, hearing them, run mad.

To avoid serious injury or madness it was considered inadvisable to pull the mandrake in person. The surrounding soil was first loosened, then the plant was attached by a rope to an underfed dog or horse, food was displayed at a distance and the hungry animal, rushing towards it, jerked the mandrake from the earth [106 and 112].

Most surviving herbals are worn, soiled and often imperfect, but it must be remembered for what purpose they were produced. Practical use in surgery or kitchen is not conducive to mint copies. Anyone who has noticed what a housewife can do to a cookery book in one generation will be surprised that any herbals have survived at all after close on five hundred years. They were used in close proximity to chemicals and liquids, hastily consulted in moments of panic, of sudden illness and snake-bite, when medicine was a dark mystery and there was no doctor within miles.

BELOW 106 The *Herbal* of Apuleius Barbarus was compiled about AD 400 and embodies the transition from pagan to Christian medicine. This first edition (possibly based on a manuscript still at Monte Cassino) was published in Rome about 1483. It is probably the earliest printed book to contain illustrations of plants.
OPPOSITE 107 The *Gart der Gesundheit (Garden of Health)*, printed by Peter Schoeffer (1485), has been described as 'the most important medieval work on natural history'. It is a completely new work and the woodcuts are nearly all drawn from the living plants; not, as was previously the case, debased copies of classical originals.

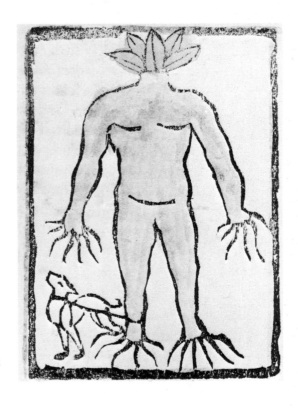

108 Since most people in the Middle Ages could not read, herbs to be used as antidotes against bites and stings were shown in conjunction with the offending animal or insect, as in this example from the *Herbal* of Apuleius Barbarus, Rome, about 1483.

OPPOSITE XX The high standard of manuscript book production achieved before the expulsion of the Jews from Spain and Portugal may be seen in this Hebrew Bible on vellum executed in Lisbon by Samuel b. Rabbi Samuel ibn Mūsā (1483–84). There are richly illuminated titles to each book and beautiful decorated supplementary leaves of Masoretic matter. British Museum, OR 2627.

The *Herbal* of Apuleius Barbarus was compiled in about the year AD 400. It is thought that the author was nicknamed Barbarus to distinguish him from the author of *The Golden Ass*. His Herbal embodies the transition from Pagan to Christian medicine. For a thousand years it had more influence on medicine than any other book of its kind. The oldest surviving manuscript, now at Leyden, was written in Provence during the seventh century. Translated into Anglo-Saxon, it brought to England the medical heritage of the ancient world. But the drawings, both in the manuscripts and the first printed version, were not taken direct from nature; they were endlessly copied after late Roman originals in the style that has come to be known as Dioscoridean.

Since most people in the Middle and Dark Ages could not read, herbs to be used as antidotes against bites and stings are shown in conjunction with the offending animal or insect [108]. And whereas later botanical artists have tended to concentrate on flowers and fruits, early herbalists gave great attention to the roots, as these were of prime importance in the making of drugs. Not unnaturally it was the first herbal to be printed [106 and 108]. Joannes Philippus de Lignamine was the first native Italian printer. As a Sicilian of good family, and a favourite at the court of Sixtus IV, he is hardly likely to have soiled his own hands with printer's ink. He was, perhaps, rather a publisher who employed craftsmen to work for him. He tells us in the preface to his edition of the *Herbal*, printed in Rome between 1481 and 1483, that he found a manuscript of Apuleius Barbarus in the monastery of Monte Cassino, and from this he had the illustrations copied in 131 metal cuts, subsequently partly coloured by stencil. With one possible exception, this is the earliest printed book to contain illustrations of plants. In our own time F. W. T. Hunger discovered a ninth-century codex of Apuleius Barbarus at Monte Cassino, which has a very close connection with de Lignamine's edition, though there are some puzzling discrepancies. Hunger published an edition with the manuscript drawings and the printed metal cuts in juxtaposition, providing an ideal opportunity to study this fascinating problem.

There are two issues of the *editio princeps*. The first is dedicated to Francesco de Gonzaga, the cardinal who was so beautifully portrayed by Mantegna in the palace at Mantua. Gonzaga died in 1483, and since he was no longer in a position to forward the career of de Lignamine at court he was replaced, as a dedicatee, by Cardinal Giulio della Rovere, later Julius II, painted by Botticelli, Raphael, Titian and others. Seldom, or never, can a pair of dedicatees have been portrayed with greater genius.

Three herbals were printed at Mainz in the fifteenth century. The *Latin Herbarius* was printed by Peter Schoeffer in 1484; this is a collection of simple remedies for simple people, based entirely on the German plants that they could find in the woods and fields, or grow in their own gardens. Nearly all the quotations are derived from authors who wrote before AD 1300, certainly none later than the mid-fourteenth century, from which we may conclude that the text was compiled about a hundred

ויהי אחרי מות משה עבד

 יהוה ויאמר יהוה אל יהושע בן
נון משרת משה לאמר משה עבדי מת
ועתה קום עבר את הירדן הזה אתה וכל
העם הזה אל הארץ אשר אנכי נתן להם
לבני ישראל כל מקום אשר תדרך כף
רגלכם בו לכם נתתיו כאשר דברתי אל
משה מהמדבר והלבנון הזה ועד הנהר
הגדול נהר פרת כל ארץ החתים ועד
הים הגדול מבוא השמש יהיה גבלכם
לא יתיצב איש לפניך כל ימי חייך כאשר
הייתי עם משה אהיה עמך לא ארפך ולא
אעזבך חזק ואמץ כי אתה תנחיל את העם

רבמ
אבא רעיא
שמשא
נילבא

הפטרה
לפרשת
וזאת
הברכה

ב
פסו

ב
וזאת

ב ד
ז
ז

ר א
פסו
בסם

Rosa centifolia Bullata.
Rosier à feuilles de Laitue.

P. J. Redouté pinx.   Imprimerie de Remond   Langlois sculp.

years before the book was printed, although no manuscript is known to have survived. The illustrations are not derived directly from nature but copied from older drawings. Although their botanical value is not high, they do have a certain vigour and attraction of their own [109].

The *Gart der Gesundheit (Garden of Health)*, also printed by Peter Schoeffer, in 1485, is an immense advance on its predecessors. Indeed John Ludwig Choulant described it as 'the most important medieval work on natural history'. It is a completely new book compiled under the auspices of a wealthy patron who engaged Dr Johann von Cube to write the medical sections. In the preface the anonymous compiler gives us an engaging account of his motives and, without realizing it, of his attractive personality. He praises and gives thanks to the Creator for providing so many antidotes to the troubles of this world.

By virtue of these herbs and created things the sick man may recover the temperament of the four elements and the health of his body. Since, then, man can have no greater nor nobler treasure on earth than bodily health, I came to the conclusion that I could not perform any more honourable, useful or holy work or labour than to compile a book in which should be contained the virtue and nature of many herbs and other created things, together with their true colours and form, for the help of all the world and the common good. . . .

When he came to illustrate the plants described by the great medical authorities of the classical world they could not be found in Germany. Nothing daunted, he laid aside his work and, combining spiritual salvation with earthly achievement, set out on a pilgrimage to the Holy Land, taking a botanical artist with him.

All this effort resulted in close on four hundred woodcuts, many of them direct drawings from the living plant, something that had not been done for over a thousand years. They were so superior to the debased copies of Dioscoridean originals that Arnold Klebs called them the greatest single step ever made in the art of botanical illustration. Even though some of the cuts were not up to the standard of the best, they dominated the field for two generations and were outmoded only when the advance of Renaissance science produced a new conception in the herbal of Brunfels, printed in 1530 [107 and 112].

The text embodies a great part of what was known and believed regarding medicine and botany in late fifteenth-century Germany. But it does more than that; it is one of the longest German texts of its time and preserves much folklore and tradition, besides giving an insight into dialects and aspects of the language that would otherwise be lost.

The *Gart der Gesundheit* contains 435 chapters. In 1491 the same wealthy patron promoted a new book, *Hortus Sanitatis,* containing 1066 chapters, printed by Jacob Meydenbach. To some extent this is a Latin translation of the earlier book, but it is more than that: far more space is given to the medical qualities of herbs and there are long new sections on animals, birds, fish and minerals. The rich variety of vigorous woodcuts makes this a very attractive book. The engraver was a more skilled craftsman, but there was some botanical retrogression, since he

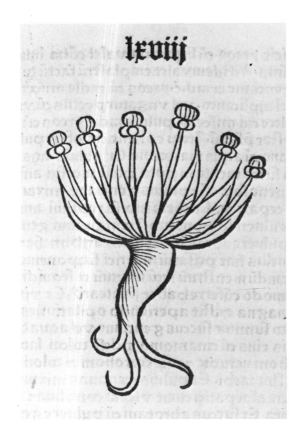

109 The *Latin Herbarius*, printed by Peter Schoeffer in 1484, is a collection of simple remedies for simple people based on German plants. The text cannot be later than the mid fourteenth century, but no manuscript has survived.

OPPOSITE ABOVE RIGHT XXI No colour-plate flower books have ever surpassed in beauty and splendour those produced by Pierre-Joseph Redouté (1759–1840). In addition to his artistic gifts, Redouté was fortunate in the brilliant engravers who created the plates and a series of rich patrons who supported him. This plate is from *Les Roses* (1817–24), the most popular of all Redouté's books.
OPPOSITE ABOVE LEFT XXII *Lilium superbum* from Redouté's *Les Liliacées*, 8 vols (1802–16).

OPPOSITE BELOW LEFT XXIII Samuel Curtis, a nurseryman in Essex, was the first gardener to promote the cultivation of the camellia as a greenhouse shrub. Anemone flowered or Watarah Camellia from *A Monograph of the Genus Camellia* (1819).
OPPOSITE BELOW RIGHT XXIV Carnations from Samuel Curtis, *The Beauties of Flora* (1820), which contains coloured aquatints based on water-colours by Clara Maria Pope who exhibited at the Royal Academy for forty years.

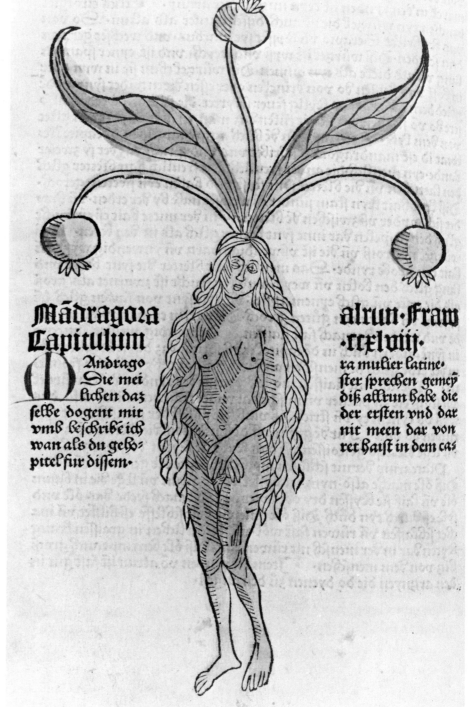

TOP, ABOVE AND OPPOSITE 110, 111 and 113
Hortus Sanitatis, printed by J. Meydenbach
(1491), is far more than a Latin translation of the
Gart der Gesundheit; more space is given to
medicine and there are new sections on animals,
birds, fish and minerals.
ABOVE RIGHT 112 A female mandrake
from the *Gart der Gesundheit* printed by
Peter Schoeffer (Mainz 1485).

did not always understand the plants he was copying from the previous
cuts. Full-page illustrations introduce each section, including the study
of disputing herbalists, an animated scene in the interior of a jeweller's
shop and doctors and patients [110, 111, 113–18].

Some qualities need to be represented by symbols, and this gives us a
charming insight into fifteenth-century life. 'Bread' is illustrated by a
housewife with her loaves; 'wine' by a man gazing at a glass; a woman
milks a cow; 'water' is represented by a fountain. Blacksmiths and
craftsmen work at their trades. One man extracts a jewel from the head
of a toad, while another sorts oysters for pearls.

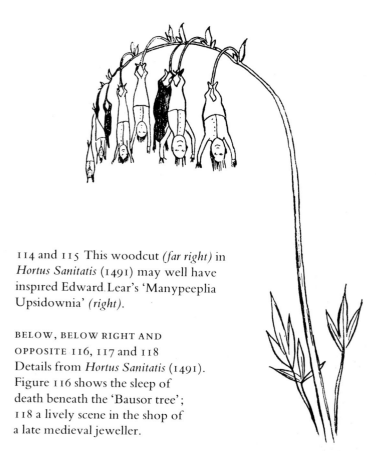

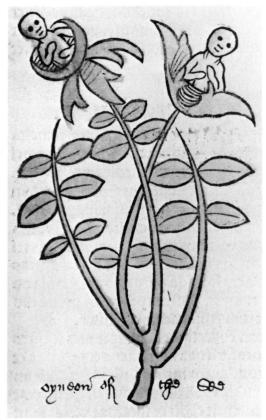

114 and 115 This woodcut *(far right)* in
Hortus Sanitatis (1491) may well have
inspired Edward Lear's 'Manypeeplia
Upsidownia' *(right)*.

BELOW, BELOW RIGHT AND
OPPOSITE 116, 117 and 118
Details from *Hortus Sanitatis* (1491).
Figure 116 shows the sleep of
death beneath the 'Bausor tree';
118 a lively scene in the shop of
a late medieval jeweller.

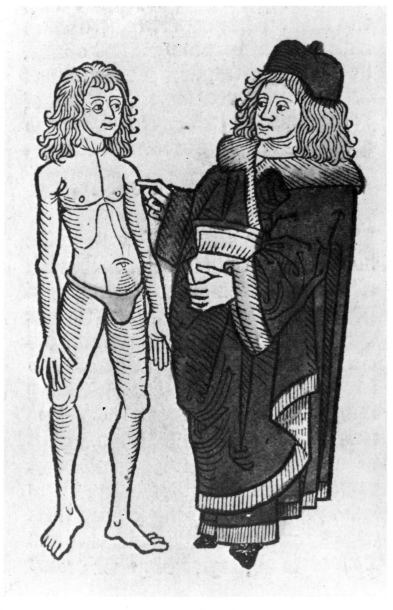

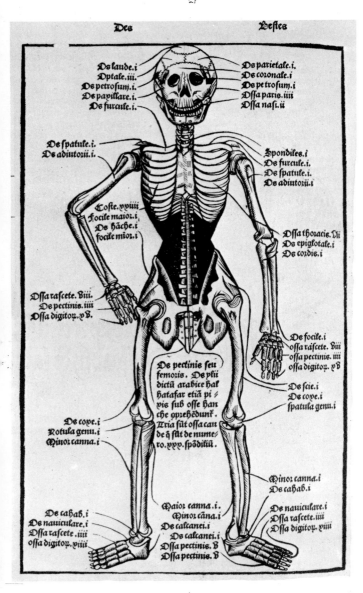

119 *Hortus Sanitatis* was shamelessly pirated by other printers; a French translation was printed in Paris by Antoine Vérard (1500). This copy was purchased by Henry VII and is now in the British Museum.

The chapters on animals include mythical creatures. The phoenix survives in the fire, the harpy flourishes its claws, while a bird, with its excessively long neck tied in a knot, is not unreminiscent of *Alice in Wonderland,* when Alice, having eaten of the mushroom, found her head projecting above the tree-tops: '. . . all she could see, when she looked down, was an immense length of neck, which seemed to rise like a stalk out of a sea of green leaves that lay far below her.' Speaking of parallels, Edward Lear's nonsense books, including *Nonsense Botany,* were created to amuse the children of the Earl of Derby. Since there was a copy of *Hortus Sanitatis* in the library at Lord Derby's seat, Knowsley, it is possible that the likeness was not mere coincidence [114 and 115].

The world of fable extends from animals to botany. It was believed that the 'Bausor tree', in common with the Upas tree, gave forth a narcotic poison, and in the woodcut two men are shown beneath it deep in the sleep of death. The ubiquitous mandrake makes another appearance here, and in another woodcut Adam and Eve are faced by a female-headed serpent.

All of these herbals were shamelessly translated and pirated by other printers and in other countries. In 1500 the French printer, Antoine Vérard, produced *Ortus sanitatis translate de latin en francois.* Henry VII hastened to order a copy and the accounts of his Treasurer of the Chamber, John Heron, contain the entry: 'Item to Anthony Vérard for two bokes called the gardyn of helth . . . £6.' This copy, I am glad to add, is now in the British Museum [119].

Probably the most famous English work in this field is Gerarde's *The Herball or Generall Historie of Plantes* (1597). John Gerarde (1545–1612) had been apprenticed to one of the leading surgeons of his day, was twice warden of the Barber-Surgeons' Company and, as the officer responsible, examined and, if he approved, licensed the young men who hoped to practise as surgeons in their turn. But Gerarde's true interest lay in botany. He cultivated a celebrated garden in Holborn and in 1596 published a list of his plants. This, the first catalogue of its kind, has survived in a single copy, once in the possession of Sir Hans Sloane and now in the British Museum.

Gerarde dedicated his herbal to Lord Burghley, whose gardens both in the Strand and at Theobalds were in his charge. It has often been stated that Gerarde's famous book is largely the work of others. According to this theory it is based on *Stirpium Historiae Pemptades Sex* (1583) an excellent work by Rembert Dodoens (the first major Belgian botanist) translated by Robert Priest who died before the completion of his work. John Norton, the publisher, is said to have handed the unfinished manuscript to Gerarde who altered the arrangement to fit the system of the French botanist Mathias de l'Obel (1538–1616). L'Obel spent the greater part of his life in England and made considerable contributions to British botany, recording more than eighty plants for the first time. Gerarde added information derived from his practical experience, such as places in England where the plants could be found. But, either through ignorance or impatience, he sometimes placed the descriptions against

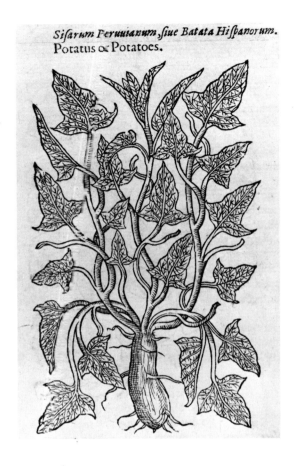

Sisarum Peruuianum, siue Batata Hispanorum.
Potatus or Potatoes.

the wrong woodcuts. There are about 2,200 of these blocks, almost all of which had been used previously at Frankfurt in the *Eicones Plantarum*, a massive series of plant illustrations by Jacob Dietrich of Bergzabern (?1520–90), better known as Tabernaemontanus.

We shall never be certain how much of the *Herball* is Gerarde's work. No doubt it is best to follow the summing up of William T. Stearn of the British Museum (Natural History):

Yet the *Herball* as published contains so much that undoubtedly came from Gerarde himself, and its production even with the possible aid of Priest's translation, was so massive a task that it seems charitable to credit him with the whole.

Gerarde gives us an interesting account of potatoes. First, of the sweet potato (*Ipomoea batates*) [120]:

The Potatoes grow in India, Barbarie, Spaine, and other hotte regions, of which I planted diuers rootes (that I bought at the exchange in London) in my garden, where they flourished vntil winter, at which time they perished and rotted. The Potatoe rootes are among the Spaniards, Italians, Indians, and many other nations common and ordinarie meate, which no doubt are of mightie nourishing parts, and do strengthen and comfort nature, whose nutriment is as it were a meane betweene flesh and fruit, though somewhat windie; but being rosted in the embers, they do loose much of their windinesse, especially being eaten sopped in wine. . . .
They are vsed to be eaten rosted in the ashes; some when they be so rosted, infuse them, and sop them in wine: and others to giue them the greater grace in eating, do boile them with prunes, and so eate them. And likewise others dresse them (being first rosted) with oile, vineger and salt, euery man according to his owne taste and liking: notwithstanding howsoeure they be dressed, they comfort, nourish, and strengthen the bodie, procuring bodily lust, and that with greedinesse.

120 Gerarde's *Herball or Generall Historie of Plants* (1597) has delighted English-speaking gardeners and botanists for almost 400 years. Here we see the sweet potato.

121 Gerarde strains our credulity with his Barnakle tree which is said to bear geese.

Gerarde then turns to the 'Virginia Potatoes [*Solanum tuberosum*] . . . It groeth naturally in America where it was first discoured, as reporteth *C. Clusius* since which time I haue received rootes hereof from Virginia, otherwise called Noremberga, which growe and prosper in my garden, as in their owne natiue countrie.' He illustrates this with one of the few original blocks in his book. Gerarde stretches our credulity by his account of the Barnakle or Goose tree [121]:

There are founde in the north parts of Scotland, & the Islands adiacent, called Orchades, certaine trees, whereon doe growe certain shell fishes, of a white colour, tending to russet; wherein are conteined little liuing creatures: which shels in time of maturitie do open, and out of them grow those little liuing things; which falling into the water doe become foules whom we call Barnakles, in the north of England Brant Geese, and in Lancashire tree Geese; but the other that do fall vpon the land, perish and come to nothing: thus much by the writings of others, and also from the mouths of people of those parts, which may very well accord with truth.

Gerarde's acceptance of old wives' tales is hardly a credit to Renaissance science. Yet from our point of view the very preservation of

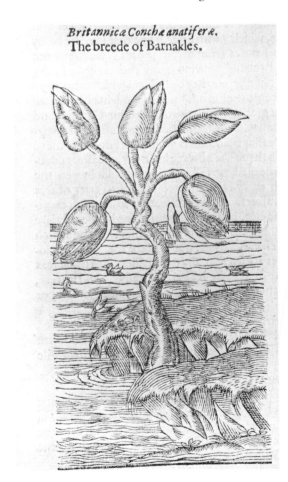

Britannica Conchæ anatiferæ.
The breede of Barnakles.

Ceres

Pomona

Ecce dedi vobis omnes herbas sementantes semen, quæ sunt. Gen. 1. 29.

Excideret ne tibi diuini muneris Author,
Præsentem monstrat quælibet herba Deum.

THE HERBALL
OR GENERALL
Historie of
Plantes.

Gathered by John Gerardê
of London Master in
CHIRVRGERIE

Very much
Enlarged and Amended by
Thomas Johnson
Citizen and Apothecarye
of
LONDON

THEOPHRASTVS

DIOSCORIDES

London Printed by
Adam Islip Ioice Norton
and Richard Whitakers
Anno 1636.

Io. Payne sculp.

folklore and old beliefs is itself of value. Gerarde and other herbalists give us the secrets of many vegetable dyes. After these recipes had been lost during the Industrial Revolution in favour of chemical substitutes, William Morris was able to turn to early herbals and revive them for the Arts and Crafts movement. Above all, both Priest and Gerarde wrote during that golden age of English literature when it seemed almost impossible not to write vivid and lively prose. As a result, Gerarde's *Herball* is a work of great value and charm that has been read and loved by generations of English gardeners and botanists.

Gerarde's book was regarded as the undoubted standard work for over a quarter of a century, until the rival herbal of John Parkinson was nearing completion. Fearing competition, the publishers resolved on a new and revised edition. For this they had the wisdom (or good fortune) to engage Thomas Johnson, and they insisted that the work should be completed within a year. Johnson added eight hundred new species and seven hundred woodcuts. His corrections to the text earned the tribute '*Gerarde emaculatus*' from no less an authority than John Ray, the father of English natural history. This handsome folio was published in 1633 and reprinted in 1636 [122].

Thomas Johnson is an attractive figure. He, too, cultivated a physic garden in what is now the centre of London, and went on plant-hunting tours through the countryside. His records of these excursions, such as *Iter Plantarum Investigationis ergo susceptum a decem Sociis in Agrum Cantianum anno Dom. 1629* are the first English local floras. But for his tragically early death, Johnson would without doubt have been a great figure in the development of English botany.

At the outbreak of the Civil War Johnson rallied to the Royalist cause and rose to be a colonel. He was foremost among the brave defenders of Basing House. On 14 September 1644, during a skirmish, he was wounded in the shoulder, 'whereby contracting a feaver, he died a fortnight after'. Anthony À. Wood described him as 'the best herbalist of his age in England', and 'no less eminent in the garrison for his valour and conduct as a soldier'. It is touching to recall that later botanists have paid their tribute to both Gerarde and Johnson by giving their names to species. Linnaeus founded the genus *Gerardia,* which now includes about thirty species, chiefly in North America. Genera dedicated to Johnson by Philip Miller and by Michel Adanson having been merged in the genera *Callicarpa* and *Cedrela,* the name *Johnsonia* now belongs to a genus of *Liliaceae.*

[Dr] Alexander Blackwell (d. 1747) was an Aberdonian adventurer who came to London in pursuit of his fortune. He was one of an active family: his brother wrote elaborate books on the classics and his sister produced nineteen children. Although at various times he practised as a doctor, there is considerable doubt as to whether he ever received any medical training. In London he abandoned medicine and worked for a printer as corrector of the press. Having married a lady who brought a fair-sized dowry, he set up as a printer in his own right, but soon found himself opposed by a closed-shop situation. The other printers, incensed

OPPOSITE 122 In 1633 Gerarde's *Herball* was enlarged, corrected and brought up to date by Thomas Johnson, an able botanist and a brave man, tragically killed in the English Civil War; here reprinted in 1636.

because Blackwell had not served a regular apprenticeship, combined in a successful effort to ruin him, and he was thrown into prison for debt.

His wife Elizabeth was one of those marvellous women of character, ability and virtue who, having become entangled with a feckless and n'er-do-well husband, devote themselves without stint to his protection and support. On learning that there was need for a medical herbal with coloured plates she took lodgings near the Chelsea Physic Garden and proceeded to paint watercolours of about five hundred plants. She carried these to the Fleet prison, where her husband added the scientific and foreign names and, with the author's consent, abridged descriptions from Philip Miller's *Botanicum Officinale*. Elizabeth then engraved the copperplates and coloured the prints by her own hand.

One would have feared that so elaborate and lengthy an enterprise, undertaken without resources, could only have increased the financial *débâcle*. Not at all. *A Curious Herbal, containing five hundred cuts of the most useful plants which are now used in the practice of Physic* was published in two volumes, folio, in 1737. The debts were paid off and Alexander Blackwell was released. What novelist would have dared to embark on such a fantastic and improbable story with the faintest hope of credence?

It would be nice if we could leave the happily reunited couple to live out peaceful and contented lives. But this would take no account of Alexander Blackwell's character. Having been placed in charge of the Duke of Chandos's princely improvements at Cannons, he defrauded his employer and lost his job in a manner, according to the *Gentleman's Magazine*, which 'kept him from other employment'. Having emigrated to Sweden, Blackwell reverted to medicine and even prescribed successfully for the king. Never a man to leave well alone, he now plunged into the shark-infested waters of political intrigue. A fatuous plot, apparently of his own devising and involving an attempt to alter the succession to the throne by the most dubious means, resulted in his arrest. He was tortured and then condemned, by a secret trial, to be broken alive on the wheel. Fortunately this sentence was commuted to decapitation.

On the scaffold Blackwell was seen at his best. Throughout his life he had been accustomed, by means of natural charm and wit, to talk himself out of awkward situations. Therefore the authorities, perhaps wisely, ordered that his speech to the assembled crowd be drowned by a roll of drums. Recklessly brave to the last, he apologized to the executioner for having placed his head on the wrong side of the block. This, he said, was not an intentional delaying tactic, but simply due to inexperience, as he had never been beheaded before. His wife lived on, for another eleven years, to the age of sixty-nine, and was buried in Chelsea Old Church, 27 October 1758.

Her book lived on and earned a fine new edition, edited by the famous doctor and botanist, C. J. Trew, at Nuremberg (1757–73). Trew drew attention to its 'superiority to the more scientific work of Morandi alike in accuracy of colouring and in the copiousness of representing exotic plants'. The original drawings were purchased by the

Earl of Bute. While I have been writing this seventy-two of them were sold by Sotheby's, who have kindly provided me with Figure 123.

The Chelsea Physic Garden had been founded by the Society of Apothecaries in 1673 on ground given to them by Sir Hans Sloane. May I digress to record that seeds sent to the Colonists from this garden formed the foundation of the vast American cotton plantations.

COLOUR-PLATE FLOWER BOOKS

Of all colour-plate flower books the most highly prized are those that were created by Pierre-Joseph Redouté [XXI and XXII]. Redouté was born in 1759 at Saint-Hubert in the Ardennes, into a family that had been producing artists for several generations. After developing his skills during a somewhat wandering youth, he went to Paris in 1782 to join a brother who was already employed in painting scenery at the Théâtre Italien. But although Redouté may have earned his bread in the theatre his heart lay elsewhere, in his passionate devotion to the flower painting to which he devoted his spare time.

Henceforth Redouté was exceptionally fortunate in his career. Quite early in life he came under the influence of two remarkable men. Gerard van Spaëndonck, a Dutch flower painter of exceptional talent, was *Professeur de peinture de fleurs* at the museum of the Jardin du Roi and as both a teacher and an exemplar he played a great part in Redouté's development as an artist. Van Spaëndonck, incidentally, produced one flower book of his own, a work of supreme quality, *Fleurs dessinées d'après Nature* (*c.* 1800).

Charles Louis L'Héritier de Brutelle (1746–1800) was a rich amateur botanist who discovered Redouté while he was painting flowers in the Jardin du Roi. He became his patron and tutor in botany and his superb botanical library enabled the young painter to examine, and learn from, the great books of the past. When L'Héritier went to London for the purpose of studying rare plants in Kew Gardens he took Redouté with him, to illustrate *Sertum Anglicum* (1786). While in London Redouté became familiar with the English technique of stipple engraving, then at its apogee.

A pre-eminent feature in Redouté's career was provided by a sequence of royal patronesses. Through the influence of L'Héritier he was appointed draughtsman to the Cabinet of Marie Antoinette. Nothing came of this post, for the Revolution broke out almost immediately, but in any case since the Queen was a complete philistine where art was concerned it is doubtful whether she would have done much for Redouté. But I cannot resist relating the story that when she was imprisoned in the Temple pending her execution she called in Redouté to paint the cactus that grew in her cell and flowered at midnight.

L'Héritier was among the many innocent victims of the Revolution. He was ruined financially, imprisoned on a baseless charge and finally assassinated. But Redouté exhibited his lifelong talent for survival and within a few years his golden opportunity arrived.

The Empress Josephine was totally devoted to flowers and resolved

123 In order to rescue her husband from the debtors' prison, Elizabeth Blackwell worked single-handed to produce *A Curious Herbal... five hundred cuts of the most useful plants now used in...Physic* (1737). All in vain, for ten years later he was decapitated in Sweden.

to gather, in the gardens at Malmaison, the greatest botanical collection in the world, to which end rare species were obtained from every quarter of the globe. Josephine was never a woman to count costs; she simply went ahead as if they did not exist. At their height the results must have been breathtaking, and it is heart-breaking that we were not there to see them. But in effect we *can* see them, for she engaged Redouté to record her flowers in several of the most beautiful flower books ever produced. In imagination we can visit Malmaison in all its glory when we turn the leaves of the two great books illustrated with colour plates after Redouté: *Jardin de Malmaison* (1803–04) and *Description des Plantes rares cultivées à Malmaison et à Navarre* (1812–17). An even greater work produced at this time was *Les Liliacées*, in eight volumes (1802–16).

As for Redouté, he had now achieved an enviable position. Josephine paid him 18,000 francs a year, in addition to which his paintings were in great demand and he was able to charge high prices. However, throughout his life his tastes ran far ahead of his means. If his patrons never practised frugality, why should he? He lived lavishly in a fine house in Paris, and owned a country estate. As a result, he was generally in financial straits.

At the fall of Napoleon and the death of Josephine, Redouté's indestructible talent for survival came into play once again and he was soon under the patronage of the Duchesse de Berry, daughter-in-law of Charles X, mother of the heir to the throne. Some of his major works were produced during this period, including the most popular of all, *Les Roses* (1817–24), *Album de Redouté* (1824), *Choix des Plus Belles Fleurs* (1827–33). There have been other flower painters who were the equal of Redouté in skill, but a fortunate combination of circumstances resulted in the creation of this series of books, which are without parallel in the history of botany: first of all Redouté was able to call on a number of brilliant stipple engravers, who recreated his drawing with exceptional sensitivity; the bottomless purses of the patrons who were ready to support such expensive works; and, finally, the restless energy of the painter himself. These books have become the prizes of the wealthiest collectors. While I have been writing this a set of *Les Liliacées* sold for £17,000. In the changed circumstances in which we now live it seems certain that no such books will ever be produced again.

Redouté died of a stroke in 1840. His friends and pupils made up a wreath of roses and lilies, symbols of his two greatest books. To it they attached the couplet:

> O Peintre aimé de Flore et du riant empire,
> Tu nous quittes le jour où le printemps expire.

THORNTON'S TEMPLE OF FLORA

More or less coeval with Redouté in France came the production of the greatest English colour-plate flower book, Thornton's *Temple of Flora* [XXVI and XXIX]. Robert John Thornton (1768–1837) inherited a competent fortune and trained as a doctor. He appears to have had considerable success in practice and was appointed both physician to the Marylebone Dispensary and lecturer in medical botany at Guy's and St Thomas's hospitals. But quite early in his career he embarked on his somewhat megalomaniac great work. What Redouté produced under the patronage of L'Héritier, Marie Antoinette, the Empress Josephine, Charles x and the Duchesse de Berry, Thornton set out to do alone. His complete lack of attention to ways and means was worthy of Josephine herself.

Numerous important artists were engaged. There were portraits by Sir William Beechey, John Opie, Sir Henry Raeburn and others; there were three emblematic frontispieces, such as 'Cupid Inspiring Plants with Love'; and, finally, twenty-eight paintings of flowers commissioned from Abraham Pether, known as 'Moonlight Pether', Philip Reinagle, son of a Hungarian who came over with Bonnie Prince Charlie and stayed, Sydenham Edwards and Peter Henderson. Thornton himself painted the most famous plate of all, 'The Roses', and he evidently infused the others with something of his own romantic genius. It must be borne in mind that many exotic oriental plants that we take for granted were then newly introduced into Europe. To Thornton it was as if they had been brought back by Coleridge from Xanadu, 'where blossom'd many an incense-bearing tree'.

One of the most noticeable features of this splendid series is the way in which plants are placed in highly romantic versions of what was held to be their natural habitat; temples, mountains, church towers with the clock at midnight, and so forth, abound. Pether added moonlight to Reinagle's Night-blowing Cereus [xxix]. It would be as pointless to complain that some of these settings are inaccurate, as to demand topographical and botanical accuracy for the forests in which Blake and the *Douanier* Rousseau placed their tigers. By good fortune this was a period of high standards of engraving, and the leading craftsmen in aquatint and mezzotint were called in to produce the plates. These were first printed in the basic colours and then finished by hand with water-colours.

When it came to the text Thornton was never at a loss for words. His prejudices were allowed full play and any hobby-horse that he happened to be riding at the moment, however remote from botany, canters through his pages. Just as Dickens's Mr Dick could never keep out King Charles's head, so Thornton had to let fly about 'the *needless and atrocious murder* of the Duke D'ENGHIEN, by torch-light, in the Bois de Boulogne' (actually at Vincennes). Most people confine themselves to looking at the plates and do not pause to read Thornton's text; Sacheverell Sitwell remarked that 'the mixture of royal and tropical flavour [of Thornton's prose] could as well be describing the chandeliers in the Brighton Pavilion'. Finally, the book was dedicated to Queen Charlotte, 'Her Gracious Majesty the Bright Example of Conjugal Fidelity and Maternal Tenderness, Patroness of Botany and of the Fine Arts'. And '. . . its progress . . . received the smile of the munificent ALEXANDER, Emperor of Russia'.

The result was almost total failure and involved Thornton in desperate financial straits. His fortune was engulfed and his family reduced to

124 Thornton commissioned William Blake to design and cut a series of charming woodcuts to illustrate his edition of Virgil for schools (1821).

penury. In an attempt to extricate himself he organized the Royal Botanic Lottery, under the patronage of the Prince Regent, but this too was a failure. When one considers that the English claim to be a nation of nature-lovers and gardeners, and when one reflects on the simply immense sums poured out during the Regency on gambling and horse racing, it is a national disgrace that Thornton's splendid enterprise did not receive the support it so richly deserved.

Thornton wrote many other books: once he took pen in hand there was no stopping him. *A New Family Herbal* was illustrated by Thomas Bewick, and for his edition of Virgil for schools Thornton commissioned a series of charming simple woodcuts by William Blake [124].

It is easy to raise one's eyebrows at Thornton's unworldly and injudicious approach to publishing and to be amused by his extraordinary, even ludicrous, style. But he produced 'with little assistance of the learned, and without any patronage of the great', the most strikingly beautiful set of flower plates ever to be printed in England, one of the loveliest books in the world, and he had the perception to promote illustrations by Thomas Bewick and William Blake. Which of us can claim as much?

Not every flower painter could boast a series of glamorous patrons like Redouté, suffer so dramatic a catastrophe as Thornton, or provide exemplary devotion like Elizabeth Blackwell. If the happiest country is that which has no history, the same may be true of artists. A quiet life devoted to flower painting provides few remarkable incidents, so I shall be brief regarding the other books illustrated, leaving the reader to enjoy the beauty of the plates.

Samuel Curtis, a nurseryman in Essex, was the first gardener to promote the cultivation of the camellia as a greenhouse shrub. He was a cousin of William Curtis, who founded the *Botanical Magazine* and whose only daughter he married. Two of his books are illustrated here: *A Monograph of the Genus Camellia* (1819) [XXIII], and *The Beauties of Flora* (1820) [XXIV]. These consist of coloured aquatints by H. Weddell based on watercolours by Clara Maria Pope (d. 1838), who exhibited at the Royal Academy for forty years.

J. L. Prevost's beautiful paintings of flowers are to be found in *Collection des Fleurs et des Fruits* (1805) [XXV]. George Brookshaw produced some of the finest colour-plate pictures of fruit in *Pomona Britannica* (1804–12) [XXVIII].

The nineteenth century was a splendid age for noble gardeners. With large estates and immense, virtually untaxed incomes (in mid-century, when the first British census was taken, there were more gamekeepers than bureaucrats) their opportunities seemed limitless. None of them surpassed the 'Bachelor Duke' of Devonshire.

Just as in the sixteenth century Trissino spotted Palladio when he was working as a stonemason, so, in the nineteenth century, the Duke of Devonshire had the perception to select Joseph Paxton at a time when the latter was working as a gardener for 18 shillings a week. At Chatsworth Paxton organized vast extensions to the gardens and built the celebrated glasshouse (three hundred feet in length) that foreshadowed his Crystal Palace, the first really modern building created from a multiplicity of identical parts.

Noble gardeners vied with one another to be the first to raise a new plant in England, or they clubbed together in sending plant-hunters to remote and tropical lands in search of new species. It is notable that so many of the species in James Bateman's *The Orchidaceae of Mexico and Guatemala* (1837–43) [XXVII] are named after English noble families or their estates, on which the first example in Europe was brought to flower. It is, however, pleasant to observe that one horticulturalist, instead of giving his own name to an orchid, called it *Galeandra Baueri* after 'Mr Bauer . . . well known to the botanical world as the *facile princeps* of microscopical draughtsmen. Although now between eighty and ninety years of age, he retains all his early fondness for his early science, and not unfrequently plies his pencil with no unsteady hand.'

(Ferdinand and Francis Bauer, to digress for a moment, must always take their places in the first rank of flower painters. They were born in Vienna but spent the greater part of their working lives in England, where they were brought, in the first place, by Sir Joseph Banks. Ferdinand accompanied John Sibthorp to Greece and drew the plates for *Flora Graeca* (1806–40); Francis remained quietly at Kew for fifty years.)

To return to Bateman, his book brings us to the new world of coloured lithography, the plates being drawn by Mrs Withers and Miss Drake. In the text Bateman included some details about life in Central America, and these are illustrated by a woodcut vignette at the end of each chapter. In addition there are a few graphic jokes. In one of these gardeners and domestic staff are chasing immense, oversize cockroaches.

This book is of great size, approximately thirty by twenty inches. Bateman made a little joke at his own expense by commissioning this woodcut:

But no species brought to Europe in the nineteenth century was more exciting than *Victoria regia*, a giant water-lily. Friedrich Haenke was the first botanist to see *Victoria regia*. The discovery took place in Bolivia in 1801, as recorded by a later traveller, Alcide Dessalines d'Orbigny.

When I was travelling in Central America [said D'Orbigny] in the country of the wild Guarayos, . . . I made acquaintance with Father La Cueva, a Spanish missionary, a good and well-informed man, beloved for his patriarchal virtues, and who had long and earnestly devoted himself to the conversion of the natives. . . . Father La Cueva and Haenke were together in a *piroque* upon the Rio Mamoré, one of the great tributaries of the Amazon River, when they discovered in the marshes, by the side of the stream, a flower which was so surpassingly beautiful and extraordinary, that Haenke, in a transport of admiration, fell on his knees and expressed aloud his sense of the power and magnificence of the Creator in his works. They halted and even encamped purposely near by the spot, and quitted it with much reluctance.

From time to time other travellers saw the marvellous plant. Then, in 1842, Dr Thomas Bridges undertook a botanical journey into Bolivia:

I made daily shooting excursions in the vicinity, and on one occasion I had the good fortune, while riding along the wooded banks of the Yacuma, a tributary of the Mamoré, to arrive suddenly at a beautiful pond, or rather small lake, embosomed in the forest, when, to my delight and surprise I descried for the first time, the Queen of Aquatics, *Victoria Regia!*

Bridges was tempted to plunge into the river, but prudently refrained as the water was full of alligators. However the Spanish governor supplied oxen to transport a small canoe so that Bridges, with the help of two Indians, brought many specimens, including leaves, blossoms and ripe seed-vessels, to the bank. In 1846 he sold the first living seeds to Kew. They germinated, but failed to survive the winter. In 1849 more seeds arrived and these were successfully raised at Kew. Plants were distributed to two ducal gardeners, Devonshire and Northumberland. At Chatsworth Paxton created a tank about nineteen feet square, which the plant filled in seventy-nine days. Single leaves reached six feet in diameter, with edges two to eight inches high. They sustained the weight, first, of Paxton's eight-year-old daughter and, subsequently, of a fully grown man. *Victoria regia* put forth its glorious blossoms, and seeds were distributed throughout Europe. One can only regret that Thornton did not live to see the plant that would have fulfilled even *his* wildest dreams.

In 1851 *Victoria regia* was celebrated in a folio volume [125 and 126] worthy in size of the plant it described. The text was by Sir William Jackson Hooker. Paxton, then busy erecting the Crystal Palace, took time off to add additional notes. The hand-coloured lithographic plates were drawn by Walter H. Fitch from the specimen at Syon and the work was dedicated to the Duke of Northumberland.

Sir William Jackson Hooker (1785–1865) made many important contributions to botany, but he is best remembered as the man who

OPPOSITE ABOVE LEFT XXV J. L. Prevost, *Collection des Fleurs et des Fruits*, with an introduction by P. M. Gault de Saint-Germain (1805).
OPPOSITE ABOVE RIGHT XXVI The most beautiful of English flower books is the *Temple of Flora* (1799–1807) by R. J. Thornton. Some of the exotic plants depicted were newly introduced into Europe and all were placed in highly romantic versions of what was held to be their natural habitat. Thornton proceeded without regard to cost and was ruined.

OPPOSITE BELOW LEFT XXVII James Bateman's *The Orchidaceae of Mexico and Guatemala* (1837–43) chronicles the introduction of orchids, so beloved by noble gardeners and frequently named after their estates.
OPPOSITE BELOW RIGHT XXVIII The smooth-leaved green Antigua pine from George Brookshaw, *Pomona Britannica* (1804–12).

VICTORIA REGIA

VICTORIA REGIA

LEFT ABOVE AND BELOW
125 and 126
Few exotic plants
created so great a
sensation on their intro-
duction into England
as *Victoria regia*
from South America;
dukes vied with one
another to produce the
first blossom and it was
celebrated in an
enormous volume
published in 1851.

OPPOSITE XXIX
Night-blowing Cereus
from the *Temple of Flora*
by R.J. Thornton.

THE

BOTANICAL MAGAZINE;

O R,

Flower-Garden Difplayed :

IN WHICH

The moft Ornamental FOREIGN PLANTS, cultivated in
the Open Ground, the Green-Houfe, and the Stove,
will be accurately reprefented in their natural Colours.

TO WHICH WILL BE ADDED,

Their Names, Clafs, Order, Generic and Specific Charaĉters,
according to the celebrated LINNÆUS; their Places of
Growth, and Times of Flowering:

TOGETHER WITH

THE MOST APPROVED METHODS OF CULTURE.

A   W O R K

Intended for the Ufe of

Such LADIES, GENTLEMEN, and GARDENERS, as wifh to become
fcientifically acquainted with the Plants they cultivate.

L O N D O N:

Printed for W. C U R T I S, at his B O T A N I C - G A R D E N,
Lambeth-Marfh; and Sold by all Bookfellers, Stationers, and News-
Carriers, in Town and Country.

M DCC LXXXVII.

created Kew Gardens as they are known and loved by the million or so people who visit them every year. The gardens had been founded in 1759 by that enthusiastic amateur botanist, Princess Augusta, mother of George III. After her death they fell into decay and were in danger of being abandoned and destroyed. When Hooker was appointed director in 1841 he revolutionized the gardens, greatly extended their size and set them upon a scientific footing.

Walter H. Fitch (1817–92) was apprenticed, as a boy, to a firm in Glasgow that designed calico. He spent his spare time helping William Jackson Hooker (at that time also in Glasgow) to mount specimens. Hooker was so impressed by the boy's abilities that he secured his freedom by repaying the apprenticeship fee, engaged him as a full-time draughtsman and, on his appointment to Kew, took Fitch with him. Contemporaries have recorded the remarkable accuracy, certainty and speed with which Fitch drew plants. He was immensely industrious and published 9,960 drawings. He illustrated many important flower books, including Joseph Hooker's *The Rhododendrons of the Sikkim-Himalaya* (1849–51) [127] and H. J. Elwes's *Monograph of the Genus Lilium* (1877–80). For many years Fitch was the sole illustrator of the *Botanical Magazine* and, at a less colourful level, he drew the illustrations for a work that has sustained generations of botanists both amateur and professional, Bentham and Hooker's *Handbook of the British Flora*.

In later years Sir Joseph Hooker (son of Sir William and, eventually, his successor at Kew), feeling that Fitch's work was worthy of national recognition, determined to secure a civil list pension for him. When approached, Disraeli was not very forthcoming, but Hooker cleverly 'played upon his imperialist feelings' by showing him a copy of *Victoria Regia*. The old prime minister was touched and granted a pension of £100 per annum.

If the British failed to support Thornton they have one remarkable publication to their credit: the *Botanical Magazine* has been published continuously since 1787, and still flourishes today.

William Curtis (1746–99), its Quaker founder, was at one time Praefectus Horti and Director of the Botanical Garden in Chelsea. Subsequently he started a garden of his own in Lambeth Fields and cultivated six thousand species of plants. The purpose of the *Botanical Magazine*, fully set out on the title-page [128], was to describe new species and illustrate them in colour [129]. William Curtis was succeeded by his nephew and son-in-law, Samuel Curtis, and by other celebrated botanists such as James Sowerby, Sydenham Edwards and John Sims. In 1826 William Hooker became editor and gave the text a more scientific basis. After William Hooker's death, in 1865, his son, Joseph Hooker, succeeded to the editorial chair.

One more word about Walter Hood Fitch. He began work for the *Botanical Magazine* in 1834 and continued until 1877, when an unfortunate row brought his connection with the magazine to an end. He was succeeded by his nephew, Joseph Nugent Fitch (1840–1927), who made 2,500 drawings for the magazine. Uncle and nephew, therefore,

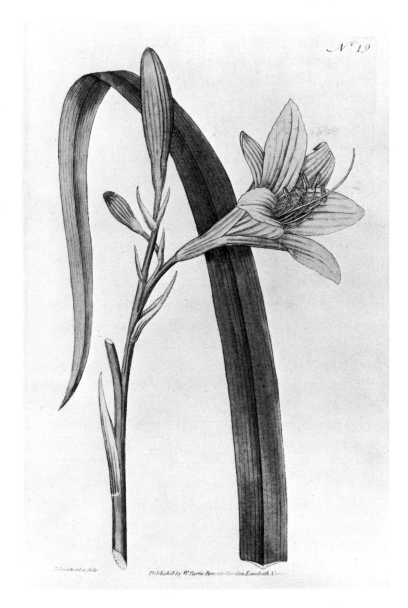

supplied drawings for the *Botanical Magazine* for over eighty-two years, during seventy-one of which they were the sole lithographers [130].

In the difficult conditions following the First World War the *Botanical Magazine* ran into great difficulties. For some years it had been published at a loss that its commercial owners felt unable to sustain. But through the energy of Henry John Elwes a body of subscribers was persuaded to buy the copyright of the magazine for £250 and present it to the Royal Horticultural Society. In the confusion no volume 147, for 1921, had been produced. To fill the gap this was published at the expense of Reginald Cory who, rather sadly, did not live to see its delayed appearance in 1938.

From 1787 until 1948 virtually every plate was coloured by hand. At that date it was realized that this beautiful process was too time-consuming and expensive for the modern world. Today the illustrations are produced by a four-colour gravure process and, even now, the artistic quality of the plates remains worthy of the magazine's high botanical and scientific status.

OPPOSITE ABOVE 127 J.D. Hooker, *The Rhododendrons of the Sikkim-Himalaya* (1849–51). The lithographs are by Walter H. Fitch who, in a lifetime devoted to botanical illustrations, published 9,960 drawings.
OPPOSITE BELOW 128 The *Botanical Magazine*, founded by William Curtis in 1787, still flourishes today. The title-page of the first volume gives a fair idea of its purpose.
ABOVE LEFT 129 From 1787 until 1948 virtually every plate in the *Botanical Magazine* was coloured by hand. This one shows the Yellow Lily from Volume I.
ABOVE RIGHT 130 Walter H. Fitch (1817–92) worked for the *Botanical Magazine* from 1834 to 1877; he was succeeded by his nephew, Joseph Nugent Fitch (1840–1927), who made 2,500 drawings for the magazine.

CHAPTER SEVEN

ENGLISH BOOKS WITH COLOURED PLATES

ENGLISH BOOKS illustrated with coloured aquatint plates are the products of one of those fortunate moments in history when, contrary to Robert Browning, the time and the place and the loved one all came together. Watercolour painting, one of England's few major contributions to the visual arts, reached the height of its creative period at the very time when the technique of aquatint printing was perfected.

It is not surprising that England, bathed in an aqueous atmosphere, should have provided the setting where, for a long time, artists in watercolour excelled those of any other country. The Romantic Movement in literature and the newborn feeling for the 'picturesque' in painting had turned men's eyes to the beauties of landscape, an interest further stimulated by the many gentlemen who devoted their leisure to antiquarian research. In a watercolour painting the light passes through the transparent colours and is reflected back from the white paper to the eye of the beholder. There are mornings in spring when, as one stands before a cathedral after early rain has brought an atmosphere of brilliant clarity, the contrast of the yellow stonework against the blue of a translucent sky and the green of immaculately kept grass reminds one, irresistibly, of a watercolour or an aquatint.

The England depicted in these engravings probably looked more beautiful than it has ever done before or since. Much of the countryside had been transformed under the influence of Capability Brown, Humphry Repton and similar landscape gardeners. In the cities most of the buildings we admire had already been built, including many that have since been destroyed, while the general aspect had not yet succumbed to that urban sprawl that was an inevitable consequence of the Industrial Revolution.

During the years preceding 1815 the Napoleonic Wars provided exciting scenes of battle on both land and sea, with picturesque uniforms and a never-ending inspiration for caricature. After Waterloo pride in a new-found national pre-eminence, expanding success in overseas trade and freedom of movement sent many expeditions to remote and exotic countries such as China, while the colourful life and landscape of India and other colonies provided endless subjects for the artists who so frequently accompanied important travellers and diplomatic missions.

The engraver who reproduces a watercolour by means of aquatint first takes a sheet of burnished copper and sprinkles it evenly with minute particles of acid-resisting resin. The portions that are to appear white are covered with a stopping-out varnish. The plate is then treated with acid, which attacks the interstices between the resin so that, in the final print, there are tiny white specks virtually invisible to the naked eye. These specks create a sense of light, while the particles of resin give a slightly sanded and pleasant texture to the surface. On to this prepared plate the engraver etches the outline of the picture, afterwards adding the form and mass by further controlled biting of different areas of the design. Two or occasionally three separate plates are made, each for a different colour: blue for sky, brown for foreground and buildings, green for grass, for example. A print made by the superimposition of these plates is given to an artist, who fills in the other colours. This exemplar is then pinned up in a workshop to be copied by a host of colourists, who complete each impression by hand.

In the late eighteenth century there were very few art schools and a number of famous painters (including Turner, Thomas Girtin and John Sell Cotman) began their careers as engravers or earned their livings as aquatint colourists. This experience gave them a natural sympathy for prints and an understanding of the engraver's problems when, in their turn, they painted original pictures. It also gave them training in technique. Cotman's marvellous capacity for putting on watercolour washes may well have been due to his experience in working as a colourist for Ackermann, just as Rouault was influenced by his early training as a worker in stained glass, and Renoir by the painting of ceramics.

Although it is obvious that not every single aquatint print was coloured by an artist of genius, none the less the standard achieved was surprisingly high. In a period where there is an upsurge of creative ability many lesser men and women are lifted by the general swell. Just as in the reign of Elizabeth I almost any statesman or adventurer seems to have been capable of writing a well-turned sonnet, so in the early nineteenth century many people whose talents did not quite enable them to stand on their own as original artists supported themselves as aquatint colourists and turned out very satisfactory work. Repton tells us in *Observations on Landscape Gardening* (1803): 'The art of colouring plates in imitation of drawings has so far improved of late that I have pleasure in recording obligations to Mr Clarke, under whose direction a number of children have been employed to enrich this volume.'

Rudolf Ackermann (1764–1834) was one of those exceptional men who, like Diaghilev, combined perception, sympathy and the ability to direct the efforts of other men of widely diverse talent and genius. He seized upon the new opportunities of his time. He co-ordinated the activities of artists, engravers, colourists and authors, provided the setting in which they could work and then organized a vast market for sale and distribution. Although he died three years before Queen Victoria came to the throne there is something almost Victorian about Ackermann's tireless energy, industry, flair, capacity and endless devotion to his business. It is safe to say that but for him many of the finest aquatint books would never have been produced.

The odd thing is that Ackermann's entry into the field of publishing was so casual that it almost seems an accident. He was born at Stolberg,

131 Ackermann's shop, 'The Repository of Arts', opened in London in 1795 roughly where the Savoy Hotel now stands. It became a fashionable *rendez-vous* where the art-loving *beau monde* selected aquatints, books, screens, fans and other novelties.

in Saxony, the son of a coach-builder. As a young man he entered the family business, but worked as a designer rather than a craftsman. In this capacity he moved first to Paris and then to London where, in 1790, he designed the state coach, built at a cost of £7,000, for a Mr Hutton, then Lord Mayor of Dublin – himself a coach-builder. Reconstructed after a fire in 1911, and known as the 'Irish state coach', this elegant carriage is still used by the Queen for the opening of Parliament and other ceremonial occasions. In 1805 he produced drawings for the fantastic and elaborate car that formed the centrepiece of Nelson's funeral.

Having married an Englishwoman and founded a family, Ackermann realized that, should he die young, his capacity for earning as a designer would die with him, leaving his dependants in want. In 1795, to provide a more lasting means of support, he opened a print shop in the Strand in London. He called this shop 'The Repository of Arts', and the venture flourished beyond all expectation.

The first volume of Ackermann's successful magazine, also called the *Repository of Arts*, contains a print illustrating the showroom [131], and the accompanying text gives us some insight into the methods of production. Many elegant but otherwise untrained French aristocrats (refugees from the Revolution) were taken on: 'Mr A. was among the first to strike out a liberal and easy method of employing them, and he had seldom less than fifty nobles, priests and ladies of distinction at work upon screens, card-racks, flower-stands, and other ornamental fancy-work of a similar nature.' When the decree allowing the return of the exiles to France was announced they hurried home (and who can blame them?). However, after 1815 a new set of refugees arrived from Spain and the good work went on.

But it would be unjust to leave a picture of Ackermann as a mere employer of sweated labour; he was a man of generous spirit, who was tireless in relieving the suffering that the ambition of Napoleon scattered over the length and breadth of Europe. After the battle of Leipzig he raised £200,000 to help the mutilated, the homeless and the bereaved.

Ackermann's *The Microcosm of London* (1808–10), three volumes quarto, with 104 coloured plates, is a book of major importance. The architectural drawings were by Augustus Charles Pugin, a French refugee who came to London in about 1798, 'driven from his country either by the horrors of the Revolution or by private reasons connected with a duel'.

At that time noblemen, inspired by the Romantic movement, were demanding that their great houses be rebuilt in the 'Gothick' manner, a style of which most architects had but a superficial knowledge. John Nash employed Pugin, not only in his drawing office but to travel about making drawings of Gothic buildings and details. Later in life Pugin set up on his own, but although he trained many architects of the succeeding generation (including his famous son), his own architectural practice was minuscule. His lasting fame rests on his consummate ability as an architectural draughtsman. By a stroke of genius Ackermann engaged Thomas Rowlandson to add human figures to the drawings that Pugin made for *The Microcosm,* so that the stately, accurate and dignified qualities of that artist are enlivened by the vitality and charm of Regency life as depicted by one of the most vigorous draughtsmen of all time. To turn the leaves of *The Microcosm* is to take a walk through London at a singularly fortunate moment, observing, as we never can in real life, the scenes of many celebrated incidents in English literature and history: the India House of Charles Lamb, the King's Bench Prison of Dickens, the Foundling Hospital of Captain Coram and Hogarth, the Guildhall bombed by the *Luftwaffe,* the Newgate of Harrison Ainsworth, the Carlton House of the Prince Regent and so forth [132 and 133].

Another of Ackermann's books, which may well be coupled with *The Microcosm,* is John Buonarotti Papworth's *Select Views of London* (1816), with seventy-six coloured plates. Many of the fine and lovely buildings depicted in these two books are still with us: Somerset House, St Paul's, St Martin-in-the-Fields. But, basically, they show us a London that has passed away. Not only are there engravings of buildings now for ever gone – the Pantheon, for example, or Carlton House or the Old Bailey, but even the settings of those that remain are now so changed as to be almost unrecognizable – the long unspoiled streets of Georgian houses, Berkeley Square and Lansdowne House before their pitiful mutilation; Charing Cross with old Northumberland House; and Oxford Street. Who would ever believe Oxford Street to have been beautiful? Yet it was, and in some ways these books are almost too heart-breaking to look through. Here, more clearly than anywhere else, we can see for ourselves how vitally and irretrievably 150 years of our brave new world have changed the London that Johnson and Wordsworth loved [134 and 135]. Three of Ackermann's important publications, each in elephant quarto, are devoted to *The History of The Colleges* (public schools) (1816),

132 The pleasure gardens which were once so great a feature of London life (Ranelagh, Vauxhall, Cremorne) have all passed away. The robust life they provided must have appealed to Rowlandson who added this lively crowd to Pugin's drawing of Vauxhall Gardens for Ackermann's *The Microcosm of London.*

ASTLEY'S AMPHITHEATRE.

OPPOSITE XXX For all its short life Carlton House exemplified the contrast between the extravagant and art-loving Prince Regent, later George IV, and his father. Pyne's *Royal Residences* is a superb record of its sumptuous decorations.

RIGHT 133 In Ackermann's *The Microcosm of London* (1808–10) the drawings were by Augustus Charles Pugin, a French refugee and brilliant architectural draughtsman. To these the irrepressible Rowlandson added lively figures.

RIGHT 134 In his *Select Views of London* (1816), J. B. Papworth shows us Oxford Street. Could anything demonstrate more clearly the degradation which has since come over London's streetscapes?

BELOW RIGHT 135 Montagu House, built by Puget in 1686 and purchased in 1753 to house the newly-founded British Museum. It was demolished in 1852 when the present south front of the Museum was completed. From J. B. Papworth, *Select Views of London* (1816).

OVERLEAF LEFT ABOVE XXXI William Beckford's fantastic Gothic Fonthill Abbey, designed by James Wyatt, only stood for a few years, to the wonder of all who saw it. Here it is before the crash, preserved for us in R. Havell's *A Series of Picturesque Views of Noblemen's and Gentlemen's Seats* (1814–23).

OVERLEAF LEFT BELOW XXXII *A Voyage Round Great Britain* (1814–25) by William Daniell and Richard Ayton is one of the most important English colour-plate books. Daniell started at Land's End and worked his way round the coast, year after year, sketching in the summer and producing finished drawings in the winter.

OVERLEAF RIGHT ABOVE XXXIII The long struggle against Napoleon provided rich material for English artists. Here, at the Battle of the Nile, Nelson destroys Napoleon's dream of conquering the Orient. From Jenkins, *The Naval Achievements of Great Britain and Her Allies, 1793 to 1817.*

OVERLEAF RIGHT BELOW XXXIV Having driven the French out of Spain, the Duke of Wellington invaded southern France. Here he repels a French sortie from Bayonne. From Jenkins, *The Martial Achievements of Great Britain and Her Allies, 1799 to 1815.*

OXFORD STREET.

MONTAGUE HOUSE, now the BRITISH MUSEUM.

Drawn by R. Carticum. from a Sketch by T. Higham.   Engraved by R. Havell & Son.

Kinnaird Head, Aberdeenshire.

Painted by Whitcombe.   Engraved by Baily

BATTLE of the NILE, Aug.ˢᵗ 1ˢᵗ 1798.

Plate II.

London Pub. April 1, 1816, at 48 Strand for J. Jenkins's Naval Achievements.

W. Heath del.ᵗ   T. Sutherland sculp.ᵗ

THE SORTIE FROM BAYONNE, at 3 in the Morning, on the 14ᵗʰ April 1814.

filled eight large quarto volumes. This book forms a wonderful panorama. Daniell was especially inspired by the wild aspects of Scotland and the Western Isles, but there are many charming pictures of ports and watering places that have since changed beyond all recognition.

The text of the first two volumes only is by Richard Ayton, who died at the early age of thirty-seven. Probably very few people read this text, but it contains some vivid and outspoken impressions of the journey which the two men made together.

While at Whitehaven Ayton descended a coalmine, and he gives an unforgettable and horrifying description of the appalling conditions in which the miners worked for thirteen hours a day – men, women and children alike. Ayton's descriptions of England and Wales in 1814–16 might well have been more highly regarded today had they not been eclipsed by the splendour of Daniell's plates [1 and XXXII].

Pride in the successful outcome of the Napoleonic Wars brought two books published by James Jenkins: *The Martial Achievements of Great Britain and Her Allies, 1799 to 1815*, with fifty-two coloured plates after drawings by William Heath, and the even more attractive *Naval Achievements, 1793 to 1817*, with fifty-five plates after drawings by T. Whitecombe and others [XXXIII and XXXIV]. C. M. Westmacott's *The English Spy* (1825) contains seventy-one coloured plates, mostly by Robert Cruikshank, though there are two by Rowlandson. This book gives a remarkable picture of fast life under the Regency, from the court of George IV at Carlton House and Brighton through the *demi-monde* to the lowest dens and gambling hells. The striking thing about this work is the freedom with which famous people are not only mentioned but portrayed [148 and 149].

Before saying farewell to the Regent we might look at *The Coronation of His Most Sacred Majesty King George the Fourth*, by Sir George Nayler, Garter King of Arms. It was intended to issue this work in five parts. The first appeared in 1823 and the second in 1827; but Nayler died in 1831 and the work was suspended. In 1837 H. G. Bohn acquired the

150 This resplendent portrait of the Duke of Wellington in his Coronation robes, loaded with honours and orders of chivalry from every country in Europe, is outstanding even in the superb series of plates in Sir George Nayler's *The Coronation of . . . George the Fourth*.

151 The magnificent masculinity of the dignitaries in the procession at the Coronation of George IV is matched by the feminine grace of the King's Herbwoman and her six maids.

152 *Boydell's Thames* traces the river from its source to the sea in seventy-six coloured·plates by Joseph Farington.

plates and brought out a sumptuous work in large folio. If ever a book illustrated the boast of heraldry, the pomp of power, this is the one. The forty-five plates display the leading dignitaries of a coronation in full ceremonial dress [150 and 151].

Boydell's Thames takes its name from the publishers, John and Josiah Boydell. John Boydell (1719–1804) was a sort of Dick Whittington character who walked from Shropshire to London in his youth and, having made a great fortune, lived to become lord mayor. He started by selling his own engravings at six for sixpence in the windows of toyshops, later founding a successful art gallery. The original drawings for *Boydell's Thames,* which trace the river from its source to the sea in a series of seventy-six plates, were by Joseph Farington, the text by the ever-resourceful William Combe [152].

Humphry Repton (1752–1818), the celebrated landscape gardener, did much to change the aspect of the parks of gentlemen and noblemen, humanizing the rather austere style of his forerunner, Capability Brown. It was Repton's custom, having surveyed an estate, to make a series of watercolour drawings to which movable flaps were attached, showing the landscape or garden as it was and as it could be if the suggested 'improvements' were implemented. These drawings were bound up, together with a handwritten explanatory text, and given to the land-owner; they were known as 'red books' from the colour of the binding. After some years of successful practice Repton published three handsome books on landscape gardening, incorporating examples from his own 'red books' and reproducing the drawings, with hinged overslips, in coloured aquatint. Repton's books therefore not only record for us the English landscape, but also played a significant part in its improvement.

In 1806 it seemed that the climax of Repton's career had arrived when the Prince Regent invited him to submit designs for a complete remodelling of Brighton Pavilion. The large domed riding school, decorated with 'Saracenic' detail, was already in existence and this gave Repton the oriental ideas that he hoped would appeal to the exotic tastes of the Regent.

It so happened that Repton had just been to Sezincote, in Oxfordshire, where Sir Charles Cockerell, home from India, was building a country house to a pastiche oriental design. This set him on the right road and, from a combination of Cockerell's ideas and the aquatints of Thomas Daniell, he created, in imagination, a veritable pleasure-dome. These designs were accompanied by an explanatory, not to say promotional, text:

I therefore considered all the different styles of different countries from a conviction of the danger of attempting to invent anything entirely new. The Turkish was objectionable as being a corruption of the Grecian; the Moorish, as a bad model of the Gothic; the Egyptian too cumbrous for the character of a villa; the Chinese too light and trifling for the outside, however it may be applied to the interior; and the specimens from Ava were still more trifling and extravagant. Thus, if any known style were to be adopted, no alternative remained but to combine from the architecture of Hindûstan, such forms as might be rendered applicable to the purpose.

Nothing could have been better calculated to please the Prince: 'Mr. Repton, I consider the whole of this work as perfect, and will have every part of it carried into immediate execution; not a tittle shall be altered – even you yourself shall not attempt any improvement.'

But, as always, the dreams of the Prince Regent far outran his royal income. His finances were already bankrupt and there could be no question of any building at Brighton.

In 1808 Repton published his designs in a folio volume with coloured aquatint plates. His device of depicting the before and after of improvements by means of folding flaps was once more brought into play. Plates xxxv and xxxvi give us some idea of a dream that was never to be realized.

When, in 1815, the Regent was at last in a financial position to build at Brighton he ignored Repton and turned to John Nash. Repton felt the blow keenly. Many years later his biographer wrote:

Towards the close of his professional life, when his ambition was about to be gratified by the patronage of the highest personage in the kingdom, it was painful to find himself superseded by that very friend, who, in earlier life, had participated in his bright visions of future fame.

CHAPTER EIGHT

BOOKS ON ARCHITECTURE

153 In *La Italia Liberata da Go:thi* Giangiorgio Trissino expressed his hope that Italy would be freed from Gothic influence and return for inspiration to the ancient world. To proclaim that his voyage in literature would range over distant seas in search of an inestimable prize he adopted the symbol of Jason's Golden Fleece.

IN 1547 GIANGIORGIO TRISSINO, of whom more presently, published *La Italia Liberata da Gotthi*, an epic poem upon which he had been working for many years. This poem was not only historical, it was symbolic. The barbarian invaders from the North had destroyed the classical civilization of Greece and Rome; it was the self-imposed task of the 'new men' of what we now call the Renaissance to rebuild it. To Trissino, as to Gibbon, Belisarius was the hero who threw the Goths out of Italy. In the *Iliad* or the *Aeneid*, the gods protect their human protégés; so, in Trissino's epic, God sends an angel to protect Belisarius, and his name is Palladio [153].

To us the words 'Gothic architecture' evoke visions of Chartres. We forget that the word Gothic, when applied to architecture, was originally a term of contempt. Further, it must be realized that what the Humanists eventually created was no mere antiquarian or pagan revival.

How then were men like Trissino, surrounded by buildings they despised, to realize this dream and rebuild the classical world? Firstly, they had, all over Italy, the ruins of Roman buildings. Secondly, they had the one architectural book that had survived from the ancient world: Vitruvius' *De Architectura Libri Decem*.

Of Vitruvius himself we know nothing apart from what we can glean from his book. He was a military architect who also designed civil buildings, among them a basilica, and he dedicated his work to Augustus. The theoretical part of his work is gathered from older writers, now lost, some of them Greek; the practical sections are based on his own experience. All this was unknown during the Middle Ages, but a manuscript of Vitruvius was rediscovered at St Gall during the fifteenth century – just when it was needed. The first edition, without woodcuts, was published in Venice. It is undated but the British Museum catalogue suggests 1495. The first illustrated edition (Venice 1511) was edited by Fra Giocondo da Verona, who may have supplied the illustration himself for, as an architect, he was subsequently in charge of the work at St Peter's.

In his passage on proportion Vitruvius laid down that the design of temples should be related to the proportions of the human figure. He pointed out that a man with extended arms and legs fits perfectly into a circle or, if the arms are extended horizontally, into a square. This precept, which had immense influence on Renaissance architecture, is illustrated by a woodcut in the 1511 edition [154]. The first translation into Italian was issued in an illustrated edition of even greater importance at Como in 1521, with magnificent woodcuts by the editor, Cesare

Cesariano. Cesariano was a pupil of Bramante, some say of Leonardo. At any rate he was a member of the Milanese circle dominated by these supremely great men, and his very full commentary embodies their ideas. Indeed the woodcut of man as the embodiment of proportion bears a striking resemblance to a drawing by Leonardo now in the Accademia at Venice [155 and 158].

Vitruvius had addressed his book to advanced readers; he dealt with sophisticated theories and difficult constructions, such as aqueducts. Naturally he took for granted the basic grammar of architecture: the five orders, proportions of columns, pediments and so forth, since every architect in the age of Augustus had been familiar with these from his youth. But these basic concepts were just what the practising Renaissance architect needed most. It was necessary that the surviving Roman buildings be examined, their proportions and details measured and reduced to an exact system. Sebastiano Serlio (1475–1554) supplied this need with his book, *Il Primo (-Quinto) Libro d'Architettura*. Written in Italian (and shortly translated into French, German, Dutch and English), it was published over a number of years and became the standby of architects and builders for generations [156 and 157].

It is significant that the fourth book, dealing with the practical application of the five orders and so on, was published *first*, in 1537; the complete

154 Vitruvius's *De Architectura*, the sole architectural work to have survived from the ancient world, became the Bible of Renaissance architects. He laid down that the proportions of buildings should be related to the human figure; a man with outstretched arms fits perfectly into a circle. (First illustrated edition, Venice 1511).

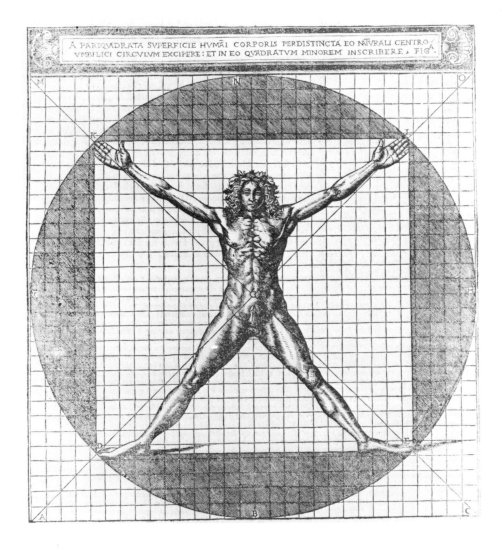

155 The first edition of Vitruvius in Italian (Como 1521) was produced in the artistic circle dominated by Leonardo da Vinci and Bramante. Indeed, this woodcut of man as the embodiment of proportion bears a striking resemblance to a drawing by Leonardo.

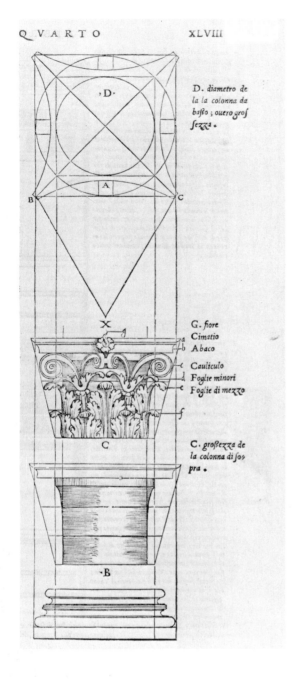

work in 1551. Serlio sent a copy of the fourth book to François 1er, asking to be taken into the French king's service. He was promised three hundred crowns and he dedicated Book Three to François. As a result he was called to Fontainebleau and put in charge of building operations.

Giangiorgio Trissino, a man who, in my opinion, has never received the posthumous fame he deserves, was born at Vicenza in 1478, of a wealthy and noble family. He studied Greek in Milan under the veteran Demetrius Chalcondyles, and formed a fine collection of Greek manuscripts. He made a profound study of Aristotle's *Poetics* and took Sophocles as a model when writing his tragedy *La Sophonisba*. This was the first play in any modern language to be written in blank verse, and thus is the ancestor of Elizabethan drama and of Shakespeare himself.

Keenly interested in linguistics, Trissino, like Bernard Shaw, hoped to found a new system of spelling. For this work he secured a typographer of genius, a fellow citizen of Vicenza, Ludovico Arrighi. The resulting italics surpass all others in beauty of form, in some of the most lovely books ever printed. In his villa at Cricoli, Trissino founded an academy embodying high and original ideals of education, where many noble youths from Vicenza were educated. An appalling quarrel with his son Giulio darkened the end of his life, and he died at Rome in 1550.

As an architectural conception Trissino's design for his Villa Cricoli was far in advance of its time. We know this was his own work, for some of his drawings have survived. Among the workmen engaged on the construction was a young stonemason and sculptor, Andrea di Pietro. Trissino, perceiving that here was a young man of exceptional ability, befriended him and carried him off to Rome. Then, since it was the custom in Humanist circles to bestow classical names (and remembering the angel who had guided Belisarius) Trissino renamed his protégé Palladio.

They stayed in Rome for two years. Palladio studied both the precepts of Vitruvius and antique and modern Rome under the tutelage of Trissino. As a result he wrote two guides to Roman antiquities, which replaced the medieval guides to the city. But, far more important, he became an architect and designed a wonderful series of churches, palaces and country villas in Venice and the Veneto. But before turning to his book one more influence must be discussed.

Daniele Barbaro (1513–70) was a perfect example of the Renaissance *huomo universale,* mathematician, poet, philosopher, theologian, historian and diplomat, Aristotelian scholar, member of the Council of Trent and patriarch of Aquileia. He was the first of those Venetian ambassadors to London who have left such vivid accounts of Tudor times. For him, in conjunction with his brother, Marcantonio, Palladio designed one of the most beautiful of his villas, the Villa Maser, decorated with frescoes by Veronese. And here, for two centuries, were to lie, undiscovered, all Palladio's drawings of Roman antiquities.

Barbaro published an edition of Vitruvius, accompanied by an exceptional commentary. His was one of the most perceptive minds ever to have dwelt upon architecture and those who, like myself, find his subtleties beyond them, will find an admirable summary in Rudolf

OPPOSITE ABOVE 156 In order that classical architecture be revived, it was necessary to examine surviving Roman buildings so that their proportions and details might be reduced to an exact system. This was done by Sebastiano Serlio in *Regole Generali di Architettura* (Book Four, Venice 1537).

OPPOSITE BELOW 157 Serlio's *Il Primo (-Quinto) Libro d'Architettura* (1537–51) was written in Italian and soon translated into French, German, Dutch and English. By means of its woodcuts architects and patrons throughout Europe became aware of classical architecture.

LEFT 158 This illustration from the Como Vitruvius of 1521 exemplifies the deep thought which Renaissance architects gave to perspective and proportion.

BELOW 159 Daniele Barbaro, a perfect example of the Renaissance *huomo universale*, published an edition of Vitruvius accompanied by an exceptional commentary. For the illustrations he engaged the help of Palladio (Venice 1556).

I DIECI LIBRI
DELL'ARCHITETTVRA DI M.
VITRVVIO TRADVTTI ET
COMMENTATI DA MONSIGNOR
BARBARO ELETTO PATRIARCA
D'AQVILEGGIA.

IN VINEGIA PER FRANCESCO MARCOLINI CON PRIVILEGGI. M D LVI.

Wittkower's *Architectural Principles in the Age of Humanism.* For the illustrations Barbaro engaged the help of Palladio, of whom he speaks with moving praise in the introduction. Here, then, must have been the interplay of two exceptional minds. Barbaro was fortunate indeed to have a genius to help him but, equally, it must have been of infinite advantage for Palladio to have Barbaro's Aristotelian training as a guide through the intricacies of the Vitruvian world [159].

In 1570 Palladio published his own book, *Quattro Libri dell'Architettura*, lavishly illustrated with woodcuts [160]. This deals with every aspect of architecture from proportions to town-planning, the whole imbued with the *gravitas* that Palladio had derived from the study of ancient Rome, refined through discussions with Trissino and Barbaro. No architectural book has ever had wider influence, more especially in England. It was swiftly translated into other languages and went through numerous editions. There can be no major city in Europe that does not contain a building influenced by Palladio, and there are a great many more in America.

160 No book has had greater influence on architecture in Europe and America than Andrea Palladio's *Quattro Libri dell'Architettura* (Venice 1570). His original and practical genius was grounded in Humanist principles and a wide knowledge of Roman architecture.

OPPOSITE ABOVE 161 In this view of the Forum, G. B. Piranesi (1720–78) gives a wonderful picture of a world of great beauty which has gone for ever: the remains of Rome, as they' inspired Gibbon, before the nineteenth-century excavations.
OPPOSITE BELOW 162 The scale and magnificence of the ancient world is given added grandeür by the ignoble clutter of contemporary life in this engraving from Piranesi's *Vedute di Roma* (1762).

The appearance of the Roman monuments as seen by Palladio *et al.* differed in a number of ways from what we can still see today. Firstly, there has been a certain amount of destruction. Secondly, the ruins were then partly buried by the accumulated rubbish of centuries. An English clergyman, who wrote a botanical guide to the Colosseum, was able to distinguish over two hundred species. During the nineteenth century most of the monuments were dug out and we can now examine them in far more detail than Palladio was able to do; but what archaeology has gained the romantic and picturesque have lost. Fortunately, thanks to a marvellous series of engravings, we are still able to see, in great detail, how Rome looked in the eighteenth century and before.

Of all the etchers and engravers who depicted Rome (and they were legion), one man towers above the rest in artistic genius. Giovanni Battista Piranesi (1720–78) was the son of a Venetian stonemason. Having first trained as an architect he set up in Rome in 1744 as an engraver and print seller. An impetuous and irascible man, he quarrelled with his relations, his teachers, his patrons and his clients. He threatened one employer with death and was only just restrained from killing his doctor. A whirlwind courtship resulted in his marrying a girl whom he had met, by chance, five days earlier. The same passionate vitality that was so pronounced a feature of his private life (if such a tornado can be called private) provided the driving force for his work. He was so totally devoted to his art that he gave up going out to eat and cooked enough rice on Sunday to last the rest of the week. He etched over a thousand plates, nearly all of them large and full of detail [161 and 162].

Examining these plates we find ourselves back in a world of great beauty that has gone for ever, and we share the experience that inspired Gibbon to write the *Decline and Fall*. The remains of Rome, depicted with the utmost grandeur, sometimes buried up to the capitals of the columns like Gulliver pegged down by the Lilliputians, seem to be struggling for release. Trees and all manner of vegetation sprout from crannies and interstices. The scale and magnificence of the ancient world is given added grandeur by the poignant contrast of contemporary life. Temples have been turned into tenements. All manner of ignoble sheds and stables clutter the arches, while pigmy layabouts loiter where Cicero and Augustus once trod.

In addition to his topographical engravings Piranesi produced, quite early in his career, one work of uncanny imagination, *Invenzioni Capric de Carceri*, 'The Prisons' [163]. These engravings depict a nightmare world set in Cyclopean halls and galleries built with stone blocks of a size greater than any ever used in real architecture. Vast vaults rise about ten times as high as Durham Cathedral. At various levels there are windlasses, pulleys, ropes and immense engines serving no apparent purpose. Oppressed Kafka-like characters, dwarfed into insignificance, climb giant stone staircases or rickety ladders, precarious gangways and wooden cat-walks, each leading to a sickening drop into the abyss. Can we be surprised that when De Quincey was shown these engravings by Coleridge he recognized his own opium-inspired nightmares?

scattered with skulls and lumbered with ponderous and ugly medieval buildings [167].

De l'Orme had intended to write a second volume, but he was recalled by Catherine de' Medicis, the Queen Mother, to build the Tuileries. This occupied his time fully until his death in 1570.

INIGO JONES AND THE PALLADIANS

The Renaissance moved northwards slowly in its journey from the Mediterranean and took a considerable time to reach England. Italians had started to erect classical pediments while the English were constructing the fan-vaulting of Henry VII's chapel. At first the Renaissance was little understood; strapwork and grotesques were applied to buildings that were almost medieval in conception. But as interest grew in advanced circles foreign architectural books were imported and consulted. Then, in 1550, the Duke of Northumberland sent John Shute to Italy in order that he might 'confer with the doings of skilful masters in architecture, and also to view such ancient monuments thereof as are yet extant'. Shute's book, *The First and Chief Groundes of Architecture*, dedicated to Queen Elizabeth, was printed in the year of his death, 1563. It is a work of such rarity (less than ten copies have survived) that I hesitate to use the word 'published'. Some believe that its circulation was confined to a small circle of noblemen.

In 1611 Serlio was first translated into English, from the Dutch, by Robert Peake [168]. For a long period this was the only major work on classical architecture in English. It is dedicated to Henry, Prince of Wales, the elder brother of Charles I, and marks the Continental style of the Renaissance-type court that the prince, so briefly, gathered round him. Salomon de Caus, the French garden designer (who afterwards laid out the gardens at Heidelberg Castle), was summoned to instruct the prince in mathematics; Constantio de Servi, a Medicean architect, came from Florence to design 'fountains, summer-houses, galleries and other things' for the palace at Richmond; Peake was his 'picturemaker' and Inigo Jones his surveyor.

Inigo Jones (1573–1652) was the first Englishman really to grasp the underlying principles of the classical ideal and to create a building in which the details grew organically out of a totally new conception. We know very little about his youth, but it appears that he was in Italy from 1598 to 1603 and mastered the new draughtsmanship that had been developed during the Renaissance. His talents came to the notice of a Roman Catholic peer, Thomas Howard, second Earl of Arundel, who became an understanding and influential patron, taking his protégé on a tour of Italy in 1613. In Rome during this visit Inigo Jones made a practice of taking his copy of Palladio to the classical sites, comparing the woodcuts with the monuments, and making notes [169]. By good fortune this precious volume has survived among the considerable proportion of Jones's library now preserved at Worcester College, Oxford. These books show that he read and annotated the classic and Renaissance authors as no other English architect or artist had done before.

BELOW 168 In 1611 Serlio's *The First (–Fifth) Books of Architecture* was translated into English by Robert Peake.

OPPOSITE 169 Inigo Jones (1573–1652) was the first Englishman to grasp the underlying principles of the classical ideal in architecture. He went to Italy, compared the buildings with the woodcuts and made notes in his copy of Palladio which survives in the library of Worcester College, Oxford.

The second Booke.   The third Chapter.   Fol. 17.

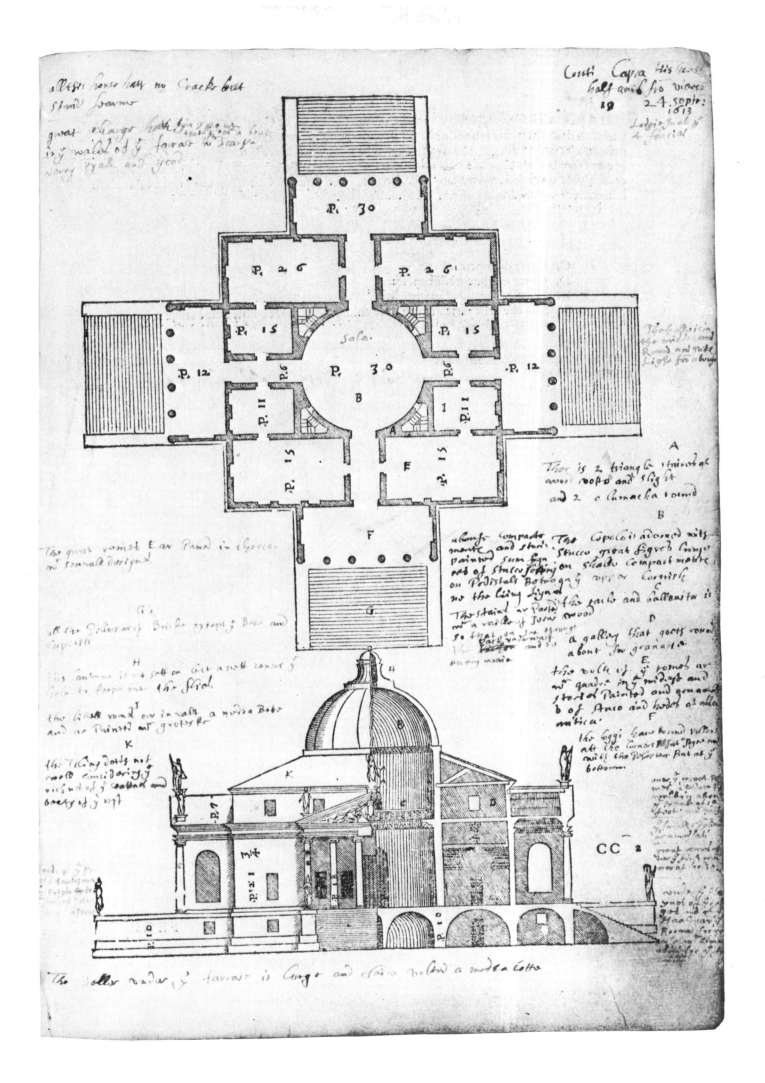

La grande Chambre D'audience.

The BANQUETTING House at WHITEHALL, by Inigo Jones.
To The R.t Honourable IOHN Earl of MAR, &c Hereditary Governour of Sterling Castle,
principal Secretary of State, and Knight of the most ancient Order of the THISTLE.

170 In 1619–22 Inigo Jones built his masterpiece, the Banqueting House in Whitehall. By some personal alchemy he transmuted Italian forms into a truly English building. From Campbell, *Vitruvius Britannicus* (1715).

On their return to England Inigo Jones was appointed Surveyor of the King's Works, a post he held until the outbreak of the Civil War in 1642. In 1616 he began to build the Queen's House at Greenwich. This, the first English classical domestic building, was to have immense influence for several hundred years, not only in England but in America (the White House is a descendant of the Queen's House), the West Indies and other erstwhile Colonies. The Queen, Anne of Denmark, died in 1619. Work was suspended for ten years and only completed in 1635, so that the final building reflects a later stage in Jones's career.

In 1619–22 he built his masterpiece, the Banqueting House in Whitehall, one of the most serene and beautiful buildings in London [170]. In this he made use of all that he had absorbed in his studies of Palladio and the Roman monuments. The remarkable thing is that, by some personal alchemy, he transmuted these Italian forms into a truly English building. This, too, was to have incalculable influence on English architecture. The ceilings were gloriously painted by Rubens to display the Apotheosis of James I and other splendid allegories.

From about 1637 Jones, in conjunction with his pupil John Webb, began to draw up plans for a vast palace in Whitehall. Whether, in view of the straitened circumstances of the English monarchy, this could ever have been built it is now idle to speculate, for all hopes were extinguished by the outbreak of the Civil War. We can only contemplate, sadly, the vision of a beautiful English building that might have been.

Inigo Jones was among the Royalist defenders at the siege of Basing House. When it fell numerous 'papist' pictures were burned, four priests were hanged and the old architect was ignominiously stripped of his clothes by the Roundheads and 'carried away in a blanket'. His estate was sequestered, but eventually restored after the payment of a savage fine. It is not surprising that the Cromwellian Puritans, with their hatred of all forms of beauty, should have chosen the Banqueting House (the very symbol of his love for and perceptive patronage of the arts) as the scene of Charles I's execution.

Owing to the confusion of the Civil War and the Commonwealth, and the Baroque tastes of the Restoration, none of Inigo Jones's drawings were published during his lifetime, but the Palladians of the early eighteenth century who looked back to him as their founding father produced several sumptuous volumes in his honour. It must be mentioned that their piety outran their perception, and a number of buildings and drawings by John Webb and others were wrongly attributed to Jones. Indeed it is only now, through the scholarly researches of John Harris, that the *oeuvre* of Inigo Jones has been finally separated from that of his followers.

The Whig nobility, who by the 'Glorious Revolution' of 1688 had thrown out the Stuarts and prevented any immediate revival of the Roman Catholic Church, were, although themselves an oligarchy of about two hundred families, among the true founders of a parliamentary democracy that actually worked. Their fathers having solved the problem of government, the second generation turned to providing a rational basis for philosophy and the arts. It was from this setting that the English revival of Palladian architecture was to spring. They rejected the Baroque of Wren and Vanbrugh not only because it was connected with the Stuarts but because it was tainted by Catholic influence. Their heroes were Palladio and Inigo Jones. A classical education had given them a feeling for the virtues of Greece and Rome. The Grand Tour had enabled them to see the Roman remains and the Palladian buildings in and round Vicenza, and they collected, avidly, those paintings of Claude and Poussin that looked back, through a golden glow, to a world of 'the Ancients' – more noble than 'the Ancients' had, in fact, been.

The difference between France and England lay in this: France was an absolute monarchy: '*L'Etat c'est Moi.*' The hearts and ambitions of the French aristocracy were centred on the court at Versailles. The Whig aristocrats of England could regard the Hanoverian monarchy as an institution that they had brought in, and their hearts were not set upon London or Windsor but in their own country estates.

It must be admitted that there were occasions when these architectural ideals demanded the sacrifice of comfort to splendour; 'Proud to catch cold at a Venetian door,' sneered Pope. And when General Wade's town house (with its perfectly balanced Palladian façade) proved almost uninhabitable, Lord Chesterfield advised him to buy the house opposite.

The study of architecture was considered an essential part of a gentleman's education and most country house libraries contained a selection of splendid folios on the subject. The early part of the eighteenth century saw the publication of two books that were to be of crucial importance. The *Architecture in Four Books* of Palladio was translated into English and provided with a fine set of plates, specially redrawn by a Venetian architect, Giacomo Leoni. This, published in 1715, may be regarded as the most handsome of all editions. *Vitruvius Britannicus* was by Colen Campbell (d. 1729), a Scottish architect with a considerable English practice who had built a number of Palladian houses that he illustrated, together with designs by Inigo Jones [170].

Vitruvius Britannicus was the first thoroughly professional measured survey of national architecture, more professional than Jean Marot's *L'Architecture Françoise* or Eric Johnson Dahlberg's *Suecia Antiqua et Hodierna,* and with a programme lacking in, say, John Kip and Leonard Knyff's *Nouveau Théâtre De La Grande Bretagne,* a topographical compilation. Campbell began work in about 1712 and used the work both as a polemical platform and a means of propagating his own neo-Palladian designs. Volume One appeared in 1715 and two more followed in 1717 and 1725. The design for innumerable buildings all over Britain and Ireland was influenced by these two books. Two more volumes were added in 1767 and 1771 (more than a generation later) by John Woolfe and James Gandon, and we may observe the unusual, perhaps unique, spectacle of the buildings in the last two volumes having been influenced by those illustrated in the first. Finally, in 1802–10, George Richardson added two further volumes, *The New Vitruvius Britannicus.*

Within this favourable setting the English Palladian movement was already quietly under way when it received immense impetus and encouragement from a remarkable patron. Richard Boyle, Earl of Burlington (1695–1753) succeeded, at the age of nine, to great wealth and the social position that was to bring him privilege and political power. His enthusiasm for architecture developed early and on his second Grand Tour, in 1719, he not only studied the buildings of Palladio, he succeeded in buying, and bringing to England, a large cache of his original drawings, including those preserved at the Villa Maser. Having engaged Colen Campbell to remodel his Piccadilly home, Burlington House, he proceeded to establish what amounted to an architectural academy and to devote his life to the promotion of Palladian architecture.

As a patron Burlington had a sympathetic understanding for the architects he supported and their relationship was one of friendship and collaboration in creation. Further, he was no mean architect himself. Buildings he designed, such as the beautiful Assembly Room at York, or Chiswick House (which shows development from Palladio's Villa Rotunda), are thought out with very real perception. Chiswick House was not designed as an independent residence but rather as a kind of pleasure dome attached by a corridor to the earlier family house, so it hardly deserved Lord Chesterfield's quip, 'Too small to live in, too large

171 James Gibbs (1682–1754), a Roman Catholic and a Tory, was out of the mainstream of Palladian architecture; his highly personal work is often Baroque or Mannerist. Here we see one of his masterpieces, the Radcliffe Library, Oxford.

to hang on a watch-chain.' It has, happily, survived both its days as a high-class lunatic asylum and the wartime battering as an auxiliary fire station. When I first went to visit it, soon after the war, I had to sign an undertaking that I would not hold Chiswick Corporation responsible for injury, should the building collapse on top of me. It has now been beautifully restored.

In addition to his own work Burlington promoted Palladian architecture in two ways: through his social position and his reputation as a 'man of taste' he was able to influence his fellow Whig magnates when they came to build, and he promoted and subsidized a series of handsome and influential books. High on the list came *The Designs of Inigo Jones,* edited by William Kent (1727), while Burlington edited a series of engravings after Jones's Palladian drawings in his own collection, *Fabbriche Antiche* (1730).

JAMES GIBBS AND ENGLISH BAROQUE

We must now retrace our steps to consider one of the most original of the British classical architects, James Gibbs (1682–1754). He was a Scotsman, a Catholic, a Tory and, possibly, a Jacobite – characteristics that placed him outside the Whig circles from which the eighteenth-century revival of Palladianism sprang. Further, he was the only British architect of his time to have studied under a Roman master, Carlo Fontana. In conception and detail his highly personal work is often Baroque or Mannerist, in contrast to the strict Palladianism of his British contemporaries.

Gibbs built many public buildings. He also built town and country houses, mainly, but not entirely, for Tory patrons. His two masterpieces, however, are the Radcliffe Library at Oxford [171] and St Martin-in-the-Fields in London. The latter, with its superb spire rising, somewhat incongruously, from behind the pediment, is far too well known to call for description here.

In 1728 Gibbs published *A Book of Architecture* [172]. This was a promotional book. It described and illustrated, with fine plates, most of the important buildings he had designed up to that time, and went further by including all manner of designs for smaller buildings, interior and exterior details, garden ornaments, monuments and so forth. By means of this book country gentlemen or church committees, living far from any architectural help, could create very creditable buildings – and very many of them did. Probably no book has had greater influence on the architecture of the English-speaking world; not only at home but even more, perhaps, in the Colonies. How often, when entering some New England village and seeing the spire of a white wooden church rising from behind the pediment, does one murmur, with a lift of the heart, 'Ah, Gibbs.'

THE ENGLISH PATTERN BOOKS

Georgian architecture was a civilized style common to nearly every country town and house during the eighteenth century. By no means

172 By means of James Gibb's *A Book of Architecture* (1728), country gentlemen and church committees in England and America could create very creditable buildings. There is little need to stress the influence of this plate on New England architecture.

The West front of St Martins Church.

confined to the mansions of great noblemen, its spread on a national scale was due to the extraordinary phenomenon of the great publishing boom in architectural pattern books, something absolutely unique to England. Hundreds of cheap books of patterns and advice were produced by authors such as Batty Langley and William Halfpenny. These, available to every country builder and mason, made the rules of architecture easy to understand and provided not only patterns for every element of building but also charts by which to compute the right measurements and proportions. Langley, for example, produced not only the smallest English pattern book, *The Builder's Jewel* (1741) but also the largest, *Principles of Ancient Masonry* (1733). Aided by these books families of builders who created work of considerable distinction sprang up in country towns well removed from the metropolis: the Smiths of Warwick, Thomas White of Worcester, the Bastards of Blandford and so on. This form of building spread to the American Colonies, then an integral part of English civilization, where many a planter derived the plan and details of his mansion from a pattern book, and where Batty and Thomas Langley's *The Builder's Jewel* was reprinted at Charleston as late as 1800.

This state of affairs was due to the political and social development of England. In some continental countries there were 'the rich' and 'the poor', with a wide gulf in between. In England reasonable affluence was far more widely spread and, during the eighteenth century, foreign visitors were struck by the large number of 'middle people'. It was for these people that the innumerable buildings based upon the pattern books were erected.

THE ADAM BROTHERS

The Adam brothers were four more Scotsmen who came south in the cause of architecture, implementing Johnson's taunt about the finest prospect a Scotsman ever sees. Their father, William, was the most successful architect in Scotland, so when Robert Adam set out on the Grand Tour he had already formed the deliberate plan of study that was to forward his brilliant career. On the return journey, in 1757, he made a wide detour from the well-trodden route to visit the ruins of the palace of the Emperor Diocletian at Spalatro.

The Emperor Diocletian, who is rightly regarded as the refounder of the Roman Empire in the troubled times of the third century AD, was a Dalmatian soldier of humble birth. In 305, stricken by ill-health, he abdicated, retired to his native country and built a palace on the shores of the Adriatic. This was no case of retiring to a simple Horatian farm. Diocletian's palace resembled a town rather than a villa. It included accommodation for an imperial suite, every form of luxurious service in a barren countryside, barracks for the guards and, finally, an imposing mausoleum. After his death the palace had no real purpose and it fell into decay. In subsequent years it became a giant tenement, filled with refugees fleeing from towns destroyed by barbarian invaders, their little homes encrusting the imperial façades like the nests of swallows.

173 Robert Adam did not limit himself to the creation of houses and interior decoration, he completed the effect by designing furniture, fire-irons, even cutlery. This design for an urn comes from his *Works in Architecture* (1778–86).

188

To this imposing mass Robert Adam brought the brilliant French draughtsman C.-L. Clérisseau, and they spent five weeks studying, measuring and drawing.

In 1764 Adam published *Ruins of the Palace of the Emperor Diocletian at Spalatro, in Dalmatia,* illustrated with fine (sometimes double-page) engravings by Francesco Bartolozzi, Antonio Zucchi and Domenico Cunego, after drawings by Clérisseau [68 and 174]. This, like many of the splendid folios of the time, was intended to promote the author's career. The bindings Adam designed for the copies presented to potential patrons have been described in Chapter Three. However, the importance of this book does not end here, for the influence of Spalatro may be seen in some of the designs that Adam produced in later years.

In the name of nationalism, which insists on substituting ugly for beautiful names, Spalatro has now been renamed Split. Further down the coast the ancient seaport of Ragusa, which gave us the word 'argosy', is now called Dubrovnik and, even worse, the Turks have replaced the lovely, historical and evocative Halicarnasus with Budrum. Credit, however, must be given to the work done on Diocletian's palace in recent years. Much of the ignoble encrustation has been stripped away and we can see a great deal more than Adam ever saw. The enormous

174 Robert Adam deviated from the grand tour and spent five weeks at Spalatro. His *Ruins of the Palace of the Emperor Diocletian at Spalatro, in Dalmatia* (1764), a splendid folio, was designed to promote his career. For the superb binding which covered some copies, see Figure 68.

underground vaults, as moving as Norman cathedrals, have been cleared of the rubbish that had filled them for more than a thousand years.

As an original and creative genius Adam was superior to the Palladians, but his greatest achievement was to be the founder of a national style of interior decoration. He left a legacy of beautiful buildings and even more lovely rooms. Some of these are illustrated in *Works in Architecture*, by Robert and James Adam (1778–86), another volume being added in 1822 [173]. The experience of looking through these plates is like taking a walk through a civilization more exquisite than the world will ever see again.

THE GREEK REVIVAL

The revival of classical architecture had been entirely based on Roman models. At the time of the Renaissance, and for long afterwards, Greece itself was under the heel of the Turks and remained a virtually unknown land. When the first European travellers began to penetrate the mainland during the latter part of the seventeenth century they experienced difficulties due to Mohammedan prejudice against Christians and the unsettled state of the country. This is all the more regrettable because the Parthenon was then still more or less intact; one of the last foreigners to see it was an Englishman, Sir George Wheler, who wrote an interesting account of his travels. A year or two later the Turks were using it as a powder magazine. When, on 26 September 1687, the Venetians succeeded in lobbing a shell through the roof, they celebrated this feat in a number of engravings [175].

The first accurate survey of Greek architecture was the work of two Britons, James Stuart (1713–88), another Scotsman, and Nicholas Revett (1720–1804). Their journey was financed by a group of English dilettanti then living in Rome. They sailed from Venice in 1751 and arrived back in London in 1755. Revett made all the measured drawings but, since he was a gentleman of independent means, he resigned his interest to Stuart.

'Athenian Stuart', as he was to be known for the rest of his life, was extremely lazy and inclined to drunkenness. As a result publication of the first volume of their book, *The Antiquities of Athens*, was delayed until 1762, and the second, dated 1787 (but actually 1789), came out posthumously. Volumes three and four followed in 1795 and 1816. This was the first time that a really thorough and accurate picture of Greek architecture had been available in Western Europe. The impact was considerable, and would have been even greater had Stuart's indolence not caused the book to be anticipated by lesser works. It has the additional value of showing us buildings which, when recorded, were more complete than they now are [67 and 176].

For us this great book has another, and a poignant, quality. Athenian Stuart drew a number of general pictures of Athens as it was then, an Athens that has gone for ever – a tiny village nestling under the shadow of the Acropolis, with indolent, happy Turks sitting about playing strange musical instruments, or riding horses and practising with bows

175 The Parthenon remained more or less intact until the seventeenth century. The Turks were using it as a powder magazine when, on 26 September 1687, the Venetians lobbed a shell through the roof; a feat celebrated in F. Fanelli, *Atene Attica* (Venice 1707).

and arrows. In a convent garden near the Temple of the Winds an elderly monk sits in the shade, taking his ease. Otherwise the beautiful and unspoiled Greek landscape stretches away to the horizon.

I began this chapter with Trissino building his villa. He saw the beginning of an epoch; we live just after its close. In the intervening four to five hundred years what a wealth of beauty has been created – how many villas, châteaux, country houses and gardens. The greater number of those buildings were first inspired by, and then recorded in, the books described here. It seems probable that no one will ever again build a great country house or create a landscape Elysium in his park. Hardly a month passes without the destruction of a Palladian house, and how many country houses are no longer homes but schools, government or business offices, or reformatories where the unhappy inhabitants gaze from the windows at the decaying gardens.

Piranesi recorded for us the wreck of Roman civilization. So we, in our turn, gaze upon the destruction of the Palladian world.

176 *The Antiquities of Athens* (1762–1816), by James Stuart and Nicholas Revett, was the first accurate survey of Greek architecture. Here we see the Acropolis cluttered with later buildings. For the superb binding which Stuart designed for some copies, see Figure 67.

191

CHAPTER NINE

THE NEW WORLD

COLUMBUS

IT IS UNNECESSARY, here, to do more than give the barest outline of the epoch-making voyage of Christopher Columbus. Having finally won the support of Ferdinand and Isabella of Spain he set sail from Palos, on 3 August 1492, with three ships, the *Santa Maria,* the *Niña* and the *Pinta.* On 12 October a sailor aboard the *Niña* sighted what proved to be the New World. Columbus named this landing place San Salvador and took possession in the name of Ferdinand and Isabella. After further voyaging, and the setting-up of a colony on Haiti, Columbus set sail on his return voyage on 4 January 1493. On 14 February, during a fierce storm,

177 On his return from the epoch-making voyage which changed our whole conception of the world, Columbus wrote a letter describing his discoveries to Luis de Santangel. This, generally known as *The Columbus Letter*, was printed at Barcelona on two leaves by Pedro Posa in 1493. The only surviving copy, discovered in 1889, is now in the New York Public Library.

Columbus wrote what he feared might be the only record of his discoveries. He wrapped this document in waxed cloth, enclosed it in a wooden cask and consigned it to the mercy of the sea. He also wrote another description of his voyage in a letter to Luis de Santangel. His fears proved needless, however, and four days later he reached the Azores.

At some time in the spring of 1493 the letter to Luis de Santangel (generally known as *The Columbus Letter*) was printed in Barcelona, on two leaves, by Pedro Posa. Only one copy survives; this was discovered in 1889 and is now in the New York Public Library [177].

The first Latin edition, *Epistola de insulis nuper inventis,* was printed in Rome, in 1493, by Stephan Plannck, in a quarto of four leaves. This was followed, in the same year, by the Basle edition (Michael Furter for Johann Bergmann) on ten leaves with eight woodcuts, by the Paris edition of Guy Marchant, and by the Antwerp edition of Thierry Martens. Translations followed in Italian and German. Of these, the most charming is that translated into Italian verse by Giuliano Dati. Illustrated with a woodcut, it was printed at Florence (probably in 1493) by L. Morgiani and J. Petri, who printed many tracts for Savonarola [178]. The German translation was printed at Strassburg by Bartholomaeus Kistler in 1497.

In spite of the rarity of *The Columbus Letter,* the Bodleian Library owned two copies of the Marchant edition, one stemming from Archbishop Laud and one bequeathed by Francis Douce in 1834. In 1936, on the three hundredth anniversary of the foundation of Harvard, Oxford University presented the Douce copy to that University.

MEXICAN PRINTING

It is an extraordinary fact, and one that gives us a vivid insight into the vigour of Spanish colonial expansion, that there was a printing press at work in the New World less than fifty years after the landfall of Columbus – less than one hundred years after the invention of the craft itself. Indeed there was printing in Mexico before it had been introduced into several European countries.

The initiative was due, as has so often been the case, to the needs of religion. Although not the mainspring of the terrible and brutal conquest, one of the chief ambitions of the *conquistadores* was the conversion of the Indians to Christianity. This project created a need for small primers, catechisms, grammars and similar items in the native tongue. The task was entrusted to Juan Cromberger, the leading printer in Seville, but the difficulties of printing in a language totally unknown to those concerned in the work soon became evident. Encouraged by both the archbishop and viceroy of Mexico, Cromberger resolved to set up a printing house in Mexico City. For this purpose he recruited Giovanni Paoli, an Italian printer already working in Seville, who had Iberianized his name to Juan Pablos. By a piece of good fortune the legal document setting out the terms of their agreement on 12 June 1539 has come to light, and it is thus translated and summarized by Douglas McMurtrie:

178 *The Columbus Letter* was translated into Italian verse by Giuliano Dati. Illustrated with a woodcut which must rank as the first picture of Americans, it was printed at Florence probably in 1493.

herro⁊ ꝟlos idolos lee ꝟl herro⁊ ꝟlos idolos.Enla ho.rrviij
fa.j.re.rvij.do dize Se entieda dello la fe ſalua:lee po⁊ parerꝑe
ſiſQue ſe entieda dicho la fe ſalua.re.rrij.oôde dize En eſfe lee
eneſte.Enla miſma êla fa3.ij.re.j.oôde dize el Miſterio Jo⁊
dä:lee el miſterio ôl Jo⁊dan.re.riiij.oôde dize No ppria ſu⁊a
ſpecie:lee no p⁊op⁊ia ſpecie ſu⁊a.re.rrir. donde dize Aqſte ꝗ́
ppheta afirma ſer ppheta:lee aꝗ́ſto ꝗ́l ppheta ⁊ mas ꝗ́ pphe
ra.Enel miſmo re.oôde dize Demâdado lo lee ômandôdolo.
Enla hoja.rrr.fa3.j.a.iiij.re.donde dize de la Reſurrectiô:lee
de reſurrectiô.Y eñl.re.rij.donde dize Tambiê vaca ⁊ eſta ſup
fluo.Enla hoja.rrrj.fa3.ij.re.rrj.Donde dize Y los colocâ:lee
⁊ los coloca.Y eñl re.final donde dize Le penetra:lee lo pene
tra.Enla hoja.rrrj.fa3.ij.re.rj.⁊.rij.donde dize. Y el miido la
ha3aña:lee ⁊ la ha3aña.Y eñl.re.rrrij.donde dize Dia no peꞇ
ꝗ́ña:lee dia·⁊ no peꝗ́ña.Enla hoja.rrriij.fa3.j.re.j.donde dize
Le poono:lee ⁊ le perdono.Enla hoja.rrrvj.fa3.j.re.iiij.don
de dize.Enel dilatar:lee enlo dilatar.

¶ Imp⁊imiofe eſte Manual de Adultos en la grâ ciudad ô
Mexico po⁊ mâdado ôlos Reuerêdiſſimos Señores Obiſ
pos ôla nueua Eſpaña ⁊ a ſus erpêſas:en caſa ô Juâ Crom
berger.Año ôl nacimiêto ônueſtro ſeño⁊ Jeſu Chriſto ô mill
⁊ quiniêtos ⁊ quarêta.A.rriij.dias ôl mes ô De3iêbre.

ABOVE 179 Printing was established in Mexico
less than fifty years after the landfall of
Columbus. Only a single fragment of three
leaves is known of the first Mexican printed
book to survive: *Manual de adultos*, printed
by Juan Pablos (then in the employ of
Juan Cromberger), 1540.
Toledo, Biblioteca Publica Provincial.
BELOW 180 *Dialectica . . . Aristotelis*, printed in
Mexico by Juan Pablos (1554). The border is an
almost direct copy, except for the royal arms, of
that which Whitchurch provided for the first
issue of The Book of Common Prayer (1549).

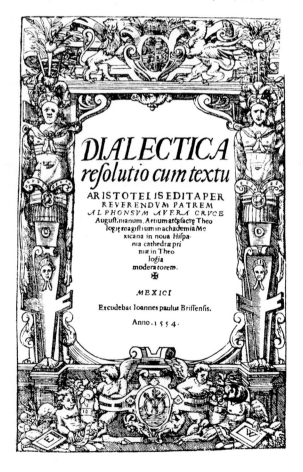

Pablos was to act as compositor and manager of the office in Mexico, but
Cromberger reserved the right to place a representative beside him to check up
on all his transactions. Neither Pablos nor his wife (who was to do the house-
keeping for the printer and his assistant) was to receive any salary, nor were they
to spend a cent of the income of the office in excess of bare living expenses. The
printer was to print three thousand sheets daily and was to be held responsible
for all errors in the original composition or in the correction of proofs. He was
to seek out and procure the personnel requisite to the organization of the
office, but at first must content himself with a pressman and a negro as helpers.
He was prohibited from entering into partnership for any business whatever,
and any emoluments which he might receive personally were to go into the
common fund. He was required to act as agent for the sale of books and mer-
chandise sent to Mexico by his principal, but was entitled to no commission on
such sales. . . . The traveling expenses were to be defrayed by Cromberger, who
also assumed the cost of shipping the printing press, materials, and equipment.
The partnership was to last for ten years, and at the expiration of that term there
was to be a settlement, to be made in Spain, in which Pablos was to receive
one-fifth of the net profits.

The impression of Cromberger that we derive from this document is of
a grasping employer who might have stepped out of the very harshest
pages of Dickens; and any sensitive reader must find himself whole-
heartedly on the side of Pablos. It is pleasant to record, therefore, that – as
happens quite frequently in Dickens, but less often in real life – all came
right in the end. Within a year after Pablos landed in Mexico, Cromberger died. Pablos, left in possession of the equipment, continued to
operate the press under his own name, flourished, gained citizenship and
was granted land on which to build his house.

On arrival in Mexico Pablos had first set to work on the primers for
which there was such a demand, but, not unnaturally, none of these has
survived.

The first Mexican printed book of which anything remains is *Manual
de adultos* (13 December 1540) surviving only in a single fragment consisting of the last two leaves which turned up among some miscellaneous
papers in the Biblioteca Provincial in Toledo. Two of the three pages
consist of errata, the last of which refers to sheet thirty-six, from which
we may conclude that the book was of a considerable size. Fortunately
the colophon survives and reads: 'In the great city of Mexico by order
of the reverend bishops of New Spain, and at their expense in the house
of Juan Cromberger' [179].

In 1550 Pablos engaged Diego de Montoya, a type-founder, and
Antonio de Espinosa, a punch-cutter and engraver of considerable
distinction. By 1554 italic type made its first appearance in the New
World and some books were illustrated by engravings. One intriguing
feature was the woodcut title border that decorated the *Dialectica* of
1554 [180]. This is an almost direct copy, except for the royal arms, of the
border that Edward Whitchurch had provided for the first issue of
The Book of Common Prayer (7 March 1549). Who would have expected the major liturgical book of the extreme Protestant world of Edward
VI to influence the rigidly Roman Catholic civilization in Mexico?

In 1559 Espinosa obtained the right to set up on his own and carried on a highly successful career as a printer until his death in 1576. His masterpiece was the *Missale Romanum* in 1561.

FIRST DESCRIPTION OF THE NEW WORLD IN ENGLISH

The first book in English to describe America was published in Antwerp, probably in 1520, by John of Doesborowe. This printer produced a few other books in English, most of them now very rare, such as *Mary of Nemeguen* (probably printed in 1518), which survives only in the Roxburghe-Heber-Britwell-Huntington copy.

Of the newe landes & ye people founde by the messengers of the kynge of Portyngale named Emanuel is hardly more than a pamphlet. The woodcut, Figure 181, shows us some of the inhabitants of Brazil. They can hardly claim to be numbered among the noble savages hymned by Rousseau, since according to the text they both copulate with and consume their nearest relations:

> . . . there we at ye laste went a lande but that lāde is not nowe knowē for there haue no masters wryten therof nor it knoweth and it is named Armenica/there we sawe meny wōders of beestes and fowles yt we haue neuer seen before/the people of this lande haue no kynge nor lorde nor theyr god But all thinges is comune/this people goeth all naked But the men and women haue on theyr heed necke/Armes/Knees/and fete all with feders boūden for there bewtynes & fayrenes. These folke lyuen lyke bestes without any resonablenes and the wymen be also as comon. And the men hath conuersacyon with the wymen/who that they ben or who they fyrst mete/is she his syster/his moder/his daughter/or any other kȳdred. And the wymen be very hoote and dysposed to lecherdnes. And they ete also on a nother. The man etethe his wyfe his chylderne/as we also haue seen and they hange also the bodyes or persons fleeshe in the smoke/as men do with us swynes fleshe.

SIR FRANCIS DRAKE: *THE WORLD ENCOMPASSED*

There is no more need to describe the circumnavigation of Sir Francis Drake than there was to describe, in detail, the voyage of Columbus. Drake sailed from Plymouth with five ships in 1577. In 1579 he plundered Valparaiso and on 17 June of that year he anchored in a 'convenient and fit harborough' on the California coast, taking possession of the new land in the name of Queen Elizabeth and naming it New Albion. Here he reconditioned his ship and established friendly relations with the local Indians whose chieftain was persuaded to crown Drake as 'King'. 'Then,' wrote Drake's chaplain, Francis Fletcher:

> . . . before we went from thence, our generall caused to be set vp, a monument of our being there; as also of her maiesties, and successors right and title to that kingdome, namely, a plate of brasse, fast nailed to a great and firme post; whereon is engrauen her graces name, and the day and yeare of our arriuall there, and of the free giuing vp, of the prouince and kingdome, both by the king and people, into her maiesties hands: together with her highnesse picture, and armes in a piece of sixpence current English monie, shewing it selfe by a hole made of purpose through the plate; vnderneath was likewise engrauen the name of our generall. . . .

181 The first book in English to describe America was published at Antwerp, probably in 1520, by John of Doesborowe. The woodcut shows some of the inhabitants of Brazil who are described in a somewhat unflattering manner.

182 In 1579 Drake took possession of what is now a part of California and set up a 'plate of brasse' to record the fact. In 1936 this plate was dramatically discovered on the shore of Corte Madera Creek, an inlet of San Francisco Bay: the first surviving piece of writing done by an Englishman in what is now the United States. See transcription below. The Bancroft Library, University of California, Berkeley.

Three hundred and fifty-seven years later, in 1936, this brass plate was found by a family enjoying a picnic on the north shore of Corte Madera Creek, an inlet that opens on the east into the main San Francisco Bay about $1\frac{1}{2}$ miles north of San Quentin. The plate was identified by Professor Herbert E. Bolton, Director of the Bancroft Library, University of California at Berkeley, as Drake's 'plate of brasse' which, even before his departure, the natives had worshipped 'as if it had bin god'. It is the first known piece of writing done by an Englishman within the present United States [182]. The inscription reads as follows:

BEE IT KNOWNE VNTO ALL MEN BY THESE PRESENTS
IVNE.17.1579.
BY THE GRACE OF GOD AND IN THE NAME OF HERR
MAIESTY QVEEN ELIZABETH OF ENGLAND AND HERR
SVCCESSORS FOREVER I TAKE POSSESSION OF THIS
KINGDOME WHOSE KING AND PEOPLE FREELY RESIGNE
THEIR RIGHT AND TITLE IN THE WHOLE LAND VNTO HERR
MAIESTIES KEEPING NOW NAMED BY ME AN TO BEE
KNOWNE VNTO ALL MEN AS NOVA ALBION
G   FRANCIS DRAKE

(Hole for
silver
sixpence)

From the journals of Francis Fletcher another Sir Francis Drake (a nephew of the admiral) printed an account of the voyage, *The World Encompassed* (1628) [183].

RICHARD HAKLUYT: *PRINCIPALL NAVIGATIONS, VOIAGES, AND DISCOVERIES*

No Englishman has ever felt greater enthusiasm for voyages of exploration than Richard Hakluyt (1552?–1616) and no man did more to inspire the early adventurers who settled in America. His first book, *Divers*

THE VVORLD
Encompassed
By
Sir FRANCIS DRAKE,

Being his next voyage to that to *Nombre de Dios* formerly imprinted;

Carefully collected out of the notes of Master
FRANCIS FLETCHER *Preacher in this imployment, and diuers others his followers in the same*:

Offered now at last to publique view, both for the honour of the actor, but especially for the stirring vp of *heroick spirits, to benefit their Countrie, and eternize their names by like noble attempts.*

LONDON,
Printed for NICHOLAS BOVRNE
and are to be sold at his shop at the
Royall Exchange. 1628.

Voyages Tovching The Discoverie of America (London 1582) [184 and 185] is the first book written by an Englishman, and directed to his fellow-countrymen, relating to what is now the United States.

Consumed with interest in the New World, he dedicated *Divers Voyages* to Sir Philip Sidney:

183 During his voyage of circumnavigation Sir Francis Drake was accompanied by a literate chaplain, Francis Fletcher, who kept a journal. From this a nephew of the admiral, another Sir Francis Drake, produced *The World Encompassed.*

I Maruaile not a little that since the first discouerie of America (which is nowe full fourescore and tenne Yeeres) after so great conquests and plantings of the Spaniardes and Portingales there, that wee of Englande could neuer haue the grace to set fast footing in such fertill and temperate places, as are left as yet vnpossessed of them. . . . But againe when I consider that there is a time for all men . . . I conceiue great hope, that the time approcheth and nowe is, that we of England may share and part stakes (if wee will our selues) both with the spaniarde and the Portingale in part of America, and other regions as yet vndiscouered. And surely if there were in vs the desire to aduaunce the honour of our Countrie which ought to bee in euery good man, wee woulde not all this while haue foreflowne the possessing of those landes, whiche of equitie and right appertaine vnto vs, as by the discourses that followe shall appeare most plainely. Yea if wee woulde beholde with the eye of pitie howe al our Prisons are pestered and filled with able men to serue their Countrie, which for small roberies are dayly hanged vp in great numbers euen twentie at a clappe out of one iayle (as was seene at the last assises at Rochester) wee woulde hasten and

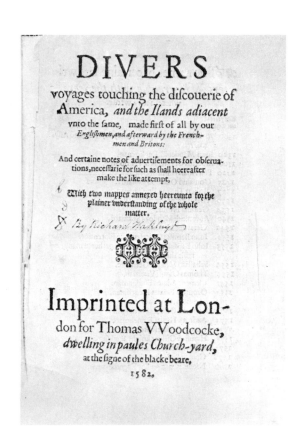

further euery man to his power the deducting of some Colonies of our superfluous people into those temperate and fertile partes of America, which being
within six weekes sayling of England are yet vnpossessed by any Christians:
and seeme to offer thenselues vnto vs, stretching neerer vnto her Maiesties
Dominions, then to any other part of Europe. Wee read that the Bees, whē
they grow to be too many in their own hiues at home, are wont to bee led out
by their Captaines to swarme abroad, and seeke themselues a new dwelling
place.

Hakluyt begins his book with a list of authorities from '1300 Abelfade
Ismael, prince of Syria, Persia and Assyria' to '1582 Humfrey Gilbert
knight, Edward Heyes, and Antonie Brigham Englishmen'. Then
comes the first printing, in both Latin and English, of the Letters Patent
of Henry VII (5 March 1495) granted to John Cabot and his three sons
for the discovery of new and unknown lands. This is followed by 'The
true and last discouerie of Florida made by Captain Iohn Ribault in the
yeere 1562', notes on what to take with you and advice on how to deal
with the natives, and 'The names of certaine commodities growing in
part of America'. At the front of the book, as a kind of stop press,
Hakluyt adds 'A verie late and great probabilitie of a passage by the
Northwest part of America in 58. degrees of Northerly latitude'.

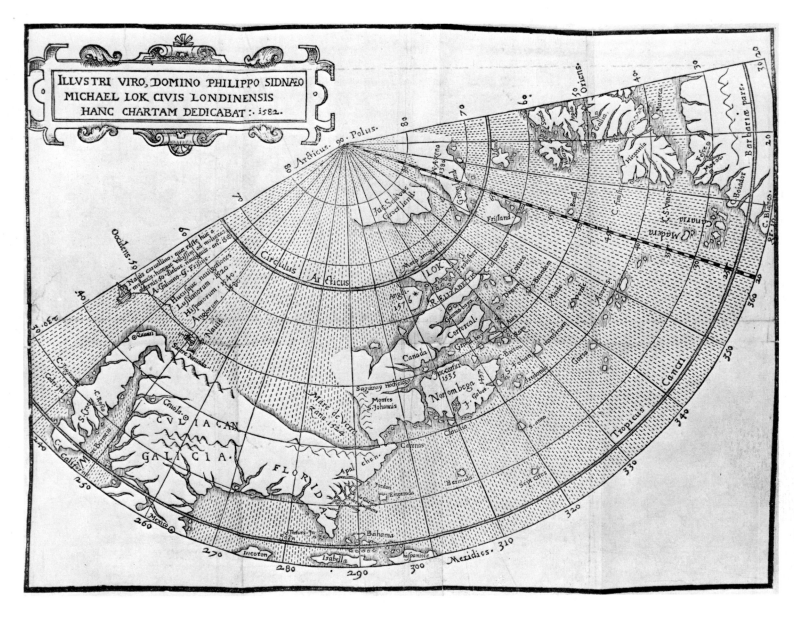

This book made such an impression on Lord Howard of Effingham, the lord admiral, that he persuaded his brother-in-law, Sir Edward Stafford, then ambassador in Paris, to appoint Hakluyt chaplain to the embassy. While in Paris, Hakluyt had further opportunities for geographical research, 'making diligent enquiry of such things as might yield any light unto our western discovery in America'. The fruit of this was a second book, *A particular Discourse concerning Western Discoveries.*

Although written in 1584, this was not printed until 1877, by the Maine Historical Society. However, a manuscript copy came into the hands of Queen Elizabeth and prompted her to set Hakluyt on the road to ecclesiastical preferment, so that he was successively prebendary of Bristol, prebendary of Westminster and, finally, in 1603, archdeacon of Westminster.

Spurred on by a natural desire to proclaim the past achievements of Englishmen and, perhaps even more, to inspire future activities, Hakluyt engaged in 'huge toil' until, in 1589, he published *The Principall Navigations, Voiages, and Discoveries of the English Nation made by Sea or over land to the most remote and farthest distant quarters of the earth, at any time within the compass of these 1500 yeares,* dedicated to Sir Francis Walsingham. Over the next ten years Hakluyt continued to add to this work, so that the final edition (1598–1600) filled three folio volumes. Well-printed modern editions fill twelve volumes. The book, one of the great classics of exploration, makes splendid reading and has been an inspiration to generations of Englishmen. J. A. Froude described it as 'the prose epic of the modern English nation ... the heroic tales of the exploits of the great men in whom the new era was inaugurated'. No other book in English, nor perhaps in any language, can be compared with it. In this field Hakluyt stands alone.

THOMAS HARIOT:
THE NEW FOVND LAND OF VIRGINIA

The second original work in English relating to America is Thomas Hariot's *A Brief and True Report of the New Fovnd Land of Virginia* (London 1588) [186]. Thomas Hariot (1560–1621) was a man of the new civilization, a mathematician and astronomer. Born and educated at Oxford, he was chosen by Sir Walter Ralegh as his resident mathematical tutor.

It had long been Ralegh's ambition to establish a colony in Virginia and in 1585 he was at last able to put his plan into action. Since Queen Elizabeth would not permit his own departure, Ralegh appointed his cousin, Sir Richard Grenville, to take charge of the little fleet that set sail in May.

Hariot accompanied the expedition as a surveyor and on his return produced the book that has made him famous. Compared with 'the messengers of the kynge of Portyngale', Hariot has progressed from the Middle Ages into the Renaissance. A trained scientist, he observed keenly and accurately before organizing his material into a work

OPPOSITE ABOVE 184 This is the first book written by an Englishman, Richard Hakluyt, and directed to his fellow countrymen, relating to what is now the United States.
OPPOSITE BELOW 185 A map from Hakluyt's *Divers Voyages Touching the Discoverie of America* (1582), dedicated to Sir Philip Sidney.

186 Thomas Hariot accompanied the expedition despatched by Ralegh in 1585 and wrote a remarkably well-organized, lucid and able book *A Brief and True Report of the New Fovnd Land of Virginia* (1588).

&⅋ A briefe and true report of the new found land of Virginia: of t̄e commodities there found and to be rayſed, as well marc̄iantable, as others for victuall, building and other neceſſarᴂ vſes for thoſe that are and ſhalbe the planters there; and of the nat̄re and manners of the naturall inhabitants : Diſcouered by the Engliſh Colony there ſeated by Sir Richard Greinuile Knight in the yeere 1585. which remained vnder the gouernment of Rafe Lane Eſquier, one of her Maieſties Equieres, during the ſpace of twelue moneſhes : at the ſpeciall charge and direction of the Honourable SIR WALTER RALEIGH Knight, Lord Warden of the ſtanneries ; who therein hath beene fauoured and authoriſed by her Maieſtie and her letters patents:

Directed to the Aduenturers, Fauourers, and Welwillers of the action, for the inhabiting and planting there:

By *Thomas Hariot*; ſeruant to the abouenamed Sir Walter, a member of the Colony, and there imployed in diſcouering.

Imprinted at London 1588.

OPPOSITE XXXVII George Catlin (1796–1872), realizing that the tribal life and culture of the Indians was fast disappearing, devoted his life to recording them. He visited forty-eight tribes and painted many pictures. This one is from *The North American Portfolio* (1844).

187 The impact of Hariot's book was not limited to England; a more elaborate edition with this splendid title-page was printed in Frankfurt in 1590.

'remarkable for the large views it contains in regard to the extension of industry and commerce'. It is divided as follows:

The first part of Marchantable commodities.

The second part of such commodities as Virginia is knowne to yeelde for victuall and sustenance of mans life.

The third and last part of such other things as is behoofull for those which shall plant and inhabit to know of; with a description of the nature and manners of the people of the countrey. Of commodities for building and other necessary uses.

No aspect of this expedition has remained more vividly in the popular imagination than the introduction of tobacco into England:

There is a herbe which is sowed a part by itselfe & is called by the inhabitants Vppówoc: In the West Indies it hath diuers names, according to the seuerall places & countries where it groweth and is vsed: The Spaniardes generally call it Tobacco. The leaues thereof being dried and brought into powder: they vse to take the fume or smoke thereof by sucking it through pipes made of claie into their stomacke and heade; from whence it purgeth superfluous fleame & other grosse humours, openeth all the pores & passages of the body: by which meanes the vse thereof, not only preseureth the body from obstructiōs; but also if any be, so that they haue not beene of too long continuance, in short time breaketh them: whereby their bodies are notably preserued in health, & know not many greeuous diseases wherewithall we in England are sometimes afflicted.

This Vppówoc is of so precious estimation amongst them, that they thinke their gods are maruelously delighted therewith: Whereupon sometime they make hallowed fires & cast some of the pouder therein for a sacrifice: being in a storme vppon the waters, to pacifie their gods, they cast some vp into the aire and into the water: so a weare for fish being newly set vp, they cast some therein and into the aire: also after an escape of danger, they cast some into the aire likewise: but all done with strange gestures, stamping, sometimes dauncing, clapping of hands, holding vp of hands, & staring vp into the heauens, vttering therewithal and chattering strange words & noises.

We ourselues during the time we were there vsed to suck it after their maner, as also since our returne, & haue found maine rare and wonderful experiments of the vertues thereof; of which the relation woulde require a volume by itselfe: the vse of it by so manie of late, men & women of great calling as else, and some learned Phisitions also, is sufficient witnes.

The impact of Hariot's book was not limited to England: a more elaborate edition with a rather splendid architectural title-page was printed in Frankfurt in 1590, and it was translated into Latin for De Bry's *Americae Descriptio* (also 1590) [187], while Hakluyt embodied it in his *Voyages* (1600).

JOHN SMITH:
THE GENERALL HISTORIE OF VIRGINIA

No figure among the early English colonists is more colourful than John Smith (1580–1631) who came from Willoughby in Lincolnshire. At the age of sixteen he crossed into Europe, where he spent ten years as a soldier of fortune, returning to England in 1605. In his own works, written

MAH - TO - TOH - PA

PLATE LXII.

Passenger Pigeon,
COLUMBA MIGRATORIA, Linn.
Male, 1. Female, 2.

Drawn from Nature & Published by John J. Audubon, F.R.S. F.L.S.

Engraved, Printed & Coloured by R Havell.

many years later, Smith has left us vivid glimpses of his early career.

We can easily understand the appeal which the prospect of further adventure in the unknown land of America would make to a man like Smith. He joined a party of 105 emigrants who set sail from Blackwall on 19 December 1606 to found, in Virginia, the first permanent English American colony. The colonists arrived at Chesapeake Bay on 26 April 1607 and founded Jamestown. Looking back in later years Smith recorded:

All this time we had but one Carpenter in the Countrey, and three others that could doe little, but desired to be learners; two Blacksmiths; two saylers; and those we write Labourers were for the most part Footmen, and such as they that were Adventurers brought to attend them, or such as they could perswade to goe with them, that neuer did know what a dayes worke was: except the Dutchmen and Poles, and some dozen other. For all the rest were poore Gentlemen, Tradsmen [sic], Serving-men, libertines, and such like, ten times more fit to spoyle a Commonwealth than either begin one, or but helpe to maintain one. For when neither the feare of God, nor the law, nor shame, nor displeasure of their friends could rule them here [England] there is small hope ever to bring one in twentie of them to be good there [Virginia]. Notwithstanding, I confess divers amongst them, had better mindes and grew much more industrious then was expected: yet ten good workmen would haue done more substantial worke in a day, than ten of them in a weeke. Therefore men may rather wonder how we could doe so much, than vse vs so badly because we did no more, but leaue those examples to make others beware; and the fruits of all, we know not for whom.

Unable to grow their own food, the colonists were forced to exist on what they could beg, borrow or steal from the Indians. From this chaotic situation Smith soon emerged as a natural leader. He negotiated with the Indians, inspired or enforced discipline, organized the building of houses and fortifications and planted crops. In 1608 he became the official (having long been the actual) leader of the colony.

In his voyages of discovery around Chesapeake Bay and its tributaries Smith is said to have covered three thousand miles and explored the Potomac as far upstream as the present site of Washington. He observed, made notes and, from these, drew the remarkable map [190] that was engraved and inserted in his books.

Smith's first book, *A Trve Relation of Svch Occvrrences and Accidents of Noate as Hath Hapned in Virginia*, was published in London in 1608 [188]. It is the earliest book relating to the colony at Jamestown and a fundamental work in the history of English-speaking America.

Finally, in 1624, there appeared *The Generall Historie of Virginia, New-England, and the Summer Isles* [189 and 191]. This work is a compilation that contains substantially all of Smith's previous works on America, with abstracts from other writers. All copies lack pages 97–104, but it has been deduced that the work was given to two printing houses (there are variations in initial letters and the style of the headings) and the gap is due to a miscalculation. There are large engravings, vignettes of Smith's adventures and also the map [190].

OPPOSITE XXXVIII It is agreed that J.J. Audubon's *The Birds of America* is one of the largest and most splendid of all ornithological books. It is less generally known that this stupendous work, involving 100,000 hand-coloured plates, was undertaken privately, with no outside backing, by a man who earned his living as a hack painter, supported by a wife who worked as a governess to maintain the family. It is a noble story without equal in the whole history of publishing.

188 This book, which gives a vivid picture of the first colony at Jamestown, is not by Watson but by John Smith (1580–1631). No figure among the early English colonists in America was more colourful and none more able.

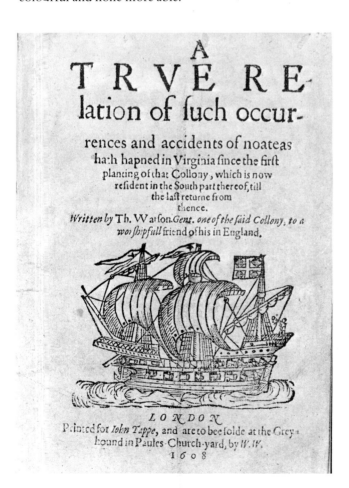

189 *The Generall Historie of Virginia, New England, and the Summer Isles* (1624) contains substantially all of John Smith's previous writings on America, with abstracts from other writers.

THE BAY PSALM BOOK

The Pilgrim Fathers landed at Plymouth Rock in 1620. Within about fifteen years they were sufficiently established to contemplate the foundation of the college that was to become Harvard University – an expansion into further education that would necessitate the establishment of a printing press.

Meanwhile over in England there was a clergyman, the Rev. Jose Glover, whose extreme Puritan views had brought him into such conflict with the Church of England that he had been suspended from his benefice at Sutton. In common with many men of like opinions he turned his eyes to the Puritan community in New England. In 1634, being a rich man, he sailed over in his own ship, the *Planter,* to evaluate the spiritual situation for himself. Having, like G. K. Chesterton, 'looked round in America', he found himself in tune with the life there. He

decided to emigrate, bought land and ordered the erection of a house – then returned home to collect his family.

It has been suggested that he had his eye on the presidency of the proposed college. At any rate while in England he bought printing equipment with his own money and type with funds raised by well-wishers. He then engaged a locksmith from Cambridge, England, Stephen Day (or Daye). Day was not himself a printer, though his technical ability would doubtless prove useful, but his two young sons had been apprenticed to a printer in Cambridge. Having resigned his benefice, Glover turned his back on the England of Archbishop Laud and, together with his family, the Days and the printing equipment, set sail in July or August 1638. It is sad that this proto-printer failed to reach the promised land, for he died of smallpox while still at sea.

The rest of the party arrived safely and the press was set up with

190 In his voyages of discovery around Chesapeake Bay John Smith is said to have covered 3,000 miles and explored the Potomac upstream to the present site of Washington. He drew this remarkable map from notes made on the spot and inserted it in his books.

205

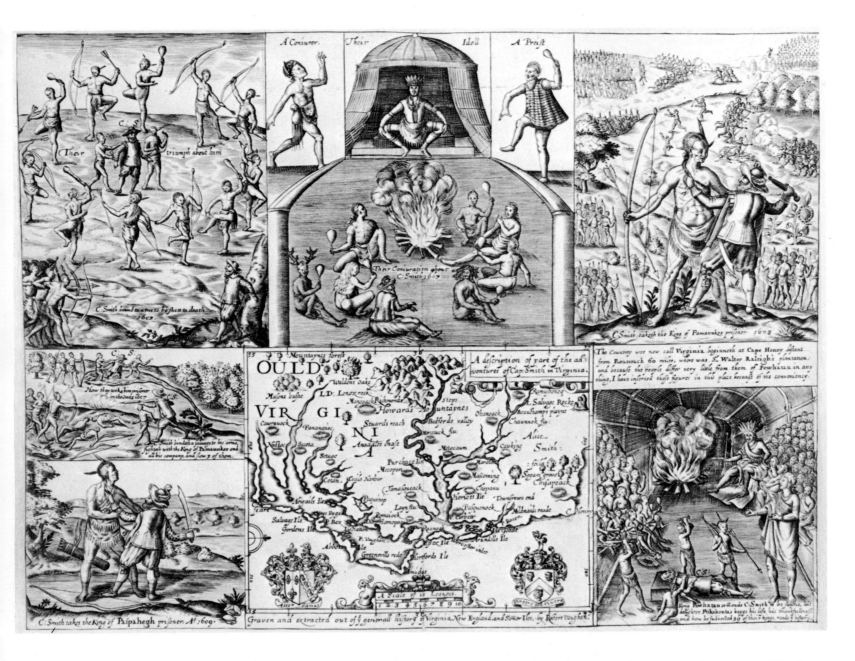

191 John Smith's adventures in Virginia are
dramatically illustrated in *The Generall Historie*.

Matthew Day, then aged nineteen, as the practical printer. Winthrop
wrote in his journal: '1639, Mo. I. A printing house was begun at
Cambridge, at the charge of Mr. Glover, who died on the seas hither-
ward.' The first two items that we know to have been printed have not
survived: *The Freeman's Oath,* on a half-sheet of small paper; and *An
Almanack for 1639, calculated for New England, by Mr. William Pierce,
Mariner.*

The first book printed on the North American continent of which
copies have survived is generally known as *The Bay Psalm Book* or, more
accurately: *The Whole Book of Psalmes faithfully Translated into English
Metre . . . Imprinted 1640* [192]. Edited by Richard Mather, this was a new
metrical translation of the *Psalms* from Hebrew into English, with a
preliminary discussion on the *Psalms* in public worship. As in the case
of the first Mexican printing, the first book embodied the religious
needs of the new community. Ten copies have survived, six of them
imperfect. The title-page makes no mention of the place of printing or

the name of the printer, so there is still a chance for some sharp eye to make a fortune by detecting an unregarded eleventh copy.

JOHN ELIOT'S INDIAN BIBLE

The Protestants in New England, like the Roman Catholics in Mexico, experienced a 'call' to convert the Indians (whose lands they had seized) to Christianity. Among the most devoted and able of the missionaries was the Rev. John Eliot (1604–90). Born in Hertfordshire, he graduated at Jesus College, Cambridge, and took orders in the Church of England; but his religious beliefs inevitably led him to New England, where he landed, in Boston, in 1631. He was soon deeply involved in the religious life of the community and was one of the three translators of *The Bay Psalm Book*; but his whole heart lay in the care for and conversion of the Indians.

His success in winning their confidence has been universally ascribed to his saintly character, and to his sincere devotion to their practical, as well as to their spiritual, needs. He learned their language and founded a school. Here, he tells us:

The Master daily . . . instructeth them in Catechisme, for which purpose I have compiled a short Catechisme, and wrote it in the Master's book, which he can read. . . . We aspire to no higher learning yet but to spell, read, and write, that so they may be able to read for themselves such Scriptures as I have already, or hereafter may (by the blessing of God), translate for them.

This endeavour was greeted with a good deal of sympathy in England now that the Puritans were in power, and Parliament appointed 'A Corporation for the Promoting and Propagating the Gospel of Jesus Christ in New England'.

By now Eliot had organized the Indian language to a point where it could be printed in roman type. Matthew Day had died and the press had been taken over by Samuel Green. Green was not a trained printer, but being a man of natural ability he became capable of turning out simple work in English and coped with the first efforts to print in the Indian language. The *Catechism* was printed before September 1654, and reprinted in 1662 and 1669. Of these editions only one copy has survived, the third, in the library of Edinburgh University. *Genesis* followed in 1655; the *Psalms in Metre* in 1658; Pierson's *Catechism* in 1658–9, and Baxter, *Call to the Unconverted* in 1664 [245].

Meanwhile Eliot had pushed on with his task and translated the whole Bible. One feels humble contemplating this extraordinary achievement: first to master and then to use the language of a simple, illiterate, taciturn people – a language mainly concerned with the practical needs of every-day life in the wilds – and, with it, express the complex and manifold teachings of the Bible.

The task of printing the whole Bible in the Indian language was deemed too complex, too beset with technical difficulties, for Green to tackle alone, so on 28 December 1658 Eliot wrote to the Corporation in London:

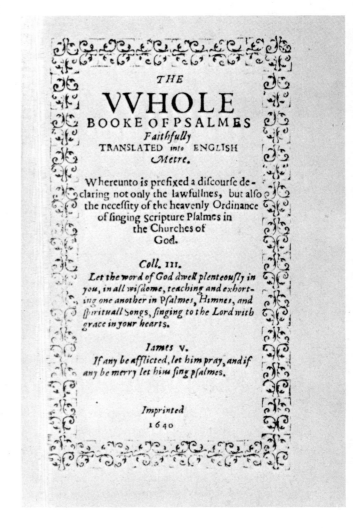

THE **WHOLE** BOOKE OF PSALMES *Faithfully* TRANSLATED *into* ENGLISH *Metre*.

Whereunto is prefixed a difcourfe declaring not only the lawfullnes, but alfo the neceffity of the heavenly Ordinance of finging Scripture Plalmes in the Churches of God.

Coll. III.
Let the word of God dwell plenteoufly in you, in all wifdome, teaching and exhorting one another in Pfalmes, Himnes, and fpirituall Songs, finging to the Lord with grace in your hearts.

Iames V.
If any be afflicted, let him pray, and if any be merry let him fing pfalmes.

Imprinted 1640

192 The first book printed on the North American continent which has survived is general y known as *The Bay Psalm Book*. A new metrical translation, edited by Richard Mather, it was printed at Cambridge, Massachusetts, in 1640, only twenty years after the landing of the Pilgrims.

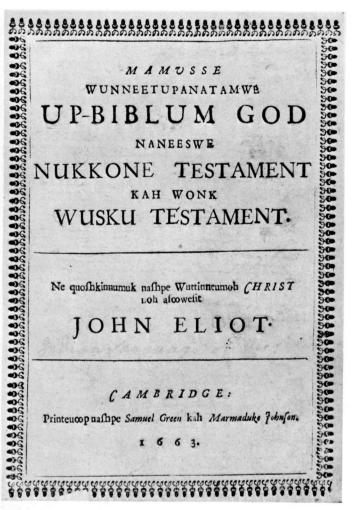

MAMUSSE
WUNNEETUPANATAMWE
UP-BIBLUM GOD
NANEESWE
NUKKONE TESTAMENT
KAH WONK
WUSKU TESTAMENT.

Ne quoſhkinnumuk naſhpe Wuttinneumoh *CHRIST*
ɴoh aſooweſit

JOHN ELIOT.

CAMBRIDGE:
Printeuɶp naſhpe *Samuel Green* kah *Marmaduke Johnſon.*
1 6 6 3.

193 The Rev. John Eliot, who landed at Boston in 1631, devoted his life to the Indians; he mastered their language into which he translated the whole Bible. This was printed by Marmaduke Johnson and Samuel Green, a task they completed within three years.

I proposed this expedient for the more easie prosecution of this work, viz. that your selves might be moved to hire some honest young man who hath skill to compose, (and the more skill in the other parts of the work, the better) send him over as your servant, pay him there to his content, or ingage payment, let him serve you here in New-England at the presse in Harvard Colledge, and work under the Colledge printer, in impressing the Bible in the Indian language, and with him send a convenient stock of Paper to begin withal.

The minutes of the Corporation for 21 April 1660 record an agreement with Marmaduke Johnson, a skilled London master-printer, who undertook to go to New England for three years. The payment to be £40 a year, plus board, lodging and washing. Further, 'for his encouragement', his name was to appear on the title-page.

Immediately on his arrival in 1660 Johnson joined Green. They worked with such expedition that the New Testament was finished by 1661 and issued with its own title. The Old Testament was completed in 1663, whereupon the two Testaments were joined and the complete Bible issued – the first Bible in any language to be printed in North America [193].

Samuel Green was the founder of a dynasty of American printers. For more than two hundred years his descendants are found printing in Massachusetts, Connecticut, Maryland and Virginia.

AITKEN'S BIBLE

No complete edition of the Bible in English was printed in America before the Revolution. This was probably because English law limited the printing of Bibles to a small number of licensed printers. The law did not stand in the way of annotated editions and several were planned, although none received sufficient support to achieve publication. Cotton Mather worked for years (in vain as things turned out) on his annotated *Biblia Americana,* while the publisher William Bradford (the first printer in New York and Philadelphia) received little response to his prospectus proposing an annotated Bible, price 20 shillings, half to be paid in silver and half in produce. In 1693, while working as Royal Printer in New York, Bradford published a pamphlet by the controversial Scottish Quaker, George Keith (1639–1716), which ranks as the first Quaker attack on slavery: *An Exhortation & Caution to Friends concerning the Buying or Keeping of Negroes.* Wing records only the single copy in the library of Friends' House, London.

During the Revolutionary War Americans were cut off from (and were no doubt disinclined to patronize) English printers. American printers saw the opportunity and seized it. The first edition of the New Testament to be printed in America came from the press of Robert Aitken, Printer to Congress, in Philadelphia in 1777. Eleven others were printed in Philadelphia, Boston, Trenton and Wilmington before the end of the war.

In 1782 Robert Aitken published the first complete Bible to be printed in America. This is sometimes known as the 'Congress Bible', as the second leaf bears the recommendation of Congress, dated 12 September

1782 [194]. The New Testament was presumably printed first, since the title is dated 1781.

BOOKBINDING IN AMERICA

The study of American bookbinding is still a young discipline; it was long held that almost all such binding was the work of immigrants working in the styles they had learned as apprentices in their home countries. With the gathering of numerous examples in one place, such as the Baltimore Loan Exhibition, 1957–58, and the remarkable private collection of Michael Papantonio (shown at Princeton, the Morgan Library and elsewhere, 1972–73) it has become evident, even to non-specialists, that towards the end of the eighteenth century a distinct American style, as different from British binding as Russian differs from German, can be perceived.

The early introduction of printing into New England created a need for bookbinders, so John Ratcliff was brought over from London to bind Eliot's *Indian Bible*. A sidelight on early colonial life is given by the payment which he received from the Colony of Massachusetts Bay in 1680 for binding an edition of *A Confession of Faith*: £9, one cord of wood and 11 shillings. Even fifty years later the Maryland Assembly, having passed an act for the publication of the Laws of the Province, ordered each county to pay William Parks, the Annapolis printer and binder, 2,000 pounds of tobacco 'for printing, stiching and Delivering a Copy of the *Publick Laws* . . . to every Member of the Assembly . . . and a Copy (bound in leather) to the Publick and each House of Assembly, and to each County-court'.

The Puritans were concerned to promote the word of God; they would probably have regarded handsome gilt-tooled bindings as being virtually sinful. The Pennsylvania Germans worked in a style which was almost medieval in its austerity; but Christopher Hoffman (a Schwenk-felder minister who bound books for his own church), working in the middle of the eighteenth century, appears to have bought a cache of second-hand Irish tools.

Not long before the Revolution a group of Scots binders emigrated to Philadelphia, led by Samuel Taylor who had learned his craft at Berwick-upon-Tweed where he had taught, as apprentices, several of his fellow immigrants.

But more important than these was Robert Aitken, already mentioned as a printer. He was yet another Scot, born in Dalkeith, who opened his bookshop in Philadelphia in 1769. Almost at once he returned home for two years, and either learned bookbinding himself or engaged a binder to go to Philadelphia with him. Very handsome work was produced in his shop where he was assisted by James Muir, an able craftsman. Indeed, by this time, the work of the best American binders can well stand comparison with their European contemporaries. In the 1840s and 1850s embossed bindings were produced in Boston, Philadelphia and New York which not only equal but sometimes surpass European work of the same period.

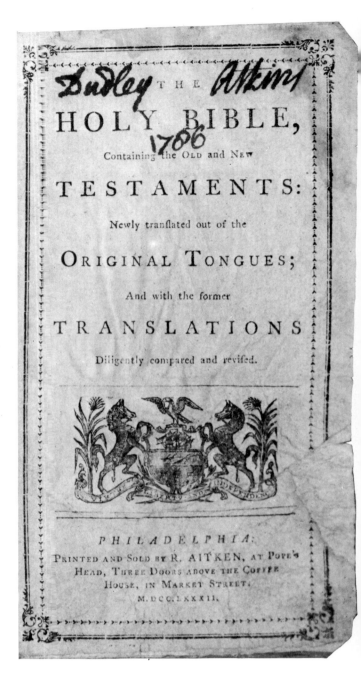

194 No complete Bible in English was printed in America before the Revolution. The first New Testament came from the press of Robert Aitken at Philadelphia in 1777. Aitken also printed the first complete Bible, known as the 'Congress Bible', published in America (1782).

I cannot leave American bookbinding without mentioning the march held in New York in 1825 to celebrate the completion of the New York Canals. One hundred and forty-four bookbinders formed the twenty-fourth body in the line of march, preceded by the printers and followed by the booksellers and stationers. A huge volume in red morocco, measuring 4 feet 8 inches by 3 feet and labelled 'Erie Canal Statistics', finished by John Bradford and Isaac Peckham, was mounted on a hand-barrow. To any modern collector, desperate to get his treasured book bound or repaired, the idea of one hundred and forty-four binders in one procession is almost too poignant to contemplate.

GEORGE CATLIN: *THE NORTH AMERICAN INDIANS*

Early in this chapter we looked at two rather fanciful woodcuts of natives, and most of the early books discussed contain some account of the Indians as seen by the early explorers. That civilization has now been destroyed almost completely but, fortunately, at almost the last possible moment one man devoted himself to observing and recording Indian life.

George Catlin (1796–1872) was born in Pennsylvania. He qualified as a lawyer and practised for a few years but, being more interested in art, he abandoned the law and set up as a professional portrait painter. Impressed by the 'silent and stoic dignity' of a party of Indian braves seen in Philadelphia (and acutely aware that their tribal life and culture was fast disappearing), he determined to devote his life to recording and preserving 'the history and customs of such people'. This was in 1832. By 1838 he had visited forty-eight tribes and painted 320 portraits and 200 pictures of villages, hunting scenes, ceremonials and dances.

Catlin organized exhibitions of his paintings, first in America and later in Europe; they were on show in the Egyptian Hall, Piccadilly, for several years. In 1841 he published *Manners, Customs and Condition of the North American Indians,* with three hundred engravings. Then in 1844, *The North American Portfolio,* a series of fine coloured plates [XXXVII]. And later, *Last Rambles amongst the Indians of the Rocky Mountains and the Andes* (1868).

J. J. AUDUBON: *THE BIRDS OF AMERICA*

Let us close this chapter by looking at the most splendid book ever produced in relation to America, and certainly one of the finest ornithological works ever printed: Audubon, *The Birds of America from Original Drawings Made During A Residence of Twenty-five Years in The United States* (1827–38) [XXXVIII].

John James Audubon (1785–1851) was the son, by a Creole mistress, of a French sailor, sometime naval officer and merchant adventurer, who had made a fortune in Santo Domingo (now Haiti) as a planter, merchant and dealer in slaves. Born at Les Cayes, the young Audubon was taken to France as an infant and brought up in the vicinity of Nantes, where he was spoiled by his father's wife, who became, so to speak, his stepmother. Between Madame Audubon's over-indulgence and the disruption caused by the French Revolution, Audubon received little schooling, while his formal instruction in art was limited to a few months spent in the studio of Jacques Louis David.

Audubon senior lost the greater part of his fortune in the disastrous revolution that destroyed the economy of Haiti, but he had providentially, purely as an investment, purchased an estate in Pennsylvania. To this estate, Mill Grove Farm near Philadelphia, the young Audubon was sent in 1803.

In 1808 Audubon made a wonderfully fortunate choice when he married Lucy Bakewell, elder daughter of his neighbour William Bakewell. The failure of some attempted mining on Mill Grove Farm, the decline of the family fortunes and the demands of married life now induced Audubon to embark on a series of disastrous commercial enterprises. The third and final crash left him bankrupt and brought about the turning point of his life. His splendid wife insisted that his lifelong passion for ornithology and the painting of birds, hitherto a hobby, should become Audubon's *raison d'être*. She undertook to provide for the family by working as a governess or running a series of small schools, thus setting her husband free to go on expeditions that lasted for months, sometimes for more than a year. Without the unwavering support, both moral and financial, of this loyal, courageous and great-hearted woman, *The Birds of America* would never have been produced.

On his natural history expeditions Audubon lived from hand to mouth, sometimes arriving in a town without a cent in his pocket and unable to buy the notebooks and drawing paper he needed for his work. He painted panels on river boats, street signs and portraits at five dollars a head; he gave lessons in French and in dancing and, constantly, he worked on the production of his endless series of bird pictures. He insisted on drawing from life, never from stuffed specimens, and was much in advance of his time in portraying the birds (in many cases unrecorded species) in their natural surroundings:

Every moment I had to spare I drew birds for my ornithology, in which my Lucy and myself alone have faith. My best friends solemnly regarded me as a madman, and my wife and family alone gave me encouragement. My wife determined that my genius should prevail, and that my final success as an ornithologist should be triumphant.

At last, in 1826, the quantity of finished drawings was sufficient for him to contemplate publication. As it was felt that there were no engravers in America sufficiently experienced to achieve the standards he required, he sailed for England. After a brief stay in Liverpool he proceeded to Edinburgh armed with letters of introduction from prominent Americans. His reception was remarkable: an exhibition of his drawings at the Royal Institution was crowded and he became the talk of the town. He was elected to all manner of learned societies, taken up by the aristocracy and introduced to Sir Walter Scott.

There were, perhaps, two reasons for this immediate, this astonishing, success. Nature, and especially the observation of birds, is an interest that runs right through the British people, and is especially strong among the landed classes who then dominated society. Secondly, Audubon retained his long hair and wore his backwoodsman's clothes. The Romantic movement was then at its height and Audubon, it would seem, was the ideal Rousseau man – a character out of *Paul et Virginie*. Here was a man who had been born in the West Indies and moved among noble savages – and you could actually have him at your dinner party! The French journalist P. A. Cap commented, perspicuously, that Audubon produced the same effect on the British as Benjamin Franklin had on the court of Louis XVI.

Much encouraged, Audubon came to an agreement with the Scottish engraver W. Home Lizars for the production of the plates. Lizars, however, crippled by a strike among his workmen, was obliged to relinquish the commission.

Audubon now went to London and approached Robert Havell senior, whose family played such an important part, for five generations, in the production of English aquatint books. The younger Robert Havell was an artist of great ability and an engraver of the highest order. His contribution to *The Birds of America* is second only to that of Audubon himself. The ten plates which Lizars had managed to complete were brought from Edinburgh and retouched, and after that all plates received Robert Havell's personal attention. In her standard work, *Aquatint Engraving*, Miss S. T. Prideaux remarks of these plates: 'A more delicate use of aquatinting can never have been made.'

The original plan was to publish in eighty parts at 2 guineas each. Once the work of engraving and printing was well in hand Audubon returned to America for the purpose of locating and drawing new species, especially in regions that he had not yet explored, from the Republic of Texas to the coast of Labrador.

An almost equal task lay in the gathering of subscriptions. Social success, dinners at great houses, being lionized at soirées, even election to the Royal Society, are all very pleasant experiences; but any new bookseller knows that those who talk loudest about culture are often the last to put their hands in their pockets and support it. There were many disappointments. George IV failed to pay; Lord Rothschild sent his set back, saying that he would not give more than £5. Audubon and his sons travelled endlessly on this quest. It was here that Edward Harris, John Bachman and Audubon's growing circle of admirers gave loyal support, enlisting their friends and persuading American state legislatures, libraries and societies to subscribe. Even then, some subscribers were so inconsiderate as to die before the work was completed, or fell by the wayside owing to the financial difficulties of the times. The final list of subscribers contains eighty-two American and seventy-nine European names, the majority of the latter British, headed by Queen Adelaide and with a fair sprinkling of earls and dukes. It is not known exactly how many sets were produced, probably just short of two hundred. Of these some sets have been broken up by print dealers, two were destroyed in the San Francisco earthquake and it is probable that a few more have succumbed to the changes and disasters of life.

At last, in 1838, the final part was issued. Havell had become so involved in the work that he subsequently emigrated to America. The completed work consisted of 87 parts, with 435 plates representing well over 1,000 individual birds as well as thousands of American trees, shrubs and insects to provide natural settings, the latter forming an especially beautiful part of the book. Some of the largest plates comprise 5 square feet, and a good set will measure about 38 by 25 inches. The total number of plates produced, each individually coloured by hand, must be in the region of 100,000.

The original cost in England was £174; American customs duties raised this to $1,000. In 1969 a particularly fine set sold at Sotheby's for £90,000, at that time the record price for a printed book. This copy had belonged previously to the Baroness Burdett Coutts, and had been sold in the same rooms, in 1922, for £600.

The courage and faith of the Audubon family is breathtaking. This immense undertaking, this unparalleled achievement, was not the production of a great and long-established publishing house – nor was it backed by any wealthy institution. It was the work of a man of relentless energy, with no private fortune, who supported himself by hack painting, a work that could not have been achieved but for the indomitable faith of a woman who earned her living as a governess. It is a story without equal in the whole history of publishing.

CHAPTER TEN

PRIVATE PRESS BOOKS

BY THE MIDDLE of the nineteenth century standards of design in printing had reached a very low ebb. The increasing use of machinery and the relentless competition as to who could print most cheaply contributed to this situation; but printing was not alone among the nineteenth-century arts and crafts in having reached something of a nadir. In the long run the only hope of salvation lay in rethinking the whole problem from basic principles. Working master printers had little time, and perhaps less inclination, to do this – it has been said that you can tell how little printers care about printing from the typographical standards of their own trade journals – and the revolutionary impact came from outside the trade in the form of the Private Press movement. This movement owed its inception and the greater part of its impetus to William Morris.

Morris was a remarkable and lovable man of very diverse talents: a writer and poet, artist, craftsman, designer and pioneer socialist. Soon after his marriage he built, in conjunction with Philip Webb, Red House at Upton in Kent. This house, original in conception and quite out of line with the conventional architecture of the time, has had an immense influence on domestic building. When he came to furnish and decorate his home the goods available in the shops so repelled him that he decided to design and make his own. What began as the furnishing of one home developed into a very considerable business, and the firm of Morris and Co. was soon making furniture, wallpaper, fabrics of all kinds, tapestry and church furnishings.

Morris had an extraordinary genius for creating decorative patterns and the greater part of the output of his firm was designed by himself. In these activities he always began by achieving a thorough mastery of the craft involved before embarking on designs, let alone upon manufacture. In dyeing his fabrics, for example, he went back to the vegetable dyes described in old herbals, working at the dye-tub and hand loom himself. Moreover he would use only the very best materials. As a result of all this his influence upon the development of furniture, fabrics and interior decoration has been such that no less an architectural historian than Sir Nikolaus Pevsner entitled his brilliant book *The Modern Movement, From William Morris to Gropius.*

In appearance Morris looked like a Norwegian sea captain. He dressed in simple clothes of blue serge that were in striking contrast to the sartorial standards of Victorian society. He was a man of great physical strength whose violent temper was easily aroused, although swiftly dispelled by the warmth of his good nature. Dante Gabriel Rossetti, a

214

man whose reminiscences tend to be artistically rather than factually true, records that at dinner one day, just as Morris had inserted a forkful of food into his mouth someone had the temerity to criticize the work of Edward Burne-Jones, Morris's greatest friend. In a Herculean, but quite untypical, effort to control his temper, Morris bit on the fork, which emerged bent and twisted beyond all recognition.

One of the strongest passions in Morris's life was his love for the Middle Ages, and especially for Gothic architecture. Nothing enraged him more than the ignorant and ill-considered over-restoration of churches. In founding the Society for the Protection of Ancient Buildings (generally known in his circle as 'the anti-scrape') he was like some knight-errant riding forth to rescue a damsel from worse than death. Wilfrid Scawen Blunt describes in his diaries their joint visit to a country church that Morris had known and loved years before. In the interval a particularly brutal restoration had taken place. Morris, almost out of his mind with fury, stamped up and down the nave, waving his arms above his head and bellowing, 'The pigs, the swine, God DAMN their souls.'

As an author himself Morris could not but be aware of the manner in which his own books were printed. From time to time he made some effort to effect improvements in their production. Someone who walked into the composing room where the title-page for *The House of the Wolfings* was being set up protested that things were going too far when Morris changed the line 'IN PROSE AND VERSE' to 'IN PROSE AND IN VERSE' so as to balance the block of type at the head of the page. 'Too far!' roared Morris, 'Why I've just written this poem to fill the blank space in the middle' [195]. This was the sixteen-line poem that gives moving expression to his nostalgia for the Middle Ages, and he had it set up in capitals so as to give a nice rectangle of black type.

On 15 November 1888 Morris attended a lecture on printing delivered by his friend Emery Walker at the Arts and Crafts Exhibition. This finally fired him to set up his own press. It is a pleasure to pay one's tribute to Walker. He was the man whose immense practical experience, knowledge, taste and developed judgement were at the service of all the private presses. He was the man who knew how to do things and where to get things; which firm in Germany made the best ink and which firm in England might collaborate in producing the finest hand-made paper; that Edward P. Prince was the most able cutter of type punches and that the doyen of wood engravers, W. H. Hooper, might be persuaded to come out of retirement and work for the Kelmscott Press. This immensely modest man placed his life's experience at the service of the amateur printers. Morris, with his warm-hearted generosity, wanted to name Walker as a partner. How Cobden-Sanderson of the Doves Press treated him we shall see.

Morris began, as usual, by studying the best work of the past and, quite frankly, based his books on incunabula, the nearest he could get to the Middle Ages. He took as his model the roman type of Nicolaus Jenson and bought a copy of the famous Pliny [20]. He had each letter of the alphabet photographed and lantern slides made so that he could

195 When designing this title-page, William Morris (1834–96) changed the wording 'IN PROSE AND VERSE' to 'IN PROSE AND IN VERSE', and then wrote the sixteen-line poem in order to achieve a better piece of typography.

A TALE OF THE HOUSE OF THE WOLFINGS AND ALL THE KINDREDS OF THE MARK WRITTEN IN PROSE AND IN VERSE BY WILLIAM MORRIS.

WHILES IN THE EARLY WINTER EVE
WE PASS AMID THE GATHERING NIGHT
SOME HOMESTEAD THAT WE HAD TO LEAVE
YEARS PAST; AND SEE ITS CANDLES BRIGHT
SHINE IN THE ROOM BESIDE THE DOOR
WHERE WE WERE MERRY YEARS AGONE
BUT NOW MUST NEVER ENTER MORE,
AS STILL THE DARK ROAD DRIVES US ON.
E'EN SO THE WORLD OF MEN MAY TURN
AT EVEN OF SOME HURRIED DAY
AND SEE THE ANCIENT GLIMMER BURN
ACROSS THE WASTE THAT HATH NO WAY;
THEN WITH THAT FAINT LIGHT IN ITS EYES
A WHILE I BID IT LINGER NEAR
AND NURSE IN WAVERING MEMORIES
THE BITTER-SWEET OF DAYS THAT WERE.

LONDON 1889: REEVES AND TURNER 196 STRAND.

study the minute details in an enlarged form, drawing these letters over and over again until he had absorbed their spirit. Then he put the whole lot away and designed his own type. He kept these designs in a matchbox, which he carried round in his pocket, taking them out at odd moments for critical examination and showing them to perceptive friends. Walker, who was a neighbour, looked in at Morris's home every night on his way back from work to discuss and guide progress.

This was named the Golden type after the first book to be started, though not the first to be completed, the *Golden Legend* of Jacobus Voragine. While the type was being cast Morris set to work designing decorated borders and initials, printers' flowers and a colophon [196 and 215]. Here again he was influenced by the early books in his own splendid library, especially the work of Erhard Ratdolt of Venice and Johann Zainer of Ulm [x]. But he was not content to work for ever in roman. He longed to express himself in gothic and so designed the Troy type based, more or less, on the gothic types of Schoeffer, Zainer and Koberger.

Morris named his venture the Kelmscott Press after his lovely country house, Kelmscott Manor, near Lechlade in the Cotswolds. His original intention was to print only a few copies of each book and give them away among his friends; but when the new activity was mentioned in

196 The Kelmscott Golden type was based on that of the fifteenth-century Venetian printer, Jenson. This page should be compared with Figure 20.

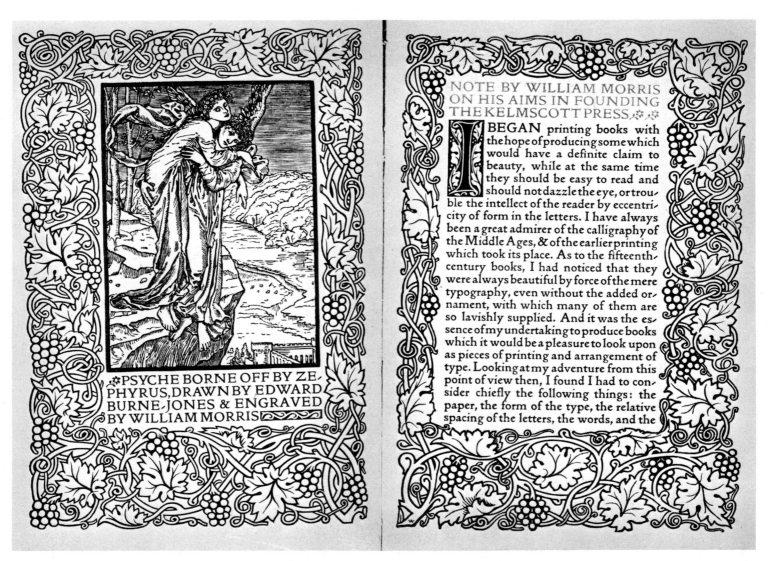

PSYCHE BORNE OFF BY ZEPHYRUS, DRAWN BY EDWARD BURNE-JONES & ENGRAVED BY WILLIAM MORRIS

NOTE BY WILLIAM MORRIS ON HIS AIMS IN FOUNDING THE KELMSCOTT PRESS.

I BEGAN printing books with the hope of producing some which would have a definite claim to beauty, while at the same time they should be easy to read and should not dazzle the eye, or trouble the intellect of the reader by eccentricity of form in the letters. I have always been a great admirer of the calligraphy of the Middle Ages, & of the earlier printing which took its place. As to the fifteenth-century books, I had noticed that they were always beautiful by force of the mere typography, even without the added ornament, with which many of them are so lavishly supplied. And it was the essence of my undertaking to produce books which it would be a pleasure to look upon as pieces of printing and arrangement of type. Looking at my adventure from this point of view then, I found I had to consider chiefly the following things: the paper, the form of the type, the relative spacing of the letters, the words, and the

the public press, and when first inquiries and then orders came flowing in, it was decided to widen the scope and print a few hundred copies for sale. Morris, who didn't really give a damn for anyone, printed his own favourite books without any consideration as to whether they were likely to be in demand with the general reading public. It is true that he included Keats, Shelley, Coleridge and, of course, Ruskin; but there is a high proportion of the medieval books dear to his heart: *The Recuyell of the Historyes of Troye, Reynard the Foxe, The Order of Chivalry, Godefrey of Boloyne, Psalmi Penitentiales* and *Beowulf.*

There was nothing new in Morris pressing medieval, or even earlier, books upon his friends. William Michael Rossetti, it will be recalled, had a rather poor reputation among his fellow Pre-Raphaelites. Dante Gabriel Rossetti, impelled by the artesian enthusiasm of Morris, endeavoured to read one of the Nibelung sagas. He got as far as Fasolt, and stuck. 'Really, Topsy,' he groaned, 'I cannot take seriously a man who has a dragon for a brother.' 'Well, Gabriel, I'd rather have a dragon for a brother than a bloody fool.'

From the very earliest days of the Kelmscott Press Morris was working up to his masterpiece, an edition of Chaucer, his favourite author and master, a tribute that would express the devotion of a lifetime [197 and

ABOVE 197 Chaucer and 'litel Lowis my sone' in his *Treatise on the Astrolabe*, from a woodcut designed by Burne-Jones in the Kelmscott Chaucer.
BELOW 198 Morris's lifelong devotion to the Middle Ages and the poetry of Chaucer found their expression in this edition, the *magnum opus* of the Kelmscott Press.

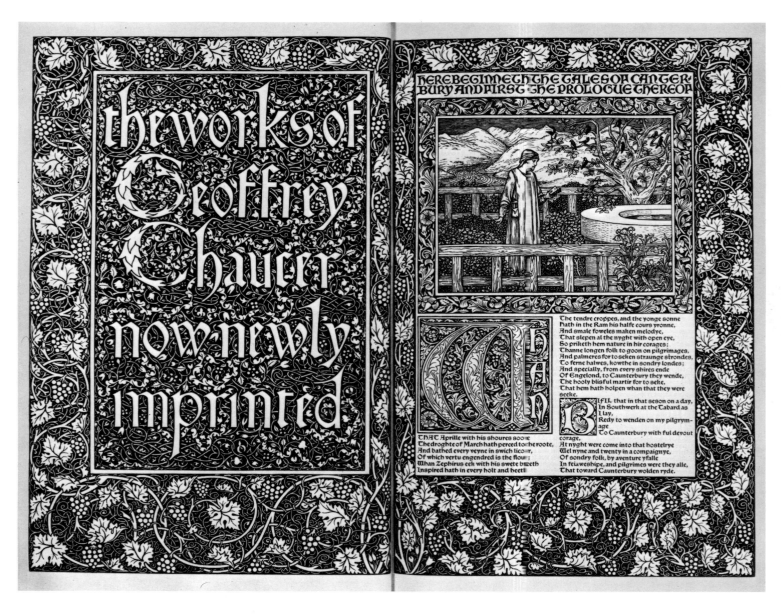

198]. Work on this book continued for five years. Morris had Chaucer in mind when he designed the Troy type and sample pages were set up; but this fount proved to be too large for the purpose, so it was recut in a smaller size as the Chaucer type. With this the first trial page was printed in July 1892 and, as it was found to be satisfactory, work went ahead. The Kelmscott Chaucer was completed in June 1896. In its final form this book contained eighty-seven woodcut illustrations designed by Burne-Jones, a decorated title, fourteen large borders, eighteen different frames round the illustrations and twenty-six large initial letters designed by William Morris and engraved on wood by C. E. Keates, W. H. Hooper and W. Spielmeyer. The Kelmscott Chaucer represents the climax of the Private Press movement. It has been chosen again and again as the most sumptuous example of English printing. Thus when the library of Tokyo University was destroyed by an earthquake in 1923 and English scholars met to decide on a worthy 'foundation stone' for presentation to the new library the Kelmscott Chaucer was their choice. Bernard Shaw, who regarded Morris as the greatest man he had ever met, ('. . . and I who say this have met most of the great men of my time . . .') gave a copy to Rodin, speaking of it as a worthy gift for a great artist.

It had been Morris's intention to follow the success of the Chaucer with a folio edition of his other medieval hero, Froissart. Sample pages had been set up and for two of these Morris designed borders and initials that show an advance on anything he had previously achieved. But death cut this work short at a very early stage and we have only a tantalizing fragment of what might have been [199].

When the productions of the Kelmscott Press first appeared in the bookshops they made an immense impact. Here were people accustomed to the grey pages of late Victorian printing, and along came those wonderful books with the rich blocks of black type on gleaming white hand-made paper, the initials and borders rioting with decoration. The copies printed on vellum must have shone like the snow of an alpine landscape in the sun.

And yet, on this side idolatry, one must listen to the devil's advocate. The chief purpose of books is to be read, and to some extent Kelmscotts are beautiful *objets d'art* rather than books. During the height of my more youthful enthusiasm I read a good many books in Kelmscott editions and, in spite of what critics say, I wasn't blinded; I have retained the use of my eyes. However, as a bookseller who has been handling them for forty-five years, I cannot help observing what a high proportion of Kelmscott Press books have never been read and, indeed, seventy-five years later remain 'unopened'.

In many ways Morris was swimming against the tide with his return to gothic type when the whole movement of Europe has been towards roman; with the over-exuberance of decoration that distracts the reader's eye from the text; the hand-made paper that is too heavy for normal use and the insistence on small editions produced by hand. Indeed this is the contradiction of Morris's later life. His immense compassion and generous character made him want all men to share more

OPPOSITE XXXIX The Golden Gospels, written by sixteen scribes at the Abbey of St Maximin's at Trier, in burnished gold 'artificial' uncials upon heavy vellum, painted purple. They were probably a gift to the Emperor Otto III (980–1002); afterwards in the possession of Henry VIII of England, the Duke of Hamilton, Theodore Irwin of Oswego, New York, and now in the Pierpont Morgan Library.

QUONIAM
QUIDEM MULTI CO
NATISUNT ORDINARE
NARRATIONEM QUAE IN
NOBIS COMPLETAE SUNT
RERU SICUT TRADIDERUN
NOBIS QUIABINITIO IPSI
UIDERUNT EMINISTRI FUE
RUN SERMONIS VISUME
DMIHI ASEQUUTO A
PRINTIPIO OMNIBUS DILI
GENTER EXORDINE TIBI
SCRIBERE OPTIME THEO
PHILE UTCOGNOSCAS EO
RUM UERBORUM OEQUI
BUS ERUDITUS ES VERITATE
FUIT INDIEBUS HERODIS
REGIS IUDEAE SACERDOS
QUIDAM NOMINE ZA
CHARIAS DEUICE ABIA
ET UXORILLI DEFILIABUS
AARON ETNOMEN EIUS
ELISABETH ERANTAUTE
IUSTI ABO ANTEDM IN
CEDENTES INOMNIBI
MANDATIS ETIUSTIFI
CATIONIBUS DNI SINE

QUERELA ETNONERAT
ILLIS FILIUS EO QUOD ES
SET ELISABETH STERILIS
ETAMBO PROCESSISSENT
INDIEBUS SUIS FACTU
EST AUTEM CUSACER
DOTIOSUO FUNGERETUR
ZACHARIAS INORDINE
UICISSUAE ANTEDM
SECUNDU CONSUETUDINE
SACERDOTII SORTE EXI
IT UTINCENSU PONERET
INGRESSUS INTEMPLUM
DNI ETOMNIS MULTITUDO
ERAT POPULI ORANS FO
RIS HORA INCENSI APA
RUIT AUTEM ILLI ANGE
LUS DNI STANS ADEXTRIS
ALTARIS INCENSI ETZA
CHARIAS TURBATUS EST
UIDENS ETTIMOR IRRUIT
SUPEREUM AIT AUTEM
ADILLUM ANGELUS NETI
MEAS ZACHARIA QUO
EXAUDITA EST DEPRECA
TIOTUA ETUXORTUA
ELISABETH PARIET TIBIFILIU
DUOCABIS NOMEN EIUS
IOHANNEM ETERITGAUDIU

fully in the good things of life, yet he fought against the machinery by which alone this end could be achieved.

All these criticisms contain a strong element of truth (though for a man to whom Morris is a hero this is hard to admit), yet none of them detracts from his key position in the history of modern printing. His work was like a hundred tons of dynamite exploding and printing, at least good printing, has never been the same again. His return to the basic principles; his insistence on the finest materials combined with the greatest possible care; his conception of the double opening (not the single page) as the unit of design – these and many other factors have extended the influence of Morris far beyond his native shores, and especially to Germany and America.

The comparatively early death of Morris brought the Kelmscott Press to a premature end. His friends and collaborators completed the books that were actually in hand, but attempted no new ones apart from a bibliography.

The closure of the Kelmscott Press fired another man to start a press of his own. T. J. Cobden-Sanderson (1840–1922), the founder of the Doves Press, was a man of different character from Morris. He began life as a barrister, a profession in which he showed considerable ability. In middle life, in 1881, he decided to abandon the bar and do creative work with his hands – a more striking decision then than today. He was in close touch with the Morris circle, whose ideals of craftsmanship and socialism he shared. Indeed it was Cobden-Sanderson who thought up the very title 'Arts and Crafts'.

Cobden-Sanderson was sixty when he entered into partnership with Emery Walker in founding the Doves Press. Between them (though Walker took the lion's share where designing was concerned) they evolved a type of superb beauty. Though also based on Jenson, it was somewhat lighter than Morris's Golden Type, a factor that enabled them to use hand-made paper that was less bulky and more suitable for book work. With this type they printed books of austere but great beauty. In contrast to the lavish black ornament of the Kelmscott Press there was no decoration unless one counts an occasional coloured, though undecorated, initial. They relied on faultless presswork, the beauty of the type and the perfect design and balance of their pages.

Their masterpiece, the Doves Bible (1903–05), in five folio volumes, ranks with the Kelmscott Chaucer as one of the twin masterpieces of the movement and, in style, it is the less dated of the two [200]. Cobden-Sanderson's pursuit of the ideals that he laid down in *The Book Beautiful* had been achieved. If Morris represented the exuberant vitality of Gothic, the Doves Press worked with a restraint that was classic.

It would have seemed impossible that any man could quarrel with the gentle-natured Emery Walker, but Cobden-Sanderson achieved this seemingly impossible feat. In 1909 the partnership was dissolved and Cobden-Sanderson continued to print alone. The question naturally arose as to who owned the Doves type that had remained in Cobden-

OPPOSITE XL English binding made for Judith (1032–94), Countess of Flanders and bride of Tostig; thick wooden boards, covered with plates of silver, with the inscription IESVS NAZAR [ENVS REX] IVDEORVM in translucent cloisonné enamel. Bequeathed to the Abbey of Weingarten, it was looted by the troops of Napoleon and is now in the Pierpont Morgan Library.

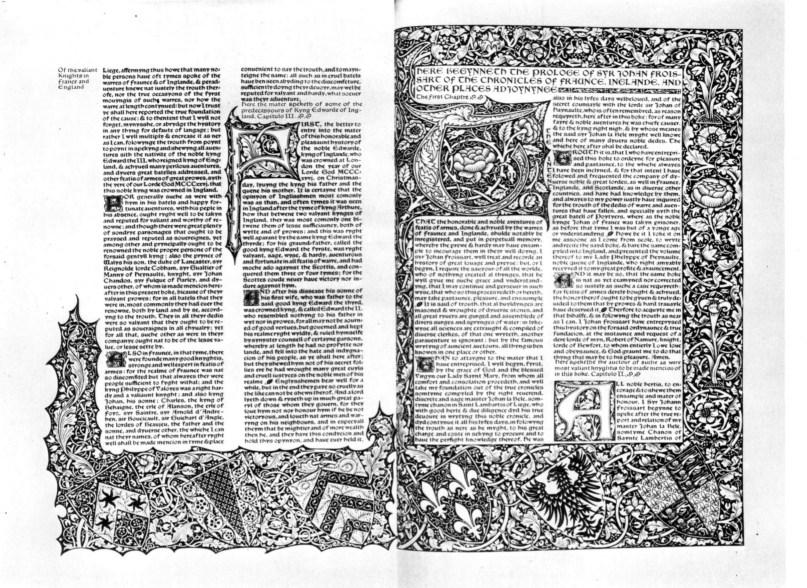

199 Morris planned to follow the Kelmscott
Chaucer with a splendid edition of his other
favourite author, Froissart, but his early death
put an end to this project.

Sanderson's possession, as he was responsible for the day-to-day conduct
of the press that operated on his premises. Sydney Cockerell, the friend
of both men, acted as a sympathetic and skilful negotiator and found a
solution. He brought both men to agree that while Cobden-Sanderson
should retain the type during his lifetime it should pass, after his death,
to Emery Walker, who was eleven years younger.

In 1916 Cobden-Sanderson printed his *Catalogue Raisonné,* the last
book to come from the Doves Press, in which appeared the following
statement:

CONSECRATIO QUAE OFFERTUR AB HOMINE NON REDIMETUR NEC VENDETUR
SED MORTE MORIETUR.

TO the bed of the RIVER THAMES, the River on whose banks I have printed all
my printed Books, I, THE DOVES PRESS, bequeath The Doves Press Fount of
Type, – the punches, matrices, and the type in use at The Doves Press at the
time of my death. And may the River, in its tides and flow, pass over them to
and from the great sea for ever and ever, or until its tides and flow for ever cease;
then may they share the fates of all the worlds and pass from change to change
for ever upon the Tides of Time untouched of other use.

This threat Cobden-Sanderson carried out, early in 1917, going night after night, 'watched only by the stars', and pitching the whole lot over Hammersmith Bridge. The first batch lodged itself on an inaccessible ledge of one of the piers; another narrowly missed a barge that was passing under the bridge – an incident that would have appealed to Morris, who loved to indulge in great swearing matches with the bargees. This extraordinary action deprived Walker of his share in the type and broke the promise given to Cockerell.

Cobden-Sanderson is a curiously mixed character. On the one hand he was an idealist who gave up what might well have become a lucrative career at the bar in order to devote himself to his ideals of craftsmanship; he was a socialist at a time when very few members of the middle classes gave themselves to that cause – yet through all this there ran a streak of ruthless selfishness and ungovernable egoism that led him to an action of which many a self-confessed money-maker would have been ashamed. This odd dichotomy of character was not unique in the Arts and Crafts movement, students of which will have no difficulty in thinking of other examples.

IN THE BEGINNING GOD CREATED THE HEAVEN AND THE EARTH. ¶ AND THE EARTH WAS WITHOUT FORM, AND VOID; AND DARKNESS WAS UPON THE FACE OF THE DEEP, & THE SPIRIT OF GOD MOVED UPON THE FACE OF THE WATERS. ¶ And God said, Let there be light: & there was light. And God saw the light, that it was good: & God divided the light from the darkness. And God called the light Day, and the darkness he called Night. And the evening and the morning were the first day. ¶ And God said, Let there be a firmament in the midst of the waters, & let it divide the waters from the waters. And God made the firmament, and divided the waters which were under the firmament from the waters which were above the firmament: & it was so. And God called the firmament Heaven. And the evening & the morning were the second day. ¶ And God said, Let the waters under the heaven be gathered together unto one place, and let the dry land appear: and it was so. And God called the dry land Earth; and the gathering together of the waters called he Seas: and God saw that it was good. And God said, Let the earth bring forth grass, the herb yielding seed, and the fruit tree yielding fruit after his kind, whose seed is in itself, upon the earth: & it was so. And the earth brought forth grass, & herb yielding seed after his kind, & the tree yielding fruit, whose seed was in itself, after his kind: and God saw that it was good. And the evening & the morning were the third day. ¶ And God said, Let there be lights in the firmament of the heaven to divide the day from the night; and let them be for signs, and for seasons, and for days, & years: and let them be for lights in the firmament of the heaven to give light upon the earth: & it was so. And God made two great lights; the greater light to rule the day, and the lesser light to rule the night: he made the stars also. And God set them in the firmament of the heaven to give light upon the earth, and to rule over the day and over the night, & to divide the light from the darkness: and God saw that it was good. And the evening and the morning were the fourth day. ¶ And God said, Let the waters bring forth abundantly the moving creature that hath life, and fowl that may fly above the earth in the open firmament of heaven. And God created great whales, & every living creature that moveth, which the waters brought forth abundantly, after their kind, & every winged fowl after his kind: & God saw that it was good. And God blessed them, saying, Be fruitful, & multiply, and fill the waters in the seas, and let fowl multiply in the earth. And the evening & the morning were the fifth day. ¶ And God said, Let the earth bring forth the living creature after his kind, cattle, and creeping thing, and beast of the earth after his kind: and it was so. And God made the beast of the earth after his kind, and cattle after their kind, and every thing that creepeth upon the

200 The austere beauty of the Doves Press typography commands the admiration of all. This type is also derived from Jenson.

27

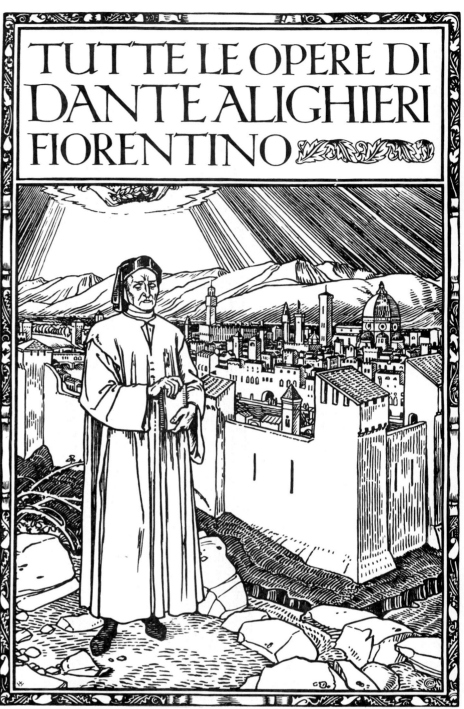

201 The woodcut title-page to the Ashendene
Dante was designed by C. M. Gere.

The third of the great trio of hand presses, the Ashendene, was founded
by C. H. St John Hornby in 1894. It was Hornby's boyhood ambition
to print fine books and his enthusiasm was inflamed when he visited
William Morris at the Kelmscott Press in 1893. At first, assisted by his
family, he printed in a summer-house at Ashendene in Hertfordshire,
using Caslon type. Then, in 1899, he moved to Shelley House on the
Chelsea Embankment. (It is curious that all three presses should have been
on the banks of the Thames within a few miles of each other.) Here he
commissioned his own type, designed by Emery Walker and S. C.
Cockerell and cut by E. P. Prince, who had cut the Kelmscott types. It
was modelled on the first type of Sweynheym and Pannartz and called,
therefore, Subiaco (the place where they first printed in Italy). It is a
rich black calligraphic semi-roman and, although rather mannered, it
combines well to make a fine black page. In this type Hornby printed his

THE PRINTER AT WORK

MORE THAN THIRTY-EIGHT YEARS have gone by since the Ashendene Press had its humble beginning in the little garden-house of happy memory shewn in the woodcut which heads this page. Now that its working days are drawing to a close it seems fitting that I should preface this 'Catalogue Raisonné' with a short account of its origin and, to others than myself, uneventful history. I do so in the hope that details unimportant in themselves may possibly have some interest for book-collectors and students of typography in days to come. The output of the Press, measured in relation to the years of its life, is small in amount compared with that of the Kelmscott and Doves Presses; but it must always be borne in mind that it has been the hobby of my leisure hours, that it was for many years worked entirely, except for some little help from my brother and sisters, by my own hands; and that it has never at any one time employed more than a single Pressman and a single Compositor. The fact that it has been the absorbing interest of an otherwise busy life must be pleaded as my excuse for this necessarily somewhat egotistical Foreword.

b   1

first really big book, a splendid folio Dante, which took three years to produce, coming out in 1909 [201].

Aldus's motto, 'Hasten Slowly', might well have been Hornby's. The Kelmscott Press lasted less than a decade, the Doves less than two, yet in forty years Hornby printed fewer books than either – about forty in all – excluding minor pieces. His books illustrate the virtues of slow work and small output, and the last productions from this press, such as the *Ecclesiasticus* of 1932, show an excellence of presswork that has never been surpassed. His choice of titles, all personal favourites, are witness to the breadth of his culture: among the classics, Virgil, Horace, Apuleius and Thucydides; among the Italians, St Francis, St Clare, Dante and Boccaccio; among English writers, Bacon, Chaucer, Malory, Milton and Spenser and, in other fields, *Omar Khayyam, Ecclesiastes* and *Don Quixote*. His last production was a *Descriptive Bibliography of Books Printed at the Ashendene Press* (1935). This contains a series of actual reprintings (not mere facsimiles) of sample pages and a selection from the woodcuts that give a fine conspectus of these noble books [202 and 203].

The Ashendene Press was the occupation of Hornby's leisure hours, for he was a director of the great firm of W. H. Smith and Sons, owner of

ABOVE LEFT AND RIGHT 202 and 203 Two pages from the Ashendene Press *Bibliography* printed in 1935: on the right, a woodcut by C. M. Gere shows the little summer-house of his father's home which sheltered St John Hornby's Ashendene Press in its early days; on the left, a portrait of C. H. St John Hornby who founded the Ashendene Press in 1895.

when he told her about the colonies
of birds who built in his wide branches
& what the winds said to him as they
waved his boughs in play or in storm
& how near his little topmost twigs were to the sun & how they could see the

ABOVE 204 Lucien Pissarro, who founded the
Eragny Press, was much influenced by Seurat and
his ideas about the division of colour.
His illustrations were printed in delicate shades
in direct contrast to the bolder reds and blues of
the other presses. This is the first Eragny book,
Margaret Rust, *The Queen of the Fishes* (1894).
BELOW 205 With this device the French artist
Lucien Pissarro (1863–1944) and his wife Esther
signed the books they printed in London.

so many bookstalls and bookshops. In the latter capacity he was not only
in a position to exert great influence for good on commercial printing,
but he was one of the very first men to employ Eric Gill, who designed
and painted the lettering on the facia boards of many WHS shops.
When one considers the vulgarity brought by so many of the multiple
shops to ruin the High Street of almost every town in England, responsi-
bility for this tiny island of beauty in a vast ocean of nauseating horror
was a public service of no mean order.

The Eragny Press stands a little to one side of the main stream of English
private presses. Its founder, Lucien Pissarro (1863–1944), was the son of
Camille Pissarro, the Impressionist painter. Being the oldest of his family
by about ten years, Lucien became almost a fellow-painter with his
father and his work was shown in the last Impressionist Exhibition of
1886. His desire to produce illustrated books met with no encouragement
in Paris, where his style of wood engraving was unacceptable to the
academic conventions then ruling. Indeed the one commission he did
receive, in the *Revue Illustrée,* brought down such a storm of protest on
the editor's head that the latter would have no more to do with him.

Feeling, rightly as it turned out, that his style of work would meet with
a more sympathetic reception in England, Pissarro moved to London,
where he was welcomed in the circle that gathered round Charles
Ricketts and Charles Shannon in their studio in The Vale, Chelsea. They
published Pissarro's woodcuts in their magazine the *Dial,* and brought
out the portfolio of woodcuts he had planned for so long. Ricketts, who
had already founded the Vale Press, generously allowed Pissarro to use
his type, so that the first sixteen books came from the Vale Press but with
the Eragny pressmark [205].

When Ricketts closed the Vale Press in 1904 – also throwing his equipment into the Thames, which must have become almost clogged with
type – Pissarro designed a fount of his own, the Brook type, named after
Stamford Brook, Hammersmith, where he lived and worked. By this
time the neglect of his fellow countrymen was a thing of the past and he
received considerable support from other parts of the Continent. However the declaration of war in 1914 cut him off from many of his patrons,
materials were hard to come by and the Eragny Press came to an end.

Both Camille and Lucien Pissarro had been greatly influenced by
Seurat and his ideas about the division of colour. Although Lucien's
woodcuts are by no means in a *pointilliste* style the influence of the
Ecole de Paris is plain to see. He was also in touch with the French
Symbolist movement in poetry, with its theories regarding the symbo-
lism of colour, and he had known Oscar Wilde, who held similar views,
during his early days in London. Pissarro and his wife Esther met with
many technical difficulties in putting these ideas into practice; but they
produced a series of little books of great charm printed in a number of
delicate colours [204].

Until the last few years these books have been curiously undervalued,
but that happy opportunity for discerning book collectors is now over

and prices have risen accordingly. Twenty years ago I was going on my knees, almost, begging my customers to buy Eragny books at absurdly low prices. In 1973 a copy of Judith Gautier, *Album de Poèmes Tirés du Livre de Jade* (admittedly printed on vellum, which spoils the story a bit) brought £560 at auction. After the sale I remarked to the purchaser that I had never expected to see an Eragny book sell for £560. 'Yes,' he replied, 'I've got a cutting from one of your old catalogues pointing out that they *really are* worth more than thirty shillings.'

Here we may diverge for a moment to consider two limited editions which, though not strictly private press books, were produced under the influence of the movement.

Aubrey Beardsley (1872–97) was, perhaps, the most extraordinary phenomenon in English art. Already tubercular at the age of seven, his only training one year's evening classes at the Westminster School of Art, he was famous at twenty and dead by twenty-five. This Keats of graphic art created an original and fantastic world entirely of his own with extreme economy of line. His reputation stands higher, and his influence has been greater, than any other English book-illustrator. Forced to earn his living, he worked as a clerk in the City of London offices of the Guardian Life Insurance Company. Many of his lunch hours were spent in the bookshop of Jones and Evans, where Frederick Evans, a cultured and sensitive man, encouraged the boy and arranged for him to swop drawings for books.

J. M. Dent was the publisher who created the Everyman Library, that series of classics for a shilling that meant so much to several generations of aspiring people from humble backgrounds at a time when neither books nor education were so readily available as they are today. Dent must have been impressed by the earliest productions of the Kelmscott Press and impelled by a desire to emulate them. He consulted Evans, who suggested Beardsley as an illustrator. It was agreed that Beardsley should illustrate the *Morte Darthur*, a scheme that involved 350 drawings, to be reproduced by line blocks. This was Beardsley's first professional commission and, on the strength of it, he left the insurance office.

It is hard to imagine two persons more dissimilar than Dent and Beardsley. Dent (who so little understood his artist that he suggested *The Pilgrim's Progress* for illustration) was earnest, worthy, rather stolid and a nonconformist. Beardsley was brilliant, a dandy, epicene, erotic and, ultimately, a Roman Catholic. The only quality they had in common was a capacity for hard work. Beardsley worked with the passionate intensity of an artist who knows he must die early. Already, when hardly more than a boy, he was utterly self-assured and created an incredible quantity of drawings. And all this was achieved while he was constantly interrupted by coughing, haemorrhages and the ensuing exhaustion.

The *Morte Darthur* was published in two volumes quarto, in 1893, the *édition de luxe* being bound in vellum with gilt cover designs by

206 Aubrey Beardsley was, perhaps, the most extraordinary phenomenon in English art; with hardly any training he was famous at twenty and dead by twenty-five. The commission by J. M. Dent to produce 350 drawings for the *Morte Darthur* (1893) enabled Beardsley to abandon work as an insurance clerk and embark on his career as an artist.

207 Aubrey Beardsley's influence on *art nouveau* was enormous. His drawings for the first edition in English of Oscar Wilde's *Salome* are the masterpiece of his early period.

Beardsley [206]. In 1894 he illustrated the first edition in English of Oscar Wilde's *Salome*, of which there was also an *édition de luxe*. These drawings, the masterpiece of Beardsley's early period, had an immense influence on Art Nouveau [207].

Although it is now seventy-five years since the death of Beardsley I feel almost as if I had touched his hand. Ernest Cooper, the bookseller under whom I trained (he was then the proprietor of Commin's bookshop in Bournemouth), had worked at Jones and Evans in the nineties and could well remember Morris showing Evans advance proofs of the Kelmscott Press, and Beardsley browsing in the shop.

Beardsley who, like D. H. Lawrence and R. L. Stevenson, was sent to Bournemouth for the sake of his lungs, had also been a customer at Commin's. When he moved from one hotel to another he asked Mr Commin to arrange the transfer of his books. Mr A. E. Cosstick, who joined the firm in 1894 and stayed until the 1940s, went round to pack the books. Forty years later he could recall the occasion vividly – Beardsley, sitting between the two tall candlesticks without which he never worked, coughing, coughing, coughing.

The Golden Cockerel Press, founded by Harold Taylor in 1920, has passed through the hands of several owners, each of whom has expressed his own personality and ideas, and it has given constant opportunities to a whole series of wood engravers: Blair Hughes-Stanton, David Jones, Paul Nash, Eric Ravilious, Reynolds Stone and many others. Its most striking period occurred in the late twenties and early thirties, when there was a remarkable collaboration between Robert Gibbings, the then owner of the press, and Eric Gill. Their masterpiece was The Four Gospels, a book that can be placed in the same group as the Kelmscott Chaucer and the Doves Bible [208]. The fact that the type and woodcuts were all the work of the same artist gives it a unity of conception rarely found. Robert Gibbings gave a delightful account of the genesis of the book in the *Book Collector* (Summer 1953): ·

Before any blocks could be cut the type had to be set. . . . I would spend hours with the compositors. . . . Eric was the perfect collaborator. . . . I would send him the proofs and on these he would build his designs, fitting his figures to the spaces determined by the type and allowing his fancy to spread into any quarter that offered itself. . . . Like many another man who is supreme at his job, Eric was essentially modest, and always ready to listen to another man's ideas . . . ready to accept a suggestion, as he was always capable of carrying it to a wonderful fruition. . . . He did some splendid work for our firm in later years, but I like to think that those engravings that he did for our edition of the Gospels were the greatest that he ever produced.

In 1923 two events occurred that profoundly affected English book production. Stanley Morison joined the Monotype Corporation and Francis Meynell founded the Nonesuch Press. The Nonesuch was to implement an entirely new conception of private presses. Hitherto every process had been carried out by hand, so that the care and labour

208 Eric Gill conceived every page of the Golden Cockerel *The Four Gospels* as an entity. He engraved the opening words of each chapter on wood, filling the lettering with stylized figures in perfect harmony with the type he himself had designed.

involved necessarily limited each edition to about three hundred copies. Moreover the scope of production was limited by the specially designed and privately owned founts of type, generally only two or three. By 1923, and increasingly as the influence of Stanley Morison was more widely felt, many commercial printers possessed fine types.

Meynell achieved success because he perceived and exploited the new opportunities. Firstly, he designed attractive books of widely differing kinds according to the individual possibilities offered by numerous printing houses. In this he used not only a variety of types but diverse ways of reproducing illustrations by Stephen Gooden, E. McKnight Kauffer, Paul Nash and other artists of striking ability. Secondly, he made full use of machine printing to issue much larger numbers – Tennyson's *In Memoriam* came in an edition of 1875 copies – thus offering Nonesuch productions at very moderate prices to a wider public than had ever bought fine books before. In the first Nonesuch prospectus Meynell proclaimed his intention 'to choose and make books according to a triple ideal; significance of subject, beauty of format and moderation of price'. Looking back, after the first hundred

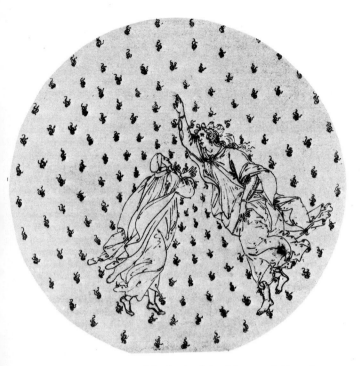

209 One of the best of the Nonesuch Press's many books is Dante's *Divina Commedia*, with the exquisite drawings by Botticelli. Italian and English texts are printed in parallel columns in the same italic type.

BELOW 210 By the intelligent application of machine printing, the Nonesuch Press, in the period between the wars, was able to publish larger editions and bring fine books within the purse of a wider public. The *Book of Ruth* was among their first publications in 1923.

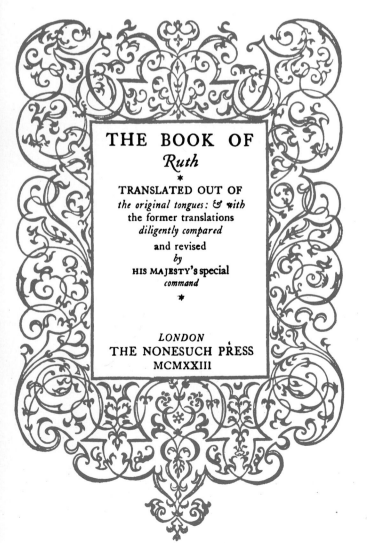

books had been published, he reflected, in *The Nonesuch Century*: '. . . our stock-in-trade has been the theory that mechanical means could be controlled to serve fine ends; that the machine in printing was a controllable tool; to be designers, specifiers, rather than manufacturers; architects of books rather than builders.'

A major factor in the Nonesuch achievement was the intelligence with which the widely varying texts were chosen. Far too many private presses content themselves with producing yet further *de luxe* editions of *Omar Khayyam* and *Daphnis and Chloe*. The directors of the Nonesuch Press were in tune with the literary tastes of the more perceptive and sensitive spirits of their own time, with the reviving interest, for example, in the seventeenth century. In this field they produced works by Donne, Hervey, Bunyan, Burton, Evelyn, Henry King, Marvell, Milton, Izaak Walton and the dramatists, Congreve, Wycherley, Vanbrugh and Dryden, edited by such scholars as Geoffrey Keynes, John Hayward, John Sparrow, Montague Summers and others. In some cases there was no really well-edited edition before the Nonesuch. In almost all cases their editions, such as Geoffrey Keynes's Blake and A. W. Lawrence's Herodotus, became the best [209, 210 and 211].

The Cresset Press produced an edition of *Gulliver's Travels* illustrated by Rex Whistler. These brilliant illustrations are far removed from the usual style of English Private Press books. Morris would have hated them, for they are Baroque or Rococo in inspiration. Each of the twelve coloured copper plates is set within a full-page border drawn in sepia pen-and-ink. The artist's brother, Laurence, tells us that these borders were probably derived from *Designs for Six Poems by Mr. T. Gray* (1753) by Richard Bentley, the friend of Horace Walpole [212].

By the time *Gulliver* was published in 1930 the world of fine books was almost submerged by the tornado of the economic depression. Although limited to 195 copies on paper and ten on vellum, it proved very difficult to sell and there was no further demand for books on this lavish scale. Rex Whistler's very popularity resulted in numerous commissions for book-jackets, menus, posters and other ephemera which, however charming in themselves, stood in the way of further major book illustrations. Then, in July 1944, while serving with the Welsh Guards, he was killed in Normandy. Had the fates decreed otherwise, what a charming and delightful series of books Rex Whistler might have created. In 1970 H. M. Fletcher issued one hundred sets of the illustrations to *Gulliver,* printed from the original plates before they were dispersed.

Outside England the Private Press movement has had most influence in Germany and North America. Indeed in Bruce Rogers, North America produced one of the most outstanding modern typographers. His greatest importance lies, perhaps, in his having managed, as Paul Beaujon puts it, 'to steal the Divine Fire which glowed in the Kelmscott Press books, and somehow to be the first to bring it down to earth'.

LEFT 212 The brilliant rococo illustrations by Rex Whistler in the Cresset Press *Gulliver's Travels* are far removed from the more sober spirit of most English Private Press books. What other charming and delightful books might Rex Whistler have created, but for his tragic and early death while serving with the Welsh Guards in Normandy?

BELOW 211 The Nonesuch Press had a lively and charming series of printer's devices. This one was designed and engraved by Stephen Gooden.

OSCAR WILDE

RECOLLECTIONS BY
JEAN PAUL RAYMOND
& CHARLES RICKETTS

THE NONESUCH PRESS
BLOOMSBURY MCMXXXII

Bruce Rogers, like Morris, designed his own ornament as well as his type, and in one respect he went even further, designing the bindings in which his books were clothed. From 1903 to 1912 he directed the Riverside Press, Cambridge, Massachusetts, where he produced a monumental three-volume edition of Montaigne, which gave its name to his Montaigne type. This type, like so many others, was based on Jenson's, the actual model being the latter's Eusebius. Bruce Rogers later designed an even finer type, the Centaur. His influence extended far beyond his own country, not only through the example of his own productions, widely though these were admired. For many years he acted as adviser to the Cambridge University Press. It was under his direction that the Oxford University Press produced one of the outstanding examples of twentieth-century printing, their Lectern Bible, a masterpiece of apparent simplicity set in Rogers's own Centaur type.

Daniel Berkeley Updike was a man in the true scholar-printer tradition. Though he was not himself a designer of type it was under his direction that the Merrymount Press, Boston, achieved the very highest standards. Perhaps his work has received less attention from connoisseurs than its merits deserve, and possibly this neglect is the result of his books not being *éditions de luxe,* printed on expensive hand-made paper in severely restricted numbers. Instead, as Mr G. P. Winship has said, '. . . his outstanding achievement was the uninterrupted production of printed matter that met the desires as well as the requirements of ordinary readers more completely as well as more satisfactorily than anyone else had done.'

Updike's name is honoured wherever printing is seriously studied because of his great book, based on the series of lectures which he delivered at Harvard, in 1911–16, *Printing Types, Their History, Forms and Use; a Study in Survivals.* This is more than a scholarly history of the types themselves; it relates the history of printing to the background and civilization from which it sprang, and it is infused throughout by the humane mind of its distinguished author. Its influence on good printers has been incalculable.

The Grabhorn Press gives us an endearing picture of achievement on a human scale in an increasingly mechanized world. It was founded in San Francisco in 1920 by two brothers, Edwin and Robert Grabhorn, who worked together in such harmony that it has been said of them: 'When Ed's away the shop goes to pieces; when Bob's away Ed goes to pieces.' Their first workshop occupied the fifth floor of humble premises in a narrow street, and they supported themselves by doing all manner of general, and even jobbing, printing until their reputation brought the support that enabled them to embark on their stately folios. Perhaps the most distinguished of these is Whitman's *Leaves of Grass,* which 'occupied the entire resources of the press for well over a year'. At one point the Grabhorns considered stating in the colophon: 'Four hundred copies printed and the press destroyed.' Oscar Lewis, who was intimately connected with the press, has written a charming memoir, to be found in *The New Colophon,* II: Part 5 (1949) [213].

On the opposite wing of modern North American fine printing lies the Limited Editions Club, founded in 1929, inspired and conducted by George Macy. This may be compared to the Nonesuch Press, for its aim has been to make fine books available at comparatively reasonable prices. Owing to the size and affluence of the United States patronage exists on a scale without precedent in the history of fine printing and in its first quarter of a century the Limited Editions Club issued 250 books for its 1,500 members. To this end it has commissioned work not only from American printers such as the Merrymount Press, the Grabhorn Press, William E. Rudge, Henry Nash and others, but also from European countries – the Golden Cockerel Press and the Oxford University Press in England, J. Enschedé in Holland, Hans Mardersteig of the Officina Bodoni in Italy and so on.

In the *Gulliver* that he designed for them Bruce Rogers was given an opportunity to display a rare sense of humour in a charming *jeu d'esprit*

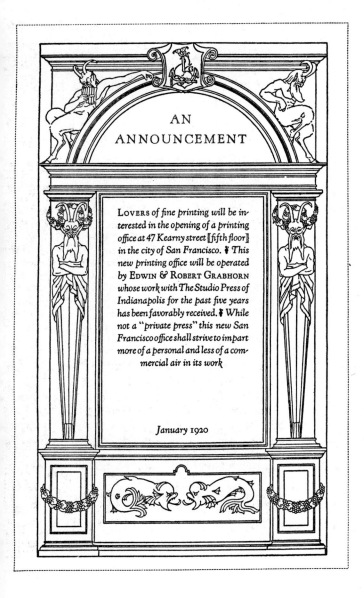

213 The first advertisement issued by the brothers Edwin and Robert Grabhorn when they opened their printing house in San Francisco in 1920.

AN
ANNOUNCEMENT

LOVERS of fine printing will be interested in the opening of a printing office at 47 Kearny street [fifth floor] in the city of San Francisco. ❧ This new printing office will be operated by EDWIN & ROBERT GRABHORN whose work with The Studio Press of Indianapolis for the past five years has been favorably received. ❧ While not a "private press" this new San Francisco office shall strive to impart more of a personal and less of a commercial air in its work

January 1920

in which *The Voyage to Lilliput* measures $2\frac{1}{2}$ by $3\frac{3}{4}$ inches, *The Voyage to Brobdingnag* $13\frac{1}{2}$ by 18 inches [214].

The illustrators commissioned by George Macy display a far more adventurous taste than that of the English private presses, which relied too parochially on the Pre-Raphaelites and the Arts and Crafts movement. In addition to American and British artists, Limited Editions Club books have been illustrated by George Grosz, Marie Laurencin, Matisse and Picasso. Picasso produced pencil drawings and etchings for the *Lysistrata* of Aristophanes (in an excellent translation by Gilbert Seldes), while Matisse illustrated James Joyce's *Ulysses*. Writing about the inception of this commission, George Macy records:

I have never been more greatly impressed with the mental facility of an artist than I was when I suggested to Matisse that he should illustrate *Ulysses*. He said, over the telephone, that he had never read it. I got Stuart Gilbert to send him a copy of Mr. Gilbert's translation into French. The very next morning, M. Matisse reported that he had read the book, that he understood its eighteen episodes to be parodies of similar episodes in the *Odyssey,* that he would like to give point to this fact by making his illustrations actually illustrations of the original episodes in Homer! I may have been taken in, of course. If I was not, it can surely be said that Henri Matisse grasped this book quicker than any other man ever did.

With the success of the Nonesuch Press and the Limited Editions Club the mission of the private presses was virtually achieved. Perceptive and sensitive publishers took note of what had been done and the standards of design and craftsmanship rose immeasurably and scores of excellent books poured into the bookshops.

Under the guidance of Stanley Morison the Monotype Corporation produced a series of fine types, including one of the greatest ever cut: Times roman. In this type attractive books of every kind have been printed and it has been extensively used in paperbacks. The same happy state of affairs is to be seen in other countries; but I hope it will not seem chauvinistic to claim that the modern movement for the betterment of printing was, in its inception, an English one. The best books of today do not look in the least like Kelmscotts, but without Morris they might never have been created at all.

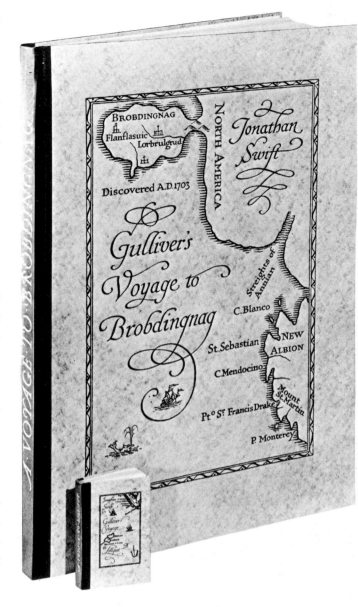

214 *Gulliver's Travels* as designed by Bruce Rogers for the Limited Editions Club (New York 1950) provides problems for those collectors who, like Samuel Pepys, arrange their books in order of size.

215 In order to emulate the early printers, Morris decided to sign his work with a woodcut device. This is the larger of his two devices and was used in books of larger format, such as *Beowulf*, from which this is taken.

CHAPTER ELEVEN

FIRST EDITIONS, FAKES AND FORGERIES

To THE OUTSIDER a collector of first editions is a man who pays an extravagant price for a modern novel because some careless pressman dropped a hammer and damaged the type, thus creating a 'first issue'. Nothing could be further from the truth.

The early collectors were devoted to the *editio princeps* of the Greek and Roman classics that represented the core of their culture. These men dominated the field for rather more than a hundred years; but by the middle of the nineteenth century other forms of collecting were coming to the fore.

The motives that impel the collecting of first editions of English literature are twofold. The austere may, perhaps, regard the first of these as sentimental. In his poem on Shakespeare, Samuel Butler wrote:

> "Men's work we have," quoth one, "but we want them –
> Them palpable to touch and clear to view."
> Is it so nothing, then, to have the gem
> But we must weep to have the setting too?

And just as, for the classical scholar, Agamemnon and Clytemnestra are never so omnipresent as when he climbs up to the Lion Gate at Mycenae or, for any sensitive person, it is impossible to walk under the walls of Constantinople without a throb of emotion, so the lover of English poetry must feel a thrill when he holds in his own hands the anonymous *A Maske presented at Ludlow Castle 1634* [Milton's *Comus*] (1637); Shakespeare's *Poems* (1640); *Lyrical Ballads* (1798); or the little volume of *Poems* by Currer, Ellis and Acton Bell, published by Aylott and Jones, the day before they went bankrupt in 1846. Equally, for the stalwarts of modern literature, copies of James Joyce's *Ulysses,* published in Paris by Shakespeare and Co. (1922), or D. H. Lawrence's *Lady Chatterley's Lover* (Florence 1928), are as oriflammes in the battle against the Philistines. These were the actual copies that went out into the world and changed the very nature of men's minds.

In all classes of fine books it has been through the enthusiasm and perspicacity of collectors, and the booksellers who serve them, that masterpieces have been sought out, treasured and preserved from every kind of destruction, whether from those who tore up (and still tear up) manuscripts to reuse the vellum, or from those who, seeing no value in unpretentious modern first editions, simply throw them away.

Secondly, it is necessary to seek out, study and compare the early editions of a masterpiece in order to establish an accurate and authoritative text. In English-speaking countries this activity has been especially underpinned by the work of the founding fathers of the Bibliographical Society, R. B. McKerrow, W. H. Gregg and A. W. Pollard, carried on to this day by their successors on both sides of the Atlantic.

In 1875 Professor Edward Dowden published *Shakespeare, a critical study of his Mind and Art*. To this he brought a unique combination of gifts, perception, sensitivity and literary style. Subsequently, however, scientific bibliographers proved that a number of pirated Shakespearean quartos had been falsely dated, and with this Dowden's hypothesis that Shakespeare's mind and work had developed in a certain order collapsed like a house of cards.

Before the introduction of power-driven presses printing was a more leisurely affair. An author who had changed his mind could wander down to the printing-house with an emended text; progress would be arrested and the pressmen could go off for a drink while the compositors altered the type. Thus a genuine 'new impression' would be created. Alternatively, if the printing of a section had been completed a whole leaf could be cancelled and a newly printed leaf pasted in its place.

This may be illustrated by the works of James Boswell. Boswell's *Life of Johnson* is rightly regarded as the greatest of all biographies. Many of its most telling passages are derived from the long and intimate conversations that took place late at night when Johnson was reluctant to go to bed and Boswell only too ready to sit up with him. Boswell's unprecedented frankness startled his contemporary readers, but within our own lifetime it has emerged, from the study of the first edition, that even while the work was being printed Boswell had second thoughts and felt it prudent to call for cancels.

Thus a very few early copies of the first edition contain an intimate discussion that was swiftly suppressed:

Sunday, 10 October 1779. I mentioned to him a dispute between a friend of mine and his lady, concerning conjugal infidelity, which my friend had maintained was by no means so bad in the husband, as in the wife. JOHNSON. 'Your friend was in the right, Sir. . . . Wise married women don't trouble themselves about infidelity in their husbands, they detest a mistress, but don't mind a whore. My wife told me I might lye with as many women as I pleased, provided I *loved* her alone.'

Boswell's earlier book, *A Tour to the Hebrides with Samuel Johnson, LL.D*, was equally frank, indeed one outraged Scotsman threatened the author with a duel. For many years it had been assumed that all of Boswell's papers were destroyed shortly after his death. In fact a great part of them had passed, through the marriage of his daughter, to his great-great-grandson, Lord Talbot de Malahide, and were preserved, if that is the word, in conditions of great neglect at Malahide Castle, near Dublin. They were discovered, or at any rate seen, in the 1920s by the American scholar and collector C. B. Tinker. Subsequently, in 1927, the delicate task of their purchase was effected by another American, of exceptional diplomatic ability, Lieutenant-Colonel Ralph H. Isham. Some time after this transaction a further cache of Boswell papers was stumbled upon at Malahide, including the original journal that Boswell kept from day to day in the Hebrides. This was found in a croquet box. Lieutenant-Colonel Isham purchased this, too, and published it. It then became clear that Boswell's published text, for reasons of tact and prudence, had been shorn of such Johnsonian dicta as his estimate of Lady MacDonald: 'This woman would sink a ninety-gun ship. She is so dull – so heavy.'

Of all rare books the hardest to find are the earliest works of subsequently famous poets. These are often produced by very minor publishers, or even jobbing printers; very few, if any, copies are sold. The author may give copies to his friends, but they, like the poet himself, are often men of little worldly substance, leading migratory lives, who slip away from their lodgings with the rent unpaid, leaving an irate landlady to destroy their possessions on a bonfire.

All of these elements may be observed in Shelley's first volume of verse, written at the age of eighteen in conjunction with his sister Elizabeth. It was published under pseudonyms as: *Original Poetry; by Victor and Cazire.* Worthing: Printed by C. and W. Phillipps, For The Authors; And Sold by J. J. Stockdale, 41, Pall-Mall. 1810 [216]. Having ordered the printing Shelley was unable to pay the bill, and he persuaded Stockdale, who dealt in remainders, to take over the stock. Elizabeth Shelley had included, as her own, a poem by 'Monk' Lewis ('Saint Edmund's Eve'), and when this became known the volume was instantly suppressed. It might have been lost completely but for the nature of the publisher, J. J. Stockdale, who was a good deal of a rogue. He is chiefly remembered for his connection with Harriette Wilson, a courtesan who had been 'protected' by a wide selection of the British aristocracy. Her *Memoirs,* a frankly blackmailing concern, were published (and possibly written) by Stockdale. Judging by an autograph letter of hers that passed through my hands, she must have been virtually illiterate. Those who paid up were omitted, while intimate and amusing details regarding those who refused entertained society. The Duke of Wellington, as is well known, replied: 'Publish and be damned.'

Encouraged by this success, Stockdale embarked on the publication of a somewhat dubious magazine, *Stockdale's Budget.* It was a failure and only one set, for 1826–27, is known to have survived; but it lasted long enough for Stockdale to print an account of his relations with Shelley and the publication of *Victor and Cazire.* In 1859 the British Museum acquired this set and Dr Richard Garnet the keeper of printed books, browsing through it, came across the Shelley story. *Victor and Cazire* was now known to Shelley scholars and collectors, but no copy of the book could be found.

Now on 17 September 1810 Shelley had presented a copy to his cousin, Harriet Grove, of Fern in Wiltshire, to whom he had been briefly engaged, a gift that she had noted in her recently discovered diary. Indeed one of the poems, 'Come – ! sweet is the hour', had been inspired by a walk she and Shelley took together. In 1898 Mr V. E. G. Hussey, grand-

ORIGINAL POETRY;

BY

VICTOR AND CAZIRE.

CALL IT NOT VAIN:—THEY DO NOT ERR,
WHO SAY, THAT, WHEN THE POET DIES,
MUTE NATURE MOURNS HER WORSHIPPER.

Lay of the Last Minstrel.

WORTHING:
PRINTED BY C. AND W. PHILLIPS,
FOR THE AUTHORS;
AND SOLD BY J. J. STOCKDALE, 41, PALL-MALL,
AND ALL OTHER BOOKSELLERS.
1810.

Given to me at Eton by the author Percy Bysse Shelley, my friend and schoolfellow – 1810.

216 *Original Poetry; by Victor and Cazire* is a juvenile publication of P. B. Shelley and his sister Elizabeth. It was suppressed and only three copies survive. This one passed to the British Museum with the library of Thomas J. Wise.

son of Harriet's brother Charles, disinterred this copy. Dr Garnet edited a reprint and the original was purchased by Thomas J. Wise at a price that he variously stated to be £155 or £225. One of the printers, Charles Phillipps, had given a copy to a Mr Perry. This was purchased for sixpence by Mr E. E. Newton, one of those omnivorous book-buyers who spend their lives browsing in bookshops, are a joy to the bookseller and who have done so much to preserve books that would otherwise have been destroyed. Newton lived at Barnesbury, a suburb of London. He kept the book for life without ever realizing what a treasure he had acquired, and bequeathed it, along with the rest of his effects, to his housekeeper. One can imagine her joy when, in 1903, this unregarded trifle sold at auction for £600. It was purchased by Thomas J. Wise.

The ensuing publicity was widespread and it brought out the third, last and most desirable copy, for it was the largest and bore the inscription: 'Given to me at Eton by the Author Percy Bysshe Shelley, my friend and schoolfellow, 1810, W. W.', i.e. William Wellesley, a relative of the Duke of Wellington. Wise secured this through Sotheby's, by private treaty.

Thus, as a reward for his unremitting determination, Wise owned, in turn, all three known copies of this rare and romantic volume. He sold his first two copies at a profit, part of his activity as an underground bookseller. The Grove copy went to J. H. Wrenn of Chicago, whose library is now in the University of Texas, the second to R. R. Halsey, whose library was purchased, *en bloc,* by Henry Huntington. The third passed, with Wise's own library, to the British Museum.

The mention of Thomas J. Wise as a collector calls for a more extended account of his multifarious activities.

THOMAS J. WISE

Thomas J. Wise (1859–1937) [217] was one of the most remarkable book collectors and bibliographical pundits who ever lived. The building of his library, the Ashley Library, was the grand passion of his life, carried on with intelligence, acumen, foresight and ruthless determination. He was one of the foremost, indeed a pioneer, among those who collected English literature subsequent to the Elizabethan period. He was one of the first to collect the Romantics, Keats, Shelley, Byron and so forth. And just as early explorers of a new continent find nuggets of gold lying on the beach, unheeded by the ignorant natives, Wise had unimaginable opportunities of acquiring the most wonderful items.

For a lifetime Wise sifted the bookshops, watched the salerooms and developed a new technique, that of seeking out the children and grandchildren of the Romantics and their friends who might still own association copies. From Leigh Hunt's daughter he purchased the copy of *Epipsychidion* that Shelley had given to her father. Other Shelley items came from Trelawny's daughter; Borrow items came from Borrow's daughter. Wise's associate, Clement Shorter, having discovered that Charlotte Brontë's widower, the Rev. Nicholls, was still alive and working as a curate for the Church of Ireland, went over and purchased a vast

217 Thomas J. Wise (1859–1937), book collector, bibliographer, pundit, secret dealer and forger, photographed at the height of his prestige – Hon. MA Oxon., Hon. Fellow of Worcester College, Oxford, President of the Bibliographical Society, Member of the Roxburghe Club, etc.

cache of Brontë manuscripts, which the two collectors shared between them. Finally, after the death of Swinburne, Wise effected a purchase from Theodore Watts-Dunton (with whom the poet had lived) that made him the virtual heir to the Pre-Raphaelite movement.

In the *Dictionary of National Biography*, Arundell Esdaile of the British Museum says this of Wise's library: 'In the sixteenth and early seventeenth century writers his library as it finally stood, was of moderate, in the late seventeenth and the eighteenth of very great and in the nineteenth century of unapproached completeness.'

Wise described this library, with full bibliographical detail, in an eleven-volume catalogue, and produced numerous bibliographies. Because of his expertise the Browning and Shelley Societies entrusted him with the production of their facsimiles. He was generous in throwing his library open to scholars. This brought him fame, and the friendship of leading scholars, such as Buxton Forman and Sir Edmund Gosse. Oxford University gave him an honorary degree, Worcester College, Oxford, made him an honorary fellow, and he had been president of the Bibliographical Society. He was even a member of the Roxburghe Club, that exclusive society of book-collecting patricians.

By the early 1930s Wise was like Alexander, with no more worlds to conquer. He was the dictatorial arbiter of the bibliographical world and students of English literature, from all over the world, flocked to Hampstead to see books in his library that they could examine nowhere else.

And then, in 1934, two brilliant young booksellers, John Carter and Graham Pollard [218] published a book with the innocent title:

218 Left to right: Percy Muir, John Carter and Graham Pollard on the terrace at Lower Througham, Stroud, Glos., the country house of Michael Sadleir, at about the time of the *Enquiry* into the activities of Thomas J. Wise. Courtesy of John Carter.

An Enquiry Into The Nature of Certain Nineteenth Century Pamphlets. This book alleged, and proved beyond all possible doubt, that about fifty first editions of nineteenth-century authors were forgeries, and the unstated implication was that the forger was Thomas J. Wise.

The effect was like a bomb exploding in the hushed and cloistered haunts of literary scholarship. It was as if Bernhard Berenson had been forging Raphaels for forty years.

What did Wise do? And how did Carter and Pollard prove it?

Wise did not forge fresh copies of books already in existence, since this leads to almost certain detection when the forgery is laid beside the genuine article. He produced books which ought to have existed, but didn't.

Poets have sometimes been loath to expose their innermost thoughts and emotions to a harsh world. Instead they print a small edition, which they distribute privately among intimate friends. On the rare occasion when this is a work of genius the friends rally round, urging that the world should not be deprived of a masterpiece. So, a year or two later, the first *published* edition is issued. These private editions are usually locally and poorly printed, hence ignorant executors and spring-cleaners throw them away. If they contain the first appearance of a work of genius they are very desirable, very rare and therefore, very valuable. Wise hit on the brilliant idea of selecting poems from the first published edition and creating a 'privately printed' edition with an earlier date. The star piece among his numerous forgeries is generally known as the 'Reading *Sonnets*'.

The strange courtship of Robert Browning and Elizabeth Barrett, morally chained to a monstrous father, and their subsequent elope-ment, is one of the most romantic stories in nineteenth-century literature. What Browning did not know is that while Elizabeth was lying on that famous sofa in her father's house in Wimpole Street she was pouring out her heart in some of the most remarkable love poetry ever written by a woman. One morning some time later, when they were living in Pisa, Elizabeth Browning pushed a packet under her husband's arm, asked him to read the sonnets it contained and, should he disapprove, destroy them. Then she rushed from the room. Browning sat there and read with ever-growing wonder. Even before he had finished he hurried to his wife and demanded their publication. To shelter her feelings it was pretended that the sonnets had been translated from the Portuguese. They first appeared in the collected edition of Elizabeth Browning's *Works,* 2 volumes (Chapman and Hall 1850).

Wise decided that there ought to have been a prior, privately printed, edition and proceeded to manufacture it. He knew that, at the relevant time, Elizabeth Browning's most intimate friend, Mary Russell Mitford, was living near Reading. For the purpose of the forgery she was deemed to have arranged the printing as a secret trust.

Wise, it will be remembered, organized the printing for the Shelley and Browning Societies. One of the activities of these societies was the publication of type facsimiles of rare first editions that would serve the

SONNETS.

BY

E. B. B.

READING:

[NOT FOR PUBLICATION.]
———
1847.

219 The 'Reading *Sonnets*', purporting to be a private issue ante-dating the genuine publication, was the *pièce de résistance* in Wise's career as a literary forger.

purpose of scholars who could not afford the expensive, or unobtainable, originals. These facsimiles were printed by the eminently respectable firm of Richard Clay and Sons. They had become accustomed to Wise ordering the printing of poetical works, the title pages of which bore dates long past. These, they knew, would subsequently be accompanied by editorial matter, bearing the imprint of the society and the true date of publication. They were all the more ready to accept the situation because the father of these societies, F. J. Furnivall, was a scholar and a gentleman of the highest reputation.

So when, at some unknown date towards the end of the century, Wise ordered the printing of Elizabeth Browning's *Sonnets,* with the imprint 'Reading, 1847' [219], they were not in the least surprised. The forgery had been manufactured; it now remained to launch it.

Among his scholarly friends, won by the fame of his library and the power of his bibliographical expertise, none was more important to Wise than Sir Edmund Gosse, a literary scholar, author of many books of essays, criticism and biography, a pundit who was to become librarian of the House of Lords and, through his weekly articles in the *Sunday Times,* a most powerful influence in the world of literature. Gosse has given an unforgettable picture of the extraordinary religious world of his youth in what is undoubtedly his masterpiece, the autobiographical *Father and Son.* Both Gosse's parents were devout Plymouth Brethren. When his father, a geologist of some eminence, was faced by the discoveries of Darwin, he opined that God had deliberately placed fossils in the rocks to ensnare arrogant geologists. This extraordinary background, so different from the world of the Establishment in which his gifts were to give him an apparently assured position, may have left Gosse with a certain insecurity, have promoted that mild and forgivable literary and social snobbery that made him a little over-eager to be first with the news. Never a very deep scholar, Gosse was rather credulous, and came to rely implicitly on Wise's infinitely superior bibliographical knowledge.

Wise now shared his exciting 'discovery' with Gosse. The poison worked. Gosse had known Browning, and had heard the story from his own lips. Prompted by the extra details supplied by Wise, Gosse rushed into print with the story in an introduction to an edition of the *Sonnets,* published by Dent in November 1894, reprinted in *Critical Kit-Kats* (1896).

In the latter year Harry Buxton Forman, whom we now know to have been implicated in the forgeries, went a step further. In *Elizabeth Barrett Browning and Her Scarcer Books* he suggested that what Elizabeth Browning pushed under her husband's arm, on that never-to-be-forgotten morning in Pisa, was not the *manuscript* of the *Sonnets,* but the private edition that Mary Russell Mitford had had secretly printed at Reading.

The next move was to give an apparently authentic provenance for a book that was to make its first appearance almost fifty years after its date of publication. Here Wise brought in the name of Dr W. C. Bennett,

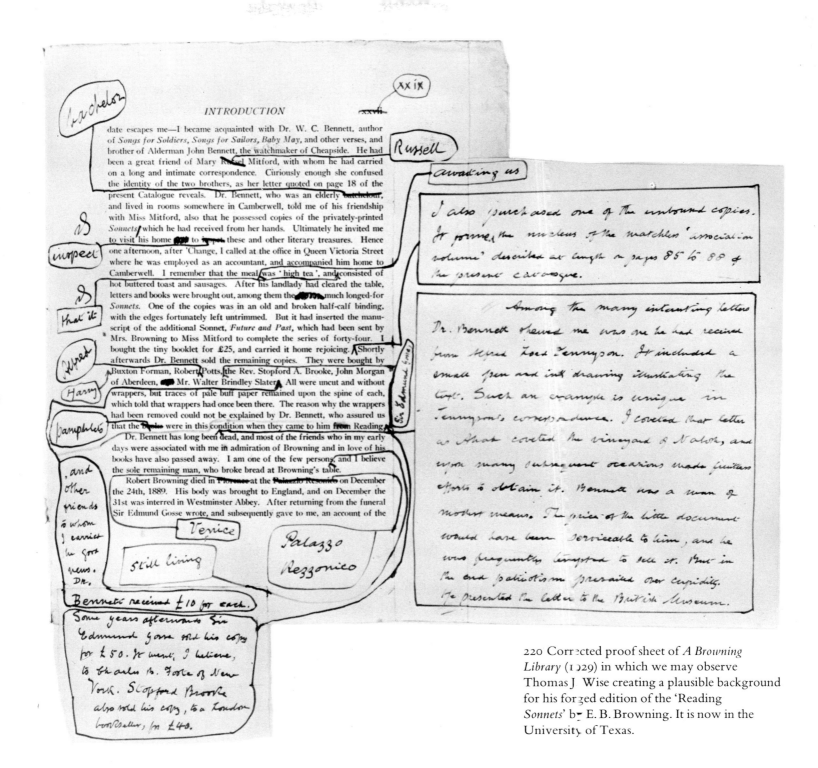

220 Corrected proof sheet of *A Browning Library* (1929) in which we may observe Thomas J Wise creating a plausible background for his forged edition of the 'Reading *Sonnets*' by E. B. Browning. It is now in the University of Texas.

who had been a friend of Miss Mitford and, according to the story, was the legatee of a small cache of the 'Reading *Sonnets*'. In the corrected proof sheets of one of his catalogues, which, fortunately enough, have survived, we can watch Wise improving on his story and adding details as they occur to him [220]:

Somewhere about 1885 – the exact date escapes me – I became acquainted with Dr. W. C. Bennett . . . [who] was an elderly bachelor, and lived somewhere in Camberwell. [He] told me of his friendship with Miss Mitford, also that he possessed copies of the privately printed *Sonnets* which he had received from her hands. Ultimately he invited me to his home to inspect these and other literary treasures. Hence one afternoon, after 'Change, I called at the office in Queen Victoria Street where he was employed as an accountant and accompanied him home to Camberwell. I remember that the meal awaiting us was 'high tea', and that it consisted of hot buttered toast and sausages. After his landlady had cleared the table, letters and books were brought out, among them the much-longed-for-*Sonnets*. [Wise bought two copies.] Shortly afterwards Dr. Bennett sold the remaining copies. They were bought by . . . and other friends to whom I hurried with the good news.

This was the final version of the story as Wise recounted it in the catalogue of his *Browning Library* (1929), but it had not always been so full, or so detailed. When the forgery was first marketed Dr Bennett was still alive, and there was no mention of him, or of his friendship with Miss Mitford. By 1905 Dr Bennett was dead, and he has become the immediate (and Miss Mitford the ultimate) source of the *Sonnets*. At the Browning sale of 1913 various manuscripts by E. B. B. came on the market, and in Wise's *A Bibliography of Elizabeth Barrett Browning* (1918), a leaf of manuscript in her hand has been inserted in his copy.

Finally, by 1928, most of the detail has been added, 'Change, high tea, hot buttered toast, sausages and the rest of what Pooh-Bah would have described as 'corroborative detail intended to give artistic verisimilitude to an otherwise bald and unconvincing narrative'.

When Wise sent his manuscript to the printer, Buxton Forman, Robert Potts, the Rev. Stopford A. Brooke, John Morgan and W. B. Slater (those fortunate purchasers to whom Wise had hurried with the good news) were all dead and in no position to deny the story. But Gosse, rather awkwardly, was still alive. Then, while Wise was still correcting the proofs, Gosse conveniently died. His name was inserted among the others and Wise rounded off his story.

If Gosse had really bought a copy from Dr Bennett, why did he never mention this treasure in his numerous renderings of the story? Why was there no copy in his sales of 1928–29? Or, since he had an elaborate book-plate that no subsequent owner is likely to have removed, where is his copy now? Thus Gosse, the innocent, credulous old goose, was led, step by step, into authenticating the 'Reading *Sonnets*'. 'The voice is Jacob's voice, but the hands are the hands of Esau.'

So Wise worked, roughly between 1886 and 1899. He produced about fifty forgeries in all. Most of the authors, like the Brownings, were dead. Of the few still alive, Ruskin was suffering from brain fever and enjoyed only occasional lucid moments; Stevenson was on the other side of the world, dying of tuberculosis in Samoa; Swinburne, generally regarded as a bit crazy, was under the thumb of Watts-Dunton down in Putney. There was William Morris, of course, but he was so full of a multiplicity of concerns, so good-natured and so careless of trifles. Indeed Buxton Forman had the impudence to go up to Morris at the end of a political meeting and get him to sign a forged copy of one of his own books.

It only remained to market the forgeries. Now Wise had gained the confidence of book collectors all over the world, and especially those in the United States whose distance from the English scene placed them at a disadvantage. As a friendly gesture, so it seemed, Wise was ready to keep watch on behalf of fellow-collectors. To no collector did he seem more friendly than to John Henry Wrenn, a Chicago stockbroker who collected, as far as such a thing was possible, a library that duplicated Wise's. Almost every Sunday morning Wise sat down to write to Wrenn, and Wrenn so treasured the letters that they have survived in their entirety. Wise did not write an autobiography, but in these letters he painted a self-portrait. It is fascinating to watch him playing Wrenn like an angler playing a trout. He has heard the rumour that a library (containing one of his own forgeries) will come on the market – Wrenn's interest is aroused – no, the owner has decided not to sell – now Wrenn wants the book more than ever. Then, by some miraculous chance, Wise discovers another copy – would Wrenn like him to secure it? And so another fish is landed by the astute angler of Heath Drive.

Finally, there was a clerk in Wise's firm, Herbert E. Gorfin, who wanted to better himself. Wise enabled him to set up as a bookseller, by providing a number of forgeries, remainders, as it were, to form the basis of his stock. Gorfin advertised these in his catalogues and, over the years, fed small groups of them into the London salerooms with the restraint and discretion necessary to avoid flooding the market.

How was it that Carter and Pollard first suspected these pamphlets to be forgeries?

First came the suspicion. As these little books were purported to have been produced for presentation to friends, it is reasonable to suppose that a large proportion would bear presentation inscriptions from the author, or at least the contemporary signature of the recipient. None did. Browning preserved his wife's books with almost religious care, and they all turned up in the Browning sale of 1913. Of all books he would surely have treasured the presentation copy of the 'Reading *Sonnets*', the most precious book of his whole life, yet where was it? Surely Elizabeth Browning would have inscribed a copy for Mary Russell Mitford in return for all her trouble. What had happened to that?

In the nineteenth century bookbinding was quite cheap and many collectors (indeed many ordinary book-lovers) had their favourite books bound in morocco gilt. The 'Reading *Sonnets*' was not only precious but extremely fragile; why had no contemporary loving owner ordered his copy to be bound in morocco? No copies of any of these books had arrived in the British Museum before 1888, and many of these, it turned out, had been presented by that generous patron, Thomas J. Wise. No copy had a pedigree that could be traced back before 1890.

But these were suspicions, not proofs.

The first step was scientific examination of the paper on which these pamphlets had been printed. Until the latter part of the nineteenth century all paper used for books had been manufactured from rags. With the spread of education and the consequent rise of the popular press there were not enough rags to go round. The difficulties of this shortage were accentuated by the American Civil War, which produced a cotton famine. In 1854 *The Times* offered a prize of £1,000 for a practical substitute for rags in the manufacture of paper. This prize

products of the workshop were placed in shop-windows at a price far too high for a reproduction, but far too low for the genuine article, and bargain hunters became regular victims. On one occasion an irate purchaser, whose eyes had been opened, returned to protest. 'You've cheated me.' 'Yes, but when you bought it, didn't you think you were cheating me?'

Curiously enough, Joni never bothered to walk the short distance to the Archivio di Stato and examine the originals. As a result his pastiches contain features that do not occur in genuine examples and are quite easy to detect. But apart from this, a forger unconsciously puts something of the spirit of his own age into his work. This may not be apparent to his contemporaries, but is evident to later generations, especially as Joni's allegorical figures of saints or the spirit of Siena, *et al.*, bear a distant resemblance to the twenty lovesick maidens in *Patience*.

THE COUNT DE FORTSAS

At times book collecting may be a rather predatory game, especially when the chance to acquire some unique or magnificent book can occur only after the death of a rival collector. 'Very well,' snapped an infuriated and embittered under-bidder to the rival who had beaten him at an auction, 'very well, I'll buy it at *your* sale.' The really important books in major collections are fairly well known in the bibliographical world, either because their history is known, or because their owners boast about them or, as is often the case, because they are generous in showing their treasures to fellow-collectors and scholars. The break up and sale of a major collection is, therefore, anticipated for years by other collectors, eager to complete their own libraries.

On the other hand there are some collectors who work in secret, who purchase through agents or buy under a *nom de guerre*. Shy and retiring scholarly men who follow the advice given by Voltaire in *Candide*, '*Pour vivre heureux vivons cachés.*' When an important but quite unknown collection emerges on to the market then there is excitement indeed.

Such an event seemed to have occurred in 1840 when the sale of the library of a Count J. N. A. de Fortsas was announced. Here, it appeared, was that exciting opportunity: a unique collection of which no one had ever before heard. The sale catalogue began with the following preface:

Almost all the libraries formed during the past fifty years have been slavishly based upon the *Bibliographie Instructive* of Debure. The consequence has been that the works presented by Debure as rare or curious have been sought for, exhumed, preserved by amateurs, and are actually everywhere met as foundations of collections; so that, in point of fact, in the matter of old books, nothing is so common as rarities.

A taste entirely opposed to this slavishness, the idea of a genuinely exclusive bibliomaniac, has, on the other hand, presided over the choice of the unique collection now offered for sale.

The Count de Fortsas admitted upon his shelves only works unknown to all bibliographers and cataloguists. It was his invariable rule, a rule from which he never departed. With such a system, it is easy to conceive that the collection formed by him – although during forty years he devoted considerable sums to it – could not be very numerous. But what it will be difficult to believe is, that he pitilessly expelled from his shelves books for which he had paid their weight in gold – volumes which would have been the pride of the most fastidious amateurs – as soon as he learned that a work, up to that time unknown, had been noticed in any catalogue.

This sad discovery was indicated upon his manuscript list in a column devoted to this purpose, by these words: "Mentioned in such or such a work," etc., and then "sold, given away" or (incredible if we did not know to what extent the passion of exclusive collectors could go) "destroyed"!

The publication of the *Nouvelles Recherches* of Brunet was a severe blow for our bibliomaniac, and one which, without doubt, contributed to hasten his end. It made him lose at once the third of his cherished library.

After that, he seemed disgusted with books and with life; he did not make a single further acquisition; but the *Bulletin* of Techener from time to time still further thinned the already decimated ranks of his sacred battalion.

Jean-Néphomucéne-Auguste Pichauld, Count de Fortsas, born the 29th October, 1770, at his Château de Fortsas, near Binche in Hainaut, died in the place of his birth, and in the chamber in which he first saw the light sixty-nine years before, the 1st September, 1839.

Devoted entirely to his books, he had seen (or rather he had not seen) thirty years of revolutions and wars pass by, without abandoning for a moment his favourite occupation – without, as it were, going out from his sanctuary. For him the device should have been: 'Vitam impendere libris'.

The sale was to take place at Binche, a small town in Belgium. Given the foregoing conditions, it may seem surprising that the sale should contain as many as fifty-two lots. Each lot held an almost irresistible appeal to some leading collector, and each of these collectors received a copy of the catalogue, unasked, through the post. The Baron de Reiffenberg, director of the Royal Library at Brussels, applied for special funds to acquire treasures of national importance, though omitting several lots that were deemed too amoral for a public library. M. F. M. Crozet was equally active on behalf of France. The princely family of de Ligne learned with horror, and for the first time, that a black sheep of their family, the outstanding roué of his day, had written his memoirs with outspoken and embarrassing detail, the manuscript of which formed a star lot in the sale. The Princesse de Ligne, anxious to destroy the record of her ancestor's amatory adventures and to protect the reputation of the grandmothers of the best families in the state, wrote to her bookseller: *'Achetez, je vous en conjure, à tout prix les sottises de notre polisson de grand père.'*

It is the dream of every bookseller, almost never realized, to find himself the only dealer present at some important but remote country auction sale. On this occasion leading booksellers attempted to make their way to the sale as inconspicuously as possible. However, all hopes were dashed when Brunet, Nodier, Techener and Renouard met one another *en route* to Belgium.

At the last moment notices appeared in two Belgian newspapers

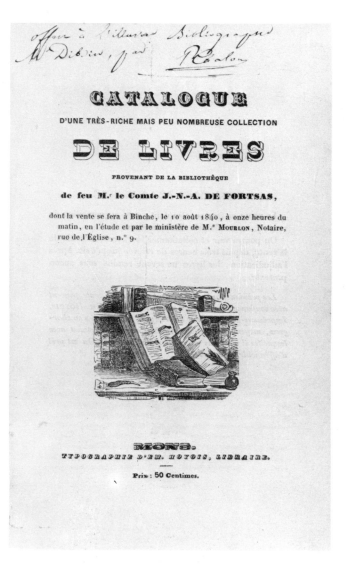

announcing the cancellation of the sale. It was stated that, with praise-worthy and virtually unique patriotism, the people of Binche found themselves unable to contemplate the dispersal of the irreplaceable collection formed by their fellow citizen. They had bought it *en bloc* for preservation in their public library.

The whole affair, need it be added, was a practical joke, the work of M. René Chalons of Brussels who, it is said, set out as though to attend the sale and entertained other bibliophiles on the journey with personal reminiscences of the mythical Count de Fortsas.

The catalogue was printed in an edition of one hundred copies. Many of these must have been torn up and thrown away in disgust, while others have disappeared over the years. Today the catalogue is a rare and desirable item in itself – so desirable that some enterprising individual has produced a forgery [224].

LOUIS HAGUÉ AND JOHN BLACKER

At roughly the same time as J. F. Joni was painting bookcovers in Siena, Louis Hagué, a bookbinder of considerable ability, was active in Belgium. Hagué took genuine sixteenth-century books and clothed them in splendid decorated leather bindings, generally with the arms and devices of popes, kings or other great Renaissance collectors. As has been elaborated in the chapter on bookbinding, romantically minded collectors have always been fascinated by Diane de Poitiers, a lady so lacking in consideration for others that she did not leave enough fine bindings to go round. Hagué proceeded to fill this lacuna [225].

In common with many fakers, he could not resist improving on the genuine article. It is this 'better than real life' quality that often gives the faker away. Another weakness in Hagué's case is the poor quality of the leather used. The joints of his late nineteenth-century bindings tend to crumble where the sixteenth-century originals hold firm.

Hagué's chief victim was an Englishman, John Blacker, who, after accumulating over a hundred examples, decided to sell his collection and sent the books to Sotheby's. They, after some hesitation, faced up to the unenviable task of informing the owner that his books were all modern fakes. The shock was so great that he blew his brains out, and when the sale took place, on 11 November 1897, the catalogue read: '*A Remarkable Collection of Books in Magnificent Modern Bindings,* formed by An Amateur *(Recently Deceased).*' That, at any rate, was how the late E. P. Goldschmidt used to give his unforgettable account of the tragedy. More recently that eminent historian of bookbinding, Howard M. Nixon (another brilliant *raconteur,* who says that he will never forgive himself for spoiling so good a story), discovered, while making some investigations at Somerset House, that Mr Blacker died of chronic bronchitis and was presumably gathered to his fathers in blissful ignorance. The books were sent to Sotheby's by his executors. The sale catalogue, incidentally, provides an illustrated record of Hagué's work.

ABOVE 224 The Count de Fortsas (it was said) would only admit books to his shelves if they were unique. The announcement of his sale in 1840 caused a sensation; each book seemed irresistible and European bibliophiles converged on Belgium only to find that the affair was a hoax.

OPPOSITE 225 This binding, purporting to have been created for Diane de Poitiers, is a fake by the Belgian binder, Louis Hagué, covering a genuine edition of *Galen* (1538). It was sold to Hagué's chief dupe, John Blacker, in the 1890s.

CHAPTER TWELVE

GREAT BOOK COLLECTORS

D. ROBERTUS COTTONUS BRUCEUS,
Eques Auratus et Baronettus,
Bibliothecæ COTTONIANÆ *Fundator.*

226 Sir Robert Cotton (1571–1631) salvaged many great manuscripts which had been scattered by the sack of the monasteries. His family virtually gave his library to the nation. Although many manuscripts were lost or damaged by fire in 1731, the Cotton manuscripts are among the most important in the British Museum.

IN MEDIEVAL ENGLAND the really important, and almost the only significant, libraries were those of the great monasteries such as Bury St Edmunds, Winchester and Canterbury. These were dispersed when Henry VIII sacked the monasteries, and the number of manuscripts destroyed is too sickening to contemplate. A few years later the cathedral and parish libraries were pillaged by the commissioners of Edward VI. In addition to the devastation caused by religious bigotry, innumerable manuscripts were doubtless scrapped as being useless and out of date.

A few collectors and antiquarians salvaged what they could from the wreck, notably Matthew Parker, Archbishop of Canterbury, who bequeathed 433 manuscripts to Corpus Christi, Cambridge, where he had once been master. A good many monks, not unnaturally, provided for their enforced leisure by taking a few favourite books from the library of their monastery before they left.

Among all those who salvaged manuscripts from the wreck of the monastic libraries no man has a greater claim on our gratitude than Sir Robert Cotton (1571–1631) [226].

He was educated at Westminster, where his enthusiasm for antiquarian research was encouraged, or perhaps inspired, by William Camden, the second master. Wealth and leisure enabled him to indulge his life-long passion for collecting antiquities, coins and especially manuscripts. His house in Westminster, on the site of the present House of Lords, became the gathering-place of scholars; a sort of Jacobean Athenaeum, Society of Antiquaries and British Museum Library rolled into one. He was equally generous in lending his manuscripts which were not always returned. Among his greatest manuscripts was the *Cottonian Genesis,* a Greek manuscript written, perhaps at Alexandria, in the first half of the fifth century. Its 250 miniatures were among the very few surviving examples of classical illumination. It had been brought to England by two refugee Greek bishops from Philippi and presented to Henry VIII; Elizabeth I gave it to her tutor who, in turn, presented it to Cotton. Cotton lent this precious codex, for four years, to the eminent French scholar and book collector N. C. Fabri de Peiresc so that it might be used in the preparation of the Paris edition of the Greek Bible (1628). (It was subsequently used by Brian Walton when working on his Polyglot.)

It is difficult to decide which manuscripts to select for mention. Plates II, III and V, and Figures 7 and 227 are all Cottonian manuscripts, but pride of place must be given to the *Lindisfarne Gospels.* There is an account of its rescue from the sea in another Cottonian manuscript, the *History of the Church of Durham,* by Simeon, a monk of Jarrow, who recorded

Christianity in Northumberland (AD 635–1096). Unique manuscripts alone preserve the texts of *Beowulf* and *The Pearl*; a tenth-century *Heliand* is almost the only Old Saxon text to have survived; the St Albans *Lives of the Offas* contains drawings believed to be by Matthew Paris (two books of maps executed in the *scriptorium* at St Albans, under the supervision of Matthew Paris, may also be in his hand); two of the four copies of *Magna Carta* (one, which is regarded as most near the original, was rescued from a tailor's shop); four leaves from the *Codex Purpureus*, a Greek manuscript of the sixth century, written on purple vellum; the *Herbal* of Apuleius Barbarus, England (eleventh century); the C text of *Piers Plowman* and the charter of the foundation of New Minster, Winchester, the earliest surviving example of the Winchester School of illumination, the *Winchester Psalter*. But one must stop somewhere.

His enthusiasm was such that on the death of Dr Dee (having heard that the old astrologer had – like Prospero – buried some of his manuscripts) Cotton bought the land and instituted excavations 'which were not without success'.

Cotton's political career proved his undoing. Siding with parliamentary reform he gained the enmity of both the crown and the government of Buckingham. He was eventually arrested and carried before the Star Chamber. On the day set for his trial an heir to the throne was born (Charles II) and the proceedings were quashed in an amnesty. But a terrible punishment remained. His library had been seized and sealed, and when he was set at liberty the library was not returned.

His friend, Sir Simonds D'Ewes, tells us that Cotton's 'ruddy and well-coloured' features changed into 'a grim blackish paleness, near to the resemblance and hue of a dead visage'. Cotton made two petitions, but he died of grief before the king relented.

The library remained in the family and was always at the service of scholars such as Sir William Dugdale and Brian Walton. At the turn of the century it was virtually given to the nation and kept in Ashburnham House, Westminster, where in 1731 there was a disastrous fire. Out of 958 manuscripts 114 were seriously injured or totally destroyed. Among the losses was the unique text of *The Battle of Maldon*. Happily, thanks to the liberal Cottonian policy, this had been transcribed by Thomas Hearne. Most tragic of all, the *Cottonian Genesis* was reduced to a pile of charred fragments [227].

In 1753 the surviving manuscripts became part of the newly founded British Museum. By 1842, the technique of restoration having made notable advances, Sir Frederick Maden organized the renovation of 100 volumes on vellum and 98 on paper.

Cotton had arranged his books in fourteen bookcases and, in accordance with a pleasant custom that may still be seen in some country house libraries, placed busts of the twelve Roman emperors and Cleopatra and Faustina above the cases. He then gave each manuscript a shelf-mark. The *Lindisfarne Gospels*, for example, is Nero, D. IV, and these marks have been retained to this day.

227 A tragic fragment of the *Cottonian Genesis*, a Greek manuscript executed, perhaps at Alexandria, in the first half of the fifth century AD. Its 250 miniatures were among the very few examples of classical illumination to survive until it was virtually destroyed in 1731. British Museum, Cotton MS Otho B VI.

In his standard work, *The British Museum Library*, Arundell Esdaile describes the Cotton manuscripts as 'perhaps the most splendid of all those of which the Museum's Department of Manuscripts has been built up'. And of Cotton himself, '[he was] an early and salient example of a class that has done great things for this country, the private gentleman with public spirit and enthusiasm'.

In the course of the next few hundred years libraries were gathered in English country houses, and here, more than anywhere else, were preserved those books that have gone forth to form the libraries of universities all over the English-speaking world. When looking at an untouched country house library that has grown over the centuries a bibliophile can observe the mental and spiritual history of the family, just as a geologist will make deductions from the strata of the earth's crust. One owner may have been the friend of poets and bought their books on publication. Another will have been interested in travel or in science, a third will have bought books while on the Grand Tour, and all these men may have been succeeded by generations of fox-hunting squires, quite unaware of what they owned. 'Poor old St George,' remarked the late Lord Lonsdale of his elder brother, 'he was the only one of us all who ever read a book.' Meanwhile the books slept on in safety. One is reminded of Sir John Henry Moore's parody of Gray's 'Elegy':

> Where groan yon shelves beneath their learned weight,
>   Heap piled on heap, and row succeeding rows,
> In peaceful pomp and undisturb'd retreat,
>   The labours of our ancestors repose.

These libraries were not 'collected', they grew as their owners entertained or informed themselves. And then in the early years of the eighteenth century a number of British dukes and earls, without warning and without much precedent, were swept up by a common urge to collect incunabula. The *Peerage* became a ready-made bookseller's list of customers; even if every book collector was not a duke, at least every duke was a book collector. Devonshire, Roxburghe, Sunderland, Pembroke, Blandford and Harley, their names roll like some speech in a Shakespearean historical play. Why did they all start to collect, simultaneously, like a flock of migrating birds heading for the Mediterranean? We don't know. They were not imitating a continental fashion. Indeed they were ahead of Europe. But for the first time all the forces of bottomless wealth, social and political power, were focused upon early printing.

Robert Harley (1661–1724), first Earl of Oxford [228], was a politician of unusual energy and ruthless determination. He rose in the service of Queen Anne and became prime minister in all but name. As a politician, Harley was interested in acquiring the papers and libraries of other men of affairs, historians and antiquarians such as Sir Simonds D'Ewes. His interest in Bibles and prayer books developed into the acquisition of superb manuscripts and he was soon involved in the rage for early printing. A large proportion of such English libraries as came on to the

228 Robert Harley (1661–1724), first Earl of Oxford, prime minister in all but name, formed a superb collection of manuscripts now in the British Museum. His printed books, including fifty Caxtons, were sold to the bookseller Thomas Osborne for £13,000. National Portrait Gallery.

market were swept into the Harleian collection and agents scoured Europe for major items. Harley's son, Edward, second Earl of Oxford (1689–1741) [229], had none of his father's restless ambition but inherited an enthusiasm for the library. He was an easy-going and generous dilettante and patron, the friend of Pope, who made wide use of the library, of Swift, who was a frequent guest, and of Prior, who died in Harley's country house, Wimpole.

Harley left no male heir. His only daughter, Prior's 'noble, lovely little Peggy', married the Duke of Portland. The Dowager Countess, 'a dull worthy woman who disliked most of the wits who surrounded her husband and hated Pope', lost little time in disposing of the library.

The manuscripts were bought by the Nation for the derisory price of £10,000, as part of the about-to-be-founded British Museum. Harley's widow had suggested the extremely modest figure of £20,000 but when the Treasury (then as now grudging where art and scholarship are concerned) offered half she, with aristocratic contempt, replied that 'she would not bargain'.

It is impossible to describe the Harley manuscripts in a few words. With the exception of Sir Thomas Phillipps, no private collector has ever gathered their equal. They alone surpass some national libraries and even now, over two hundred years later, they form one of the major glories of the British Museum. It is difficult to choose among treasures that include the seventh-century Greek-Latin gloss from Cusa, manuscripts from the court of Charlemagne (including the *Codex Aureus*), [230], the eighth-century *Paradoxa* of Cicero and the earliest text of Vitruvius. Figures 8, 15, 230 and 250 and Plate IV are Harley manuscripts.

The printed books, including over fifty Caxtons, were purchased for £13,000 (less than they had cost to bind) by the bookseller Thomas Osborne. This seems a remarkable buy to us, but they proved a heavy burden to Osborne. Then, as now, collectors complained that prices were too high; the very quantity glutted the market, and twenty years later many books were still on his hands. The young Samuel Johnson had been engaged as one of the cataloguers. Do I detect his hand in Osborne's rebuttal?

If I have set a high value upon books, if I have vainly imagined literature to be more fashionable than it really is, or idly hoped to revive a taste well-nigh extinguished, I know not why I should be persecuted with clamour and invective, since I shall only suffer by my mistake, and be obliged to keep the books I was in the hopes of selling.

Let it not be thought that book collecting was confined to dukes John Ratcliffe (d. 1776), a Southwark chandler, became interested in early books because they were commonly used as wrapping paper in his and other shops. Anyone who has used newspapers for packing knows how the printed word catches the eye. That is what happened to Ratcliffe: he started reading his wrapping paper, especially when printed with black letter. Once hooked, he devoted the next thirty years to book collecting. Every Thursday morning he kept open house in his shop and entertained the leading collectors. His sale at Christie's, on 27 March

229 Edward Harley (1689–1741), second Earl of Oxford, the friend of Pope and Swift, inherited and added to his father's great library. This is the original drawing by G. Vertue from the portrait by M. Dahl for the engraving of 1746. Dibdin reproduced this in his edition of Ames's *Typographical Antiquities*, though with typical carelessness giving the dates of the first Earl. Courtesy of Dr A. N. L. Munby.

230 The *Codex Aureus* of the Four Gospels was executed in the Imperial Schools founded by Charlemagne at Aachen about AD 800. It was purchased by Robert Harley, Earl of Oxford, in 1720 for about £100. This miniature faces the *Gospel of St Mark* and we see the Evangelist writing his Gospel, as explained in a scroll held by his symbol, a lion.
British Museum, Harley MS 2788.

1776, lasted for nine days and included over fifty Caxtons, the largest number ever to appear in one sale. They averaged £9 each [231].

If no eighteenth-century collector of manuscripts could approach Harley, George John, second Earl Spencer (1758–1834) [232], was the greatest collector of incunabula and early printed books the world has ever seen. A love of the classics and an early enthusiasm for bibliography enabled Spencer to discover some Elizabethan treasures in the family library at Althorp, and launched him on his career as a collector. But the real foundation of his collection of early printing was the purchase of the library of Count Reviczki, a wealthy Hungarian nobleman who had served as ambassador for Maria Theresa and Joseph II. Lord Spencer was unexpectedly lucky over this deal. He agreed on a down payment of £1,000 and an annuity of £500 for the life of Count Reviczki. As it happened, the count survived for only three years.

For thirty years Lord Spencer was widely known as the most generous buyer in Europe and received the first offer of every really important book that came on the market. In addition to single works he purchased whole libraries, such as that of the Duke de Cassano Serra, of Naples. When describing Lord Spencer's library the generally austere Seymour de Ricci becomes almost lyrical:

Lord Spencer's library has been rightly described as the finest private collection of books in Europe. For incunabula and Aldines it equalled – when it did not surpass them – the greatest public libraries of the world. No other collector ever owned *all* the first editions of the classics, both the Mayence Bibles (42-line and 36-line editions), both the Fust and Schoeffer Psalters (1457 and 1459),

LEFT 231 John Ratcliffe (d. 1776), a Southwark chandler, became interested in early books because they were used as wrapping paper in shops. His sale included over fifty Caxtons, the largest number ever to appear in one auction. Courtesy of Dr A. N. L. Munby.
ABOVE 232 George John, second Earl Spencer (1758–1834), the greatest collector of incunabula and early books the world has ever seen. His library remains intact in the Rylands Library, Manchester. National Portrait Gallery.

Bibliotheca Ratcliffiana.
A
CATALOGUE
Of the Elegant and truly Valuable
LIBRARY
Of JOHN RATCLIFFE, Efq;
Late of BERMONDSEY,
DECEASED,
The Whole collected with great Judgment and Expence during the laft thirty Years of his Life;
Comprehending the largeft and moft choice Collection of the rare old Englifh Black Letter, in fine Prefervation and in elegant Bindings, printed by Caxton, Lettou, Machlinia, the anonymous St. Alban's Schoolmafter, Wynkyn de Worde, Pynfon, Berthelet, Grafton, Day, Newberie, Marfhe, Jugge, Whytchurch, Wyer, R ſtell, Coplande, and the Reft of the Old Englifh Typographers; feveral Miffals and MSS. and two Pedigrees on Vellum, finely illuminated;
Amongft which are the following VALUABLE and SCARCE
BOOKS, viz.

Chaucer, 1ſt Edit.	The Proud Lady, 1485,
Game of Cheffe,	Hyftorie of Roberte the Dyvell,
The Praife of Women,	Myrrour of the World,
Godefrey of Boleyne,	Tulle of old Age,
Gower, Confeffio Amantis,	Doctrine of Sapyence,
Legenda Aurea,	Kalendayr of Shypars,
The Wydow Edyth,	Orcharde of Syon,
The Cyte of Ladyes,	Pilgrimage of Perfection,
Lyfe of St. Catherine,	Lyfe of our Lady,
Lyfe of St. Wenefrede,	Cuftomes of London,
Reynard the Fox,	The Boke called Caton,
Sayenges of Philofophers,	Polychronicon, 2 Copies,
Hyftory of Prince and King Arthur,	Booke for a Kynge,
Dives and Pauper,	Shyppe of Foles,
The Dyinge Creature,	Boke of Dyftyllacyon, &c. &c.
Dyftruccyon of Troye,	

Chronicles by Caxton, Raftell, Boece, Froffart, Grafton, Hall, Fabian, Hollinfhed, Speed, Stow, Mundy, Cooper, Hardyng, &c. &c.
Chambers's Dictionary, 2 Vols. Harris's Voyages, 2 Vols. Gerard's Herbal, 2 Vols. coloured, Atkins's Gloucefterfhire, Mr. Walpole's Pieces, Morocco, Pope's works, 5 Vols. L. P. Granger's Biography, 4 Vols. Ames's Printing, Puritan Tracts, 20 Vols. Morocco, Political State, 60 Vols. Morocco, with many others equally good.
Which will be Sold by AUCTION.
By Mr. CHRISTIE,
At his Great Room, the *Royal Academy, Pall-Mall,*
On *Wednefday, March 27,* and the 8 following Evenings (Good Friday and Sunday excepted)
To be viewed on Monday the 25th, and to the Time of Sale, which will begin each Evening at Six o'Clock.
Catalogues may be then had at the Place of Sale, and at the Bank and Garraway's Coffee Houfes
⁎ Mr. Ratcliffe's curious Manufcript Catalogues will be fold in the laft Day's Sale.

1776

ABOVE 233 The Rev. Thomas Frognall Dibdin (1776–1847) hymned the great period of patrician book collecting in epic terms. Courtesy of Dr A. N. L. Munby.

BELOW 234 The extremes of bibliomania in the nineteenth century are here caricatured in the person of Isaac Gossett: when he lay stricken with illness, he was miraculously restored to health by the mere sight of one volume of the Complutensian Polyglot on vellum. Courtesy of Dr A. N. L. Munby.

nearly all the rarest incunabula, including impressions by Pfister and no less than fifty-six Caxtons (more than the British Museum until a quite recent date), the finest Bibles, the first editions of all the great Italian authors, books in splendid bindings, the rarest English Bibles, fourteen block-books, about one hundred books printed on vellum, beautiful Elzevirs and the choicest collection of Aldines existing in any library.

Lord Spencer, his library and his activities as a collector are especially well known to us through the writings of the Rev. Thomas Frognall Dibdin (1776–1847) [233]. He prepared the sumptuous catalogue of Lord Spencer's books and also produced some handsomely printed and lavishly illustrated works of his own, including *The Bibliographical Decameron*. Never has book collecting been hymned in more high-flown or romantic terms.

His bibliographical expertise, it must be confessed, was a bit amateur even by the standards of his own day, let alone of ours. His *A Bibliographical Antiquarian and Picturesque Tour in France and Germany* (1821) was lavishly illustrated with copperplates after drawings by G. R. Lewis. It has been unkindly said that the book would have been better without any text.

Dibdin was not alone in this bibliographical enthusiasm. When his friend Isaac Gossett [234] lay stricken with illness he was miraculously restored to health by the mere sight of one volume of the Pinelli copy of the Complutensian Polyglot on vellum.

The Spencer library remained at Althorp until 1892, when it was purchased for £250,000 by Mrs John Rylands as the basis of the library that she founded in Manchester as a memorial to her husband, housed in a splendid building designed by Basil Champneys.

The apogee of patrician collecting came with the sale, by auction, of the library of John, third Duke of Roxburghe (1740–1804) [235 and 236], which took place on 18 May 1812 and continued for forty-one days. This was the greatest event in Dibdin's life, and he compared it to the *Iliad*. The time was especially favourable (the national economy was buoyant with the groundswell of a wartime boom), while the competition between ducal collectors was almost beyond control, with the Duke of Devonshire, Earl Spencer and the Marquess of Blandford (later Duke of Marlborough) in the lead. The high-point of the sale came with the edition of Boccaccio's *Decameron* printed in Venice by Christopher Valdarfer in 1471, then believed to be the only surviving copy. After a titanic battle the 'Valdarfer Boccaccio' was knocked down to the Marquess of Blandford, against Lord Spencer, for £2,260. Dibdin reports: 'At the tap of the auctioneer's hammer Boccaccio turned in his grave.' This record price held for seventy-two years until it was surpassed by the 1459 Psalter in the Syston Park sale of 1884.

Thirty-one patrician book collectors, reluctant to allow the golden glow of their enthusiasm to fade, formed the Roxburghe Club. Even if not quite equal to the Garter, the Roxburghe Club is, for a bibliophile, what the Royal Society is to a scientist or the Jockey Club to the turf.

A

CATALOGUE

OF

THE LIBRARY

OF THE LATE

JOHN DUKE OF ROXBURGHE,

ARRANGED BY

G. AND W. NICOL,

BOOKSELLERS TO HIS MAJESTY, PALL-MALL;

WHICH WILL BE

SOLD BY AUCTION,

AT HIS GRACE'S LATE RESIDENCE IN ST. JAMES'S SQUARE,

On MONDAY, 18th MAY, 1812, and the Forty-one
following Days, Sundays excepted, at Twelve o'Clock,

BY

ROBERT H. EVANS,

BOOKSELLER, PALL-MALL.

The Books may be viewed Four Days previous to the
Sale.

N. B. No person can be admitted without a Catalogue.

LONDON:

PRINTED BY W. BULMER AND CO. CLEVELAND-ROW,
ST. JAMES'S.
1812.

Among the original members of the Roxburghe Club was Richard Heber (1773–1833) [237], wealthy landed gentleman, half-brother of Bishop Reginald Heber, who wrote 'From Greenland's icy mountains, From India's coral strand'. He made an early start by producing a catalogue of his library at the age of eight, and was already buying at auction, through the agency of his father, at ten. In common with his contemporaries his early collecting was devoted to the classics, an interest that continued throughout his life. It was the chance purchase of Henry Peacham's *Vallie of Varietie* (1638) that turned his attention to what became the most important part of his library, early English poetry and drama. In this he was a pioneer, and a relentless devotion to this part of his library extracted, from dormant libraries and all manner of unexpected sources, an incredible number of exceedingly rare books – many of which he doubtless saved from destruction.

It cannot be claimed that all the major book collectors have been attractive characters, but Heber was a warm-hearted man with winning manners, generous in sharing his library with friends and scholars. '[His] volumes open as his heart,' said Walter Scott, his life-long friend.

235 and 236 The apogee of patrician book collecting came with the sale of the library of John, third Duke of Roxburghe (1740–1804), here caricatured by Thomas Patch. The 'Valdarfer Boccaccio' brought £2,260, a record which stood for seventy-two years. 'At the tap of the auctioneer's hammer Boccaccio turned in his grave,' said Dibdin. National Portrait Gallery.

ABOVE 237 Richard Heber (1773–1833) collected between two and three hundred thousand books and filled seven houses. His relentless search for early English literature saved many unique books from destruction. National Portrait Gallery.

It was Heber's axiom that 'no gentleman can be without three copies of a book; one for show, one for use, one for borrowers'. Bibliophiles who have lent some treasured volume to the kind of scholar who regards books as quarries out of which one hacks facts will appreciate the latter phrase.

Estimates vary as to the number of books finally accumulated by Heber, but the total seems to have been between two and three hundred thousand. His library filled two houses in London, one in Oxford and others in Paris, Brussels, Antwerp and Ghent – and this in addition to smaller hordes all over the Continent.

The Heber library was dispersed in sixteen sales, thirteen in London, two in Paris and one in Ghent, but the result was disaster. The books auctioned in London had cost over £100,000; they sold for £56,774. The great days seemed over. The original members of the Roxburghe Club were either dead or too old to care; the new generation of collectors had not yet got into its stride – and most of the giant American collectors, who towards the end of the century were to dominate the scene, were not yet born. John Pierpont Morgan, let it be noted, was born during the time of the last Heber sales.

One man alone appreciated the unparalleled opportunity: William Henry Miller (1789–1848) [238]. Although a member of parliament for some years, this quiet and unassuming Scotsman from Craigentinny devoted the whole of his life to book collecting. He attended all the major sales and when he was not in the auction room he was ransacking the bookshops. He earned the nickname 'Measure Miller' through his habit of always carrying a pocket foot-rule to test the tallness of any volume that he considered buying.

Miller kept his books at Britwell Court in Buckinghamshire, a name that has become immortal wherever early English books of poetry and drama are studied and treasured.

In America, two years after the death of Miller, occurred the birth of Henry E. Huntington, the man who, sixty years later, was destined to become Miller's principal bibliographical heir.

One example will serve to show the sources from which such major collections as the Britwell Library were derived.

The Isham family purchased Lamport Hall in about 1560 and have owned it ever since. Thomas Isham, who died in 1605, was a friend of the poets of his day and purchased their works on publication. In 1654 Lamport Hall was remodelled by John Webb, and is one of the most distinguished of Caroline houses. During the rebuilding Thomas Isham's books (which did not look very splendid to the untutored eye) were moved to an attic, where they remained until their rediscovery in 1867. Many of them were unique texts or editions that have not otherwise survived. Further, they were in the most remarkable condition, some of them having never been opened. This is probably due to the fact that, although a keen book-buyer, Thomas Isham was blind. His blindness was his undoing. One day his horse was frightened by the creaking of Scaldwell windmill and he was thrown to his death.

The cache in the attic included one extraordinary volume containing Shakespeare's *The Passionate Pilgrim* and *Venus and Adonis,* both of 1599 (the latter a hitherto unknown edition), together with Sir John Davies's *Epigrammes* with Marlowe's translation of Ovid's *Elegies* (Middleborough [but probably London] 1600) [239]. Bishop Bancroft had ordered the Davies/Marlowe book to be burned at the time of publication, and it seems that the same fate overtook this edition of *Venus and Adonis,* for no other copy has survived.

Towards the end of the nineteenth century the income of the Ishams, in common with many other landed families, was badly hit by the agricultural depression. In 1893 they sold the best books from the re-discovered library. A few were purchased by the British Museum, but the most important went to Britwell.

Sydney Richardson Christie-Miller succeeded to the Britwell Library in 1898, and in 1916 he decided to sell it. Sotheby's issued a catalogue of the Americana, but before the sale could take place the 346 lots were purchased *en bloc* for, it is said, £40,000, by Henry E. Huntington.

In 1919 the Isham volume containing *Venus and Adonis, The Passionate Pilgrim* and so on (by then in the Britwell Library) came up for sale and was purchased by Huntington for £15,100. Only one other copy of *The Passionate Pilgrim* has survived; this was presented to Trinity College, Cambridge, by Edward Capell, in 1779 and bears his note: 'Not quite perfect, so it cost but 1½d.'

The Britwell sales continued at steady intervals until 1927 and realized half a million pounds, the highest figure for any library up to that date. The same pattern was followed at every sale. Henry Huntington swept away all the important books, so the Huntington Library in California is in many ways the direct and final heir of the Heber, Miller, Isham and Britwell libraries.

Great books can have pedigrees as long as those of racehorses, based upon the owners through whose hands they have passed. For example, a manuscript written in about 1500 for Louis de Hédouville, Seigneur de Sandricourt (where a tournament was held in 1493), entitled: *Noms, armes et blasons des chevaliers de la Table Ronde,* is the Girardot de Préfond-Gaignat – Duc de La Vallière – Crevenna – Duke of Roxburghe – Duke of Marlborough – John Broadley – D. S. Ker – Earl of Ashburnham – John Pierpont Morgan copy.

Sir Thomas Phillipps (1792–1872) [240 and 241] was the greatest collector of manuscripts the world has ever known. It is not possible to estimate the number of manuscripts amassed by him, for a collection of over one hundred manuscripts may appear in his catalogue under a single number. I cannot, in the space available to me here, give an adequate account of the final contents of his library, of the multitudinous sources from which the books came, and of the great story of their dispersal. Fortunately all this has been documented in great detail, because Phillipps was quite incapable of throwing away any piece of paper that bore handwriting, and this vast archive has been brilliantly edited by Dr A. N. L. Munby.

VENVS AND ADONIS.

Vilia miretur vulgus: mihi flauus Apollo Pocula Castalia plena ministret aqua.

Imprinted at London for William Leake, dwelling in Paules Churchyard at the signe of the Greyhound. 1599.

239 A volume containing Shakespeare's *The Passionate Pilgrim* and *Venus and Adonis,* both 1599 (the latter previously unknown), remained forgotten at Lamport Hall until rediscovery in 1867. This passed to the Britwell Library, at the sale of which in 1919 it was purchased by Henry Huntington for £15,100. Only one other copy of *The Passionate Pilgrim* has survived, presented to Trinity College, Cambridge, by E. Capell, bearing the note: 'Not quite perfect, so it cost but 1½d.'

OPPOSITE 238 William Henry Miller (1789–1848), here painted by Lawrence, was known as 'Measure Miller' through carrying a pocket rule to test the tallness of books. The chief purchaser at the great Heber sales and a relentless ransacker of bookshops, his library at Britwell Court became the greatest private collection of early English books ever formed in England. It was augmented by his successors, then sold in 1916–17 for £500,000.
Courtesy of Major S. V. Christie-Miller.

obviously desirable that the two volumes should be reunited at Cambridge, but the chances of this happening seemed hopeless. Rather less than £20,000 was raised by public subscription and time was running out. Then another American, Eugene Power, of Ann Arbor, Michigan, came forward with a most generous suggestion. He would advance the remainder of the purchase price (over £70,000), hoping to recover his outlay by the sale of a proposed facsimile edition of the complete work. So Caxton's Ovid is now reunited, after almost four hundred years, at Magdalene College, Cambridge.

Phillipps burned with two overwhelming hatreds: his attitude to the Roman Catholic Church virtually amounted to pathological insanity and he loathed his son-in-law, James Orchard Halliwell. It seems more than probable that Halliwell stole Phillipps's copy of the first edition of ·Hamlet, tore out the title-page and sold the book to the British Museum. Phillipps's house, Middle Hill, and the estate must pass to his eldest daughter and the hated Halliwell. He could not escape the entail, but at least he could save the library. He bought a large mansion, Thirlestaine House, in Cheltenham, to which he took every portable object that he owned. He then proceeded to turn the Middle Hill estate into a desert, cutting down all the trees, removing the lead from the roof and so forth.

It was this irascibility that prevented Phillipps from making the last grand gesture of bequeathing his unparalleled library to some institution, for the glory of scholarship and as a lasting monument to himself. He always imposed impossible conditions upon prospective recipients and, inevitably, quarrelled with the librarians.

At last the dreadful old man died, but he carried his hatreds beyond the tomb. In his last will he stipulated that neither his elder daughter, James Orchard Halliwell, nor any Roman Catholic, 'shall ever be admitted to the inspection of my library of books and manuscripts'.

The library and Thirlestaine House passed to his youngest daughter, Katharine, wife of the Rev. John F. A. Fenwick. It was an embarrassing inheritance, this vast mansion with no income to keep it up. Every day brought a dozen letters from scholars all over the world, asking for information about manuscripts. At last the burden proved too great, and Fenwick decided to sell. The first sale, at Sotheby's, took place in 1886. No one now living is old enough to have taken an active part in the earliest Phillipps sale, yet they continue and the end is nowhere in sight.

John Fenwick's son, Thomas Fitzroy Fenwick, devoted his whole life to the steady dispersal of the library, a task that he carried out with shrewd and assiduous ability. Quite early on he arranged the bulk sales of large groups of manuscripts to European national libraries. The finest items did not pass through the salerooms but were the subject of private transactions with the major collectors including Yates Thompson, Chester Beatty, John Pierpont Morgan and Henry Huntington who bought the remaining incunabula *en bloc*. The dispersal was still in full flow when Thomas Fitzroy Fenwick died in 1938. Shortly after the outbreak of war, in 1939, Thirlestaine House was requisitioned by the Ministry of Aircraft Production. The great collection, with all the

literature and records relating to it, was bundled into the cellars and never returned to the place that Sir Thomas Phillipps had so lovingly provided for its preservation.

After the war, in 1945, came the greatest purchase in the history of bookselling. The trustees accepted an offer of £100,000 for the whole remaining collection from Lionel and Philip Robinson, two remarkable booksellers who deserve a whole book to themselves. Even now the library has not been exhausted. Each year sees two sales at Sotheby's and each sale contains fresh discoveries. There can be no doubt that many secrets from the library of Sir Thomas Phillipps still await disclosure.

By the middle of the nineteenth century American collectors were already making inroads into a field that, in the next century, they were to dominate. The first Gutenberg Bible to cross the Atlantic, now in the New York Public Library, was bought at auction in London by Henry Stevens, acting for James Lenox. That was in 1847. Lenox had given an unlimited commission, but when he heard the 'mad price' of £500, he almost repudiated the transaction. 'Henry Stevens of Vermont' was a remarkable character. Operating from London, he sold European books to American collectors and American books to the British Museum. On despatching the second Gutenberg Bible to George Brindley in 1873 he instructed his New York agents as follows:

243 Sotheby's sale room in 1890 at Wellington Street, The Strand, the scene of the early Phillipps' and other titanic sales. The auctioneer is E. G. Hodge, Bernard Quaritch sits just below the rostrum, Frederick Locker-Lampson sits at the extreme right.

244 Henry E. Huntington (1850–1927) collected, in rather less than twenty years, a library worthy to stand with the national libraries of Europe. Through his purchases at the Britwell sales he became the heir to the vast range of books from early English libraries that had been accumulated by Heber and Miller.

Pray ponder for a moment to fully appreciate the rarity and importance of this precious consignment from the Old to the New World. It is not only the first BIBLE, but is a fine copy of the FIRST BOOK EVER PRINTED. It was read in Europe nearly half a century before America was discovered. Therefore, in view of these considerations please suggest to your Deputy at the Seat of Customs to uncover his head while in the presence of this first Book, and never for a moment to turn his back upon it while the case is open. Let no ungodly or thieving politician lay eyes or hands upon it. The sight can *now* do him no good, while the Bible may suffer. Let none of Uncle Samuel's Custom House Officials, or other men in or out of authority, see it without first reverentially lifting their hats. . . .

When, in 1951, John Carter carried the Shuckburgh copy to New York (the first to travel by air), he insisted on declaiming Henry Stevens's eulogy to the customs official, but the latter pointed out that he wasn't wearing a hat anyway.

Of the many giant American collectors I have only space to write, in any detail, of two men who collected, in the brief space of their own lifetimes, libraries that may well stand comparison with European national libraries that have been gathering for centuries. One on the West Coast, one on the East: Henry Edwards Huntington and John Pierpont Morgan.

Henry E. Huntington (1850–1927) [244] made an immense fortune from the promotion of railways and from multiple interests in California. In about 1908 he retired from business and devoted the rest of his life to his library. Apart from one or two rather splendid side-lines, such as the Gutenberg Bible and several thousand incunabula, this was devoted to English and American literature and history. Huntington's astonishing achievement, in rather less than twenty years, was based on his practice of buying important libraries *en bloc*. He was fortunate in his time because several libraries that major collectors had started to form when more books were available came on to the market, and because European noblemen were beginning to feel the financial pinch and were prepared to part with family libraries that had been growing since the Renaissance. Because it was well known that for Huntington money was no object, he generally received the first offer, and he was aided by two of the most able and aggressive booksellers of all time, George D. Smith and, after Smith's death, Abraham Rosenbach.

At the H. W. Poor sale of 1908–09 Huntington purchased 1,600 lots – a quarter of the sale. Then in 1911 he purchased the library of E. Dwight Church for one million dollars. It was especially rich in early English literature, including twelve Shakespeare folios and thirty-seven quartos, while among the equally important Americana was the original manuscript of Benjamin Franklin's *Autobiography*.

Robert Hoe, the manufacturer of printing machinery, had collected one of the finest libraries in America. At his sale Huntington purchased the Gutenberg Bible on vellum for $50,000, and nearly all the other lots he needed.

In 1914 the Duke of Devonshire parted with twenty-five Caxtons and the Kemble-Devonshire collection of plays, and these too went to

Huntington. The latter had been started by the actor John Philip Kemble (1757–1823). It was richly augmented by the sixth Duke and contains one of the only two surviving copies of the first edition of *Hamlet* (1603) and (although it lacks the last leaf) it is the only one to contain the title-page. The library of F. R. Halsey, purchased in 1915, was especially rich in Dickens and Shelley, including one of the three known copies of *Original Poetry; by Victor and Cazire*.

The Bridgewater House library was founded by Sir Thomas Egerton, Lord Keeper of the Great Seal under Queen Elizabeth I. Many Elizabethan books had been purchased on publication and later generations made important additions. It included the Ellesmere Chaucer, one of the most lovable books in the world and, to me, the greatest treasure of the Huntington Library. This manuscript was written within a decade of Chaucer's death in 1399. It contains many unique readings, but the great attraction lies in the twenty-three pictures in the margins of mounted pilgrims and, especially, the earliest portrait of Chaucer himself [246]. Huntington purchased this collection *en bloc* in 1917.

In 1925 the Royal Society decided, very wrongly as some people thought, to sell much of its library. Among the books was a hitherto unknown translation into the Indian language, by John Eliot, of Richard Baxter's *Call to the Unconverted*, printed in Cambridge (Massachusetts) by Samuel Green in 1664 [245]. Huntington bought it for £6,800.

In my accounts of the Lamport, Heber, Britwell and, to a less exclusive extent, the Phillipps libraries, I have tried to show how a great procession of early English books and manuscripts came, finally, to rest in the Huntington Library. The library contains every one of Shakespeare's first editions published in quarto except *Titus Andronicus*, and of that it holds the second quarto, of which only one other copy is known. Of the rich collection of Americana I am less qualified to speak, but there is an almost complete collection of the rare early printed accounts from Colombus onwards; seven thousand American imprints between 1640 and 1800; letters and documents by Washington, Jefferson and Lincoln – and, as one would expect, the great majority of printed Western Americana and a wealth of manuscript material relating to the West.

Having erected a splendid building to contain it (surrounded by magnificent gardens and accompanied by a superb art collection), Huntington handed his library to the care of trustees and threw it open to scholars. In subsequent years a succession of able librarians have added to the collection until today Daniel H. Woodward presides over 5 million autographs, documents and manuscripts; 5,340 incunabula; 38,000 STC and Wing Books (English books printed up to 1701); 8,000 European books of the Renaissance; in general, 300,000 rare books.

In contrast to the majority of American tycoons, John Pierpont Morgan (1837–1913) [247] was born to wealth and power. His ancestor Miles Morgan had landed at Boston in 1636, while on the maternal side John Pierpont had arrived in America from London by 1640 – both of them, so to speak, eligible for inclusion in the STC. As early as 1851 he was

OVERLEAF 246 The Bridgewater House library, founded in Elizabethan times, was purchased *en bloc* by Henry Huntington in 1917. It contained the Ellesmere Chaucer which has twenty-three pictures of the Canterbury Pilgrims and a portrait of Chaucer.

245 Huntington's early English books are equalled by his Americana. This is the only surviving copy of Baxter's *Call to the Unconverted* (1664), written in the Indian language. It was presented to the Royal Society by Governor Winthrop of Connecticut and is still in the original boards. Sold by the Society in 1925, it was purchased by Huntington for £6,800.

collecting autographs of American presidents, but his serious and stupendous collecting commenced only after the death of his father (in a carriage accident on the Riviera) in 1890.

Pierpont Morgan's tastes were princely. He collected autograph manuscripts of great authors, the finest manuscripts, the most important incunabula and superb bindings, all in the finest state, to form a collection that is unsurpassed for quality in the western hemisphere. Early acquisitions included the Gutenberg Bible on vellum and the 1459 Mainz Psalter, for which he gave the highest price then ever paid for a printed book. The latter remained, until very recently, the only copy in the United States. Other early acquisitions included the ninth-century Lindau Gospels in a superb jewelled binding, the autograph manuscripts of Keats's *Endymion* and Dickens's *A Christmas Carol*.

In 1900 he purchased the best part of the library of Theodore Irwin, of Oswego, New York, which included the tenth-century Golden Gospels on purple vellum previously belonging to Henry VIII, Ralph Palmer of Little Chelsea and Alexander, tenth Duke of Hamilton [XXXIX]. This was written by sixteen scribes at the Abbey of St Maximin's in Trier, in burnished gold 'artificial' uncials upon heavy vellum painted purple, in shades ranging from imperial purple to rose lavender, the opposite pages carefully matched in colour. It is believed to have been a gift to the Emperor Otto III (980–1002), whose mother, Theophano, was the daughter of the emperor of Byzantium. It was subsequently presented to Henry VIII of England and his royal arms are emblazoned on the first leaf.

Another major acquisition was the sole complete copy of Malory's *Morte Darthur*, printed by Caxton in 1485 [248]. (Other than this, there is only the imperfect Spencer copy, now in the Rylands Library.) This is the Dr Bernard (1698)–Thomas Rawlinson–Earl of Oxford (Harley)–Osborne–Bryan Fairfax–Francis Child (then Earl of Jersey)–A. E. Pope–Robert Hoe–Pierpont Morgan copy.

In 1900 Morgan planned a library building that was to be worthy of his treasures, a Renaissance building based on the Palazzo del Tè, the pleasure palace of the Gonzaga family in Mantua. To walk into this building, which has been called 'one of the Seven Wonders of the Edwardian World', is like entering the library of a Renaissance prince [249]. Indeed there is a striking parallel with that *Quattrocento* family of art-loving bankers, the Medici, who also formed a great library, and especially between Cosimo de' Medici and Pierpont Morgan himself, of whom it was said, '[he] pursued the life of an unostentatious gentleman on a majestic scale'.

Pierpont Morgan engaged as his librarian a somewhat formidable lady with remarkable gifts, Miss Belle Da Costa Greene, who guided the fortunes of the library for forty-three years until her retirement in 1948. She had exceptional knowledge and taste combined with practical acumen.

After the death of Pierpont Morgan in 1913 his son J. P. Morgan (1867–1943) in conjunction with Miss Greene continued to build the

247 John Pierpont Morgan (1837–1913) collected the greatest books in superb copies, forming a library which would have been the envy of a Renaissance prince.

248 The only complete copy of Malory's *Morte Darthur*, printed by Caxton in 1485, now in the Pierpont Morgan Library.

249 The setting of the Pierpont Morgan Library in New York is worthy of the books: the chimney piece sculpted by a pupil of Desiderio da Settignano, the sixteenth-century polychromed ceiling from a cardinal's palace at Lucca, the walls hung with tapestries and old masters.

library. Among his purchases were the four manuscripts from Weingarten described in Chapter Three [XL]. Other manuscripts came from Sir George Holford, the Phillipps collection, Yates Thompson and Chester Beatty.

In 1924 J. P. Morgan transferred the library to a board of trustees with an endowment for maintenance. After the retirement of Miss Greene in 1948 the library continued under the able guidance of her successor, Frederick B. Adams Jr. He formed an association of Fellows, some of them major collectors in their own right. This broadening of the base has resulted in continued acquisitions of the highest class. The Fellows have made gifts of fine collections to the Morgan, often bequeathing their own libraries. Today the holdings of the library include tens of thousands of autograph letters and manuscripts, over a thousand early manuscripts, almost all of them of great importance and beauty, and approximately 2,275 incunabula, including sixty Caxtons, of which five are unique. The Morgan collection of Caxtons is the finest after the British Museum and the Rylands Library. Now under the direction of Charles Ryskamp, the Morgan Library continues to be, as it has been for many years, an important centre for advanced studies.

I would not like to leave the subject of J. P. Morgan without referring to an act of great generosity on his part for which every English bibliophile should be grateful.

The *Luttrell Psalter* [11 and 12] was on display in the British Museum for so long (1896–1928) and had been reproduced in so many history books that most people took it for granted that the manuscript was part of the British Museum Library. In fact it was the property of the Welds, one of the oldest English Roman Catholic families, who had deposited it on loan. In 1928 Mr Herbert Weld decided to sell the *Luttrell Psalter* and the almost equally famous *Psalter and Book of Hours* of John, Duke of Bedford, and sent them to Sotheby's.

It was obvious that J. P. Morgan would want to add these supreme manuscripts to his own library. Instead he forbore to bid himself and advanced the purchase price, £64,830, free of interest for a year, while the money was raised. Through this generous intervention both manuscripts passed to the British Museum.

Of the libraries we have discussed, Cotton intended his for public use and his heirs virtually gave it to the nation; the Harleian manuscripts went to the British Museum at an absurdly low price through a mixture of generosity and aristocratic disdain on the part of the Dowager Countess of Oxford; Lord Spencer's early printed books were given to Manchester by Mrs Rylands; T. J. Wise's library of English literature passed to the British Museum at a fraction of its value through the generosity of his widow; Pierpont Morgan and Henry Huntington founded what may well be regarded as National Collections and, quite recently, the British Museum has benefited from the Henry Davis Gift.

Alfred W. Pollard, then Principal Keeper of Printed Books at the British Museum, and one of the most highly regarded of all English bibliographers, wrote:

It is mainly by the zeal of private collectors that books which would otherwise have perished from neglect are discovered, preserved and made to yield up their secrets, with the result that almost every great library owes more on its historical side to their generosity than to the purchases from its own resources.

250 John Sieferwas, a friar of Guildford, was admitted as an acolyte in 1380. He has signed his name at the foot of the miniature and presents a lectionary to his patron John Lovell whose name appears on a scroll to the left.
British Museum, Harley MS 7026.

BIBLIOGRAPHY

ABBEY, J. R. *Scenery of Great Britain and Ireland in Aquatint and Lithography, 1770–1886. A Bibliographical Catalogue,* London, 1952

Life in England in Aquatint and Lithography, 1770–1860. Architecture, Drawing Books, Art Collections, Magazines, Navy and Army, Panoramas, etc. A Bibliographical Catalogue, London, 1953

Travel in Aquatint and Lithography, 1770–1860. A Bibliographical Catalogue, 2 vols, London, 1956

Alcuin Bible *Die Bibel Von Moutier-Grandval,* Berne, 1970

AMRAM, D. *The Makers of Hebrew Books in Italy,* Philadelphia, 1909; Photocopy, London, 1963

APULEIUS BARBARUS *The Herbal of Apuleius Barbarus, From the 12th Century Manuscript formerly at Bury St Edmunds,* Edited by T. R. Gunter, Roxburghe Club, Oxford, 1925

Herbal of Pseudo-Apuleius, Parallel MS and First Edition, Edited by F. W. T. Hunger, Leyden, 1935

ARBER, A. *Herbals, Their Origin and Evolution, A Chapter in the History of Botany, 1470–1670,* Cambridge, 1953

Ashendene Press *Descriptive Catalogue of Books Printed at Ashendene Press,* London, 1935

AUBREY, J. *Brief Lives, chiefly of Contemporaries, set down 1669–96, Edited from the Author's Manuscript by A. Clark,* 2 vols, Oxford, 1898

BERKOVITS, I. *Illuminated Manuscripts from the Library of Matthias Corvinus,* Budapest, 1964

BERKOWITZ, D. S. *In Remembrance of Creation. Evolution and Scholarship in the Medieval and Renaissance Bible.* Catalogue of a loan exhibition at Brandeis University, Waltham, Mass., 1968

Berlin *Katalog der Ornamentstich-Sammlung der Staatlichen Kunstbibliothek Berlin,* 1939; Photofacsimile, New York

BERLINER, A. *Censur und Confiscation Hebräischer Bücher im Kirchenstaate,* Berlin, 1891

Bible, Cambridge History of the, Vol 2, *The West from the Reformation to the Present Day,*

Edited by S. L. Greenslade, Cambridge, 1963

Bibliographica Essays by R. Garnett, A. W. Pollard, R. Proctor, E. M. Thompson, E. G. Duff, P. Kristeller, W. Morris, etc, 3 vols, London, 1895–97

BLAND, D. *A History of Book Illustration. The Illuminated Manuscript and the Printed Book,* London, 1958

BLUNT, A. *Philibert de l'Orme,* London, 1958

Art and Architecture in France, 1500–1700, Pelican History of Art, London, 1953

BLUNT, W. *The Art of Botanical Illustration,* London, 1950

British Museum *English Bookbindings,* with Introduction and Descriptions by W. Y. Fletcher, London, 1895

Foreign Bookbindings, with Introduction and Descriptions by W. Y. Fletcher, London, 1896

Illuminated Manuscripts in The British Museum, Miniatures, Borders, and Initials, Text by G. F. Warner; 4 portfolios, London, 1900–03

Queen Mary's Psalter, Facsimile, Introduction by Sir George Warner, 1912

Catalogue of Books Printed in the XVth century, Parts I–X, London, 1908–71

Reproductions from Illuminated Manuscripts, Series I–V, London, 1923–65

BROWN, H. *The Venetian Printing Press,* London, 1891

Brown, John Carter, Library *Bibliotheca Americana,* 3 vols in 5, Providence, Rhode Island, 1919–31

BRUNET, J.-C. *Manuel du Libraire et de l'Amateur de Livres,* 6 vols, Paris, 1860–65

BURCKHARDT, J. *The Civilisation of the Period of the Renaissance in Italy,* Basel, 1860; English translation by S. G. C. Middlemore, London, 1878

California Historical Society *Drake's Plate of Brass,* Various authors and extracts from early authorities, San Francisco, 1937

CARTER, J. *ABC for Book Collectors,* London, 1952 and revised editions

Taste and Technique in Book Collecting, Second edition with Epilogue, London, 1970

CARTER, J. and POLLARD, G. *An Enquiry into the Nature of Certain Nineteenth Century Pamphlets,* [T. J. Wise], London, 1934

CLAIR, C. *A Chronology of Printing,* London, 1969

COLE, G. W. *Catalogue of Books Relating to the Discovery of North and South America . . . E. D. Church,* 5 vols, New York, 1907

Catalogue of Books consisting of English Literature and Miscellania . . . E. D. Church, New York, 1909

COLONNA, F. *Hypnerotomachia Poliphili of 1499,* Facsimile, With an Introduction on the Dream, the Dreamer, the Artist and the Printer by G. D. Painter, London, 1963

CRAIG, M. *Irish Bookbindings,* London, 1954

DARLOW, T. H. and MOULE, H. F. *Historical Catalogue of the Printed Editions of Holy Scripture in the Library of The British and Foreign Bible Society,* 4 vols, 1903, London. Vol I, *English Bibles,* Revised and expanded by A. S. Herbert, London, 1968

DAVIES, H. W. *Devices of the Early Printers, 1457–1560. Their History and Development,* London, 1935

DAVIES, J. I. *The Italian Book, 1465–1900,* National Book League Exhibition, London, 1953

DELISLE, L. V. *Les Bibles de Gutenberg,* Paris, 1895

DE RICCI, S. *A Census of Caxtons,* London, 1909

Catalogue Raisonné des Premières Impressions de Mayence, 1445–67, Mainz, 1911

English Collectors of Books and Manuscripts, 1530–1930, Cambridge, 1930

DIBDIN, T. F. *Bibliotheca Spenceriana,* 4 vols, London, 1814–15

A Bibliographical Antiquarian and Picturesque Tour in France and Germany, 3 vols, London, 1821

The Bibliographical Decameron, 3 vols, London, 1817

DIRINGER, D. *The Illuminated Book, its History and Production,* Revised and augmented with

the assistance of Reinhold Regensburger, London, 1967

DODWELL, C. R. *The Great Lambeth Bible,* London, 1959

Doves Press *Catalogue Raisonné,* London, 1916

DUFF, E. G. 'The Great Mearne Myth', in *Papers of the Edinburgh Bibliographical Society,* 1918

EDE, C., (Editor) *The Art of the Book, 1930–50,* London, 1951

Epistole et Evangelii, Florence, 1495 Fascimile, Roxburghe Club, London, 1910

ESDAILE, A. *The British Museum Library,* London, 1946

ESSLING, PRINCE D' *Les Livres à Figures Venitiens,* 3 vols in 6, Florence and Paris, 1907–14

FANELLI, F. *Atene Attica Descritta da suoi Principii Sino All'acquisto Fatti dall'Armi Veneto nel 1687,* Venice, 1707

FRANKLIN, C. *The Private Press,* London, 1969

FREIMANN, A., and MARX, M. *Thesaurus Typographiae Hebraicae Saeculi XV, Hebrew Printing in the XVth century,* 1924–31. Type facsimile, Jerusalem. 1967–69

FURLONG CARDIFF, G. *Origenes del Arte Tipografica en América,* Buenos Aires, 1947

Gesamtkatalog Der Wiegendrucke, Vols 1–7, A-Eig., Leipzig, 1925–34

GINSBURG, C. G. *The Massorah,* 4 vols, London, 1880–1905

Introduction to the Massoretico-Critical Edition of the Hebrew Bible, 1897

Golden Cockerel Press Bibliographies *Chanticleer 1921–36,* 1936; *Pertelote 1936–43,* 1943; *Cockalorum 1943–48,* 1951; London

GOLDSCHMIDT, E. P. *Austrian Monastic Libraries,* In 'The Library' *(Transactions of the Bibliographical Society),* Vol. XXV, London, 1945

Gothic and Renaissance Bookbindings, 2 vols, London, 1928

The Printed Book of the Renaissance, Three Lectures on Types, Illustrations and Ornament, Cambridge, 1950

GRIGSON, G. *Thornton's Temple of Flora,* London, 1951

HAKLUYT, R. *Principall Navigations*, 12 vols, Glasgow, 1903–05

HARRIS, J., ORGEL, S., and STRONG, R.
The King's Arcadia: Inigo Jones and the Stuart Court, Quartercentenary Exhibition, London, 1973

HARRISON, F. *English Manuscripts of the Fourteenth Century*, London, 1937

HERRICK, F.H. *Audubon the Naturalist. A History of His Life and Time*, 2 vols, New York, 1917

HIND, A.M. *G.B. Piranesi. A Critical Study, with a List of his Published Works*, London, 1922
An Introduction to a History of Woodcut, with a Detailed Survey of Work Done in the Fifteenth Century, 2 vols, London, 1935

HOBSON, A.R.A. *French and Italian Collectors and their Bindings. Illustrated from Examples in the Library of J.R. Abbey*, Roxburghe Club, London, 1953
Great Libraries, London and New York, 1970

HOBSON, G.D. *Bindings in Cambridge Libraries*, Cambridge, 1929
English Bindings, 1490–1940, in the Library of J.R. Abbey, London, 1940

HOLME, C. (Editor) *The Art of the Book*, London, 1914

JOHNSON, A.F. *Type Designs, their History and Development*, London, 1934

Kells, Book of, *Evangeliorum Quattuor Codex Cenannensis*, Facsimile, Edited by E.H. Alton and P. Meyer, 3 vols, Berne, 1950–51

KER, N.R. *Medieval Libraries of Great Britain*, 2nd edition, London, 1964

KLINEFELTER, W. *The Fortsas Bibliohoax*, New York, 1941

KRISTELLER, P. *Early Florentine Woodcuts, With an Annotated List of Florentine Illustrated Books*, London, 1897

LEHMANN-HAUPT, H., and WROTH, L.C.
The Book in America, New York, 1952

LEHMANN-HAUPT, H. *Peter Schoeffer. With a List of his Surviving Books and Broadsides*, New York, 1950

LIPPMANN, F. *The Art of Wood-Engraving in Italy in the Fifteenth Century*, London, 1888

LOVETT, R. *The English Bible in the John Rylands Library*, Manchester, 1899

MACKAIL, J.W. *The Life of William Morris*, 2 vols, London, 1899

MCMURTRIE, D.C. *The Book. The Story of Printing and Bookmaking*, New York, 1943
The Gutenberg Documents. With translations of the texts into English, based with authority on the compilation by Dr Karl Schorbach, New York, 1941

MARX, MOSES 'On the date of appearance of the First Printed Hebrew Books', in the *Alexander Marx Jubilee Volume*, New York, 1950

MASSON, SIR I. *The Mainz Psalters and Canon Missae, 1457–1459*, London, 1954

MEISS, M., and THOMAS, M. *The Rohan Book of Hours*, London, 1973

MICHON, LOUISE-MARIE *La Reliure Française*, Paris, 1951

MILLAR, E. *The Luttrell Psalter*, London, 1932

MINER, DOROTHY *The History of Bookbinding, 525–1950 A.D. An Exhibition Held at the Baltimore Museum of Art, Organised by the Walters Art Gallery*, Baltimore, 1957

Morgan Library *Italian Manuscripts in the Pierpont Morgan Library*, Text by M. Harrsen and G.K. Boyce, New York, 1953
Central European Manuscripts in the Pierpont Morgan Library, Text by M. Harrsen, New York, 1958

MORISON, S. *Four Centuries of Fine Printing, upwards of six hundred examples, 1500–1914*, Large folio, London, 1924
Ditto. Two hundred and seventy-two examples, 1465–1924, 8vo, London, 1949

MUNBY, A.N.L. *Phillipps Studies*, 5 vols, Cambridge, 1951–60
Connoisseurs and Medieval Miniatures, 1750–1850, Oxford, 1972

NIXON, H.M. *Twelve Books in Fine Bindings From the Library of J.W. Hely-Hutchinson*, Roxburghe Club, Oxford, 1953
Broxbourne Library, Styles and Designs of Bookbindings from the Twelfth to the Twentieth Century, London, 1956
Bookbindings from the Library of Jean Grolier, A Loan Exhibition, British Museum, London, 1965
Sixteenth-Century Gold-Tooled Bookbindings in the Pierpont Morgan Library, New York, 1971
English Restoration Bookbindings, Samuel Mearne and his contemporaries, Exhibition, British Museum, London, 1974

Nonesuch Press *The Nonesuch Century, An Appraisal, a Personal Note and a Bibliography, 1923–34*. By A.J.A. Symons, Desmond Flower, Francis Meynell, London, 1936

NORTON, F.J. *Italian Printers, 1501–1520. An Annotated List with an Introduction*, London, 1958

OAKESHOTT, W. *The Artists of the Winchester Bible*, London, 1945

OVIDIUS NASO, P. *Metamorphoses*, translation by Wm. Caxton, 2 vols, New York, 1968

Oxford Dictionary of the Christian Church, Edited by F.L. Cross, London, 1957 and later revised editions

PAINTER, G.D. 'Gutenberg and the B36 Group. A Re-Consideration', in *Essays in Honour of Victor Scholderer*. Edited by D. Rhodes, Mainz, 1970

PAPANTONIO, M. *Early American Bindings from the Collection of M. Papantonio*, New York, 1972

PARTINGTON, W. *Thomas J. Wise in the Original Cloth*, Appendix by Bernard Shaw, London, 1946

POLLARD, A.W. *Italian Book Illustrations, Chiefly of the Fifteenth Century*, London, 1894

PORCHER, J. *The Rohan Book of Hours*, London, 1959
French Miniature from Illuminated Manuscripts, London, 1960

PRIDEAUX, S.T. *Aquatint Engraving*, London, 1909

Printing and the Mind of Man *A Descriptive Catalogue Illustrating the Impact of Print on the Evolution of Western Civilization during Five Centuries*, John Carter, Percy H. Muir, Nicolas Barker, H.A. Feisenberger, Howard Nixon and S.H. Steinberg, London, 1967

RENOUARD, A.A. *Annales de l'Imprimerie des Alde, ou Histoire des Trois Manuce et de leurs Éditions*, Paris, 1834

RICKERT, M. *The Reconstructed Carmelite Missal*, London, 1952
Painting in Britain: The Middle Ages, The Pelican History of Art, London, 1954

RODAKIEWICZ, DR ERLA *The Editio Princeps of Roberto Valturio's 'De Re Militari' in Relation to the Dresden and Munich Manuscripts*, Milan, 1940

ROSSI, J.B. DE *Annales Hebraeo-Typographici Seculi XV et ab Anno 1501 ad 1540*, Parma, 1776

SANDER, M. *Le Livre à Figures Italien*, 6 vols in 5, Milan, 1942

SANUTO, M. *I Diarii di M. Sanuto*, Edited by F. Stefani, 58 vols, Venice, 1879–1902

SCHAD, R.O. 'Henry Edwards Huntington' in *The Huntington Library Bulletin*, No 1, 1931. Reissued separately, 1963

SCHOLDERER, V. *Johann Gutenberg*, London, 1963

SITWELL, S., BLUNT, W., and SYNGE, P.M.
Great Flower Books, London, 1956

SMITH, CAPT. JOHN *Works*, Edited by Edward Arber, 2 vols, Birmingham, 1884

SPARLING, H.H. *The Kelmscott Press and William Morris, Master-craftsman*. This reprints *A Note by William Morris on His Aims in Founding the Kelmscott Press* and the Bibliography of the Press, London, 1924

S.T.C. POLLARD, A.W., and REDGRAVE, G.R., and others *A Short-Title Catalogue of Books Printed in England, Scotland, and Ireland, And of English Books Printed Abroad 1475–1640*, London, 1926. (A new edition, edited by F.S. Ferguson and W.A. Jackson, and, since their deaths, by Katharine F. Pantzer, is in an advanced state of preparation.)

STEVENSON, A. *The Problem of the Missale Speciale*, London, 1967

STILLWELL, M.B. *Incunabula and Americana, 1450–1800. A Key to Bibliographical Study*, New York, 1961

STRACHAN, J. *Early Bible Illustrations, A Short Study based on some Fifteenth and Early Sixteenth Century Printed Texts*, London, 1957

SUMMERSON, J. *Architecture in Britain, 1530–1830*, Pelican History of Art, London, 1953

TAYLOR, F.H. *Pierpont Morgan as Collector and Patron*, New York, 1957

THOMPSON, L.S. *Printing in Colonial Spanish America*, Hamden, Connecticut, and London, England, 1962

TOMKINSON, G.S. *A Select Bibliography of the Principal Modern Presses Public and Private in Great Britain and Ireland*, London, 1927

TOOLEY, R.V. *English Books with Coloured Plates, 1790–1860*, London, 1954

TURNER, D.H. *Early Gothic Illuminated Manuscripts in England (in the British Museum)*, London, 1965
'Two rediscovered miniatures of the Oscott Psalter' in *The British Museum Quarterly*, Vol XXXIV, No 1–2, 1969
Romanesque Illuminated Manuscripts in the British Museum, London, 1971

UPDIKE, D.B. *Printing Types, Their History, Forms and Use*, 2 vols, Cambridge, Mass., 1937

VALÉRY, P., and Eluard, P., Moutard-Uldry, R., Blaizot, G., Michon, L.-M. *Paul Bonet*, Paris, 1945

WAGNER, H.R. *Nueva Bibliografía Mexicana, S.XVI*, Mexico, 1940
The Grabhorn Press, A Catalogue of Imprints in the Collection of H.R. Wagner, Los Angeles, 1938

WANLEY, HUMPHREY *The Diary of Humphrey Wanley*, Edited by C.E. and Ruth C. Wright, 2 vols, London, 1966

WESTCOTT, B.F. *History of the New Testament Canon*, London, 1855
Introduction to the Study of the Gospels, London, 1860
History of the English Bible, London, 1868

WING, D. *Short-Title Catalogue of Books Printed in England, Scotland, Ireland, Wales and British America and of English Books Printed in Other Countries, 1641–1700*, Compiled by Donald Wing, 3 vols, New York, 1945–51. Vol I, Second, revised edition, New York, 1972

WISE, T.J. *Letters to John Henry Wrenn*, Edited by F.E. Ratchford, New York, 1944
Thomas J. Wise Centenary Studies, Edited by W.B. Todd, Essays by J. Carter, G. Pollard, W.B. Todd, Austin, Texas, 1959

WITTKOWER, R. *Architectural Principles in the Age of Humanism*, London, 1952
Art and Architecture in Italy, 1600–1750, London, 1958

WOLF, E., with FLEMING, J.F. *A.S.W. Rosenbach: A Biography*, New York, 1960

WOOD, ANTHONY À. *Athenae Oxoniensis. An exact history of all the Writers and Bishops who have had their education in the most ancient and famous University of Oxford . . . 1500–1690*, London, 1691–92

WORMALD, F. *The Benedictional of St Ethelwold*, London, 1959

WORMALD, F., and WRIGHT, C.E. Editors, *The English Library before 1700 (Including Cotton)*, London, 1958

ACKNOWLEDGEMENTS FOR ILLUSTRATIONS

The author and publishers would like to thank the following museums, institutions and photographers for permission to reproduce illustrations and for supplying photographs:

American Bible Society: 209

The Bancroft Library, University of California; reproduced by permission of the Director: 196

Bayerische Staatsbibliothek, Munich: *30*

Bibliographical Society: 237

Biblioteca Laurenziana, Florence: 13

Biblioteca Publica Provincial, Toledo: 194 *above*

Bibliothèque de Méjanes, Aix-en-Provence: 83

Bibliothèque Nationale, Paris: 32, *70, 74*

British Museum: 10, 14, 16, *18, 19, 20*, 21, 22, 24, 25, 26, 27, *29*, 31, 32, 35, 39, 40, 42 *below right*, 43 *centre*, 43 *bottom*, 46, 47, 48, 49, 50, 51, *52*, 53, 54, 55, 56, 57, 59, 62 *above right*, 63, 69, 75, 77, 78, 81 *below*, 82, 84 *left*, 85, 86, *87 above left*, 88, 92, 93, 95, 97, 99, 101, 103, 104, 106, 107, 109, 110, 111, 113, 115, 116, 117, 118, 120, 121, 125, 126, 127, 128, *129, 130 above left and right*, 131, 132, 133, 134, 135, 136, 137, 138, 144, *147, 148*, 149, 154, 155, 156, *157, 158, 159, 160*, 162, 163, 164, 165, 166, 167, 168, 169, 172, 173, 174, 175, 176, 177, 178, 179, 180, 181, 182, 184, 186, 187, 189, 190, 191, 193, 195, 197, 198, 199, *201*, 203, 204, 205, 206, 208, 217 *below*, 224, 225, 226 *below*, 227, 228, 236, 240, 245, 246, 250, 252, 253, 256, 263, 271

British Museum (Natural History): *130 below left and right*, 145, *147 below left*, 150, 151

Broxbourne Library, deposited in the Bodleian Library, Oxford: 66, 67, 80 *above*

Eton College Library (photos: John Webb): 73 *right*, 76

Fitzwilliam Museum, Cambridge: 23

Hereford Cathedral, by permission of the Dean and Chapter: 64

Michael Holford: *202*

Henry E. Huntington Library, San Marino, California: 266 *below*, 267, 268

Jewish Theological Seminary of America, New York: 114

John Rylands Library, Manchester: 44

Dr A.N.L. Munby, King's College, Cambridge: 255, 257 *left*, 258, 262

National Portrait Gallery: 254, 257 *right*, 259 *left*, 260 *above*

New York Public Library: Spencer Collection, Astor, Lenox and Tilden Foundations: *87 above right*; Rare Book Division, Astor, Lenox and Tilden Foundations: 192; 207

Pierpont Morgan Library: 73 *left*, 119, *219, 220*, 269, 270

Private Collections (photos: John Webb): 41, 42 *above*, 42 *below left*, 43 *top*, 57 *below*, 58, 60, 62 *above left*, 62 *below*, 68, 80 *below*, 81 *above*, 89, 100, 108, 123, 134 *above left*, 200, 215, 216, 217 *above*, 222, 223, 226 *above*, 229, 230, 231, 232, 233, 236, 244, 251, 259 *right*

Rothschild Collection, National Trust, Waddesdon Manor: 87 *below left*

Societe Archéologique, Avesnes: 15 *above*

Courtesy of Sotheby's: 141, 194 *below*, 265

Stonyhurst College (photo: Pye's Photo Service): 65

Trinity College, Dublin; by permission of the Board: 12, *17*

University of Texas at Austin, courtesy of the Humanities Research Center: 241

Victoria and Albert Museum (photos: John Webb): 170, 188

The Walters Art Gallery, Baltimore: 84 *right*

Winchester Cathedral Library, by kind permission of the Dean and Chapter: 15 *below*

Worcester College, Oxford: 183

Picture research by Susan Pinkus

INDEX